ARMO

A TANKIE'S TALES

Second edition 2009

First published in 2007 by

WOODFIELD PUBLISHING
Bognor Regis, West Sussex, England
www.woodfieldpublishing.com

ISBN 1-84683-029-X

ARMOURED FARMER

A Tankie's Tales

MALCOLM CLEVERLEY

Woodfield

"LULL BEFORE

CAMBRAI, 19T

In No Man's Land one early morn at fifty in the shade
From out the British lines there came the famous Tank Brigade
The Huns began to strafe 'em, couldn't make it out at all
Especially when the tanks began the Caterpillar crawl.

And the tanks went on, and they strolled along with an independent air
And their guns began to blaze, and the Huns began to swear
For they pulled the trees up by the roots, and they made the Huns look like galoots
Did the tanks that broke the tanks out in Picardy

The Huns peeped through their trenches, for they couldn't understand.
They cried "Here comes the British Navy, sailing on the land!"
The Kaiser saw them also and, as through the trench he ran,
He shouted out to Tirpitz "Hush! Here comes the bogey man!"

And the tanks went on, and they strolled along with an independent air
Said the Huns, "It isn't fair! You're not fighting on the square!"
At the fortress then they made a call and started walking through the wall
Did the tanks that broke the tanks out in Picardy.

Special Order No 6.

1. Tomorrow the Tank Corps will have the chance for which it has been waiting for many months, to operate on good going in the van of the battle.

2. All that hard work and ingenuity can achieve has been done in the way of preparation.

3. It remains for unit commanders and for tank crews to complete the work by judgement and pluck in the battle itself.

4. In the light of past experience, I leave the good name of the Corps with great confidence in their hands.

5. I propose leading the attack of the centre division.

Hugh Elles

19th Nov 1917 Commanding Tank Corps.

Dedicated to all who served with the
Third Royal Tank Regiment until
its amalgamation in 1992.

"Gone but not forgotten."

And for my young son Dominic who, when
he's older may hopefully read this and think,
"Did my Dad really do all that?"

Also to my partner Leigh and the 'kids' John and Lauren,
who have had to sit through my trials and tribulations in
getting published.

"I remember shouting to the Infantry; 'Come on you blokes, you can't expect to live forever!' and away we went... "
British tank Commander, Cambrai 1917.

"They come steadily forward and are not bound to road and track, with horror we see our wire entanglements crushed down and that fences and even garden walls do not stop them."
German Infanteer, Cambrai 1917.

"Lucy you old sod, one day I will write a book about all this!"
Author, Paderborn 1980s.

Contents

Preface

CLUNK! The carriage door slammed with an air of finality behind me. I heaved my suitcase onto the rack above a seat, turned and put my head out of the open window. There on the platform stood my father, mother and little sister Annette.

I was a naive sixteen-year-old about to take his first real step towards manhood in the service of Queen and Country as a soldier, a step that many young men in the past had taken. But they had lived in darker and more dangerous times and their decisions were made for them by powers beyond their control. They had packed their possessions into bags and had headed not only into the Army but also into the maelstrom of war...

I imagine their emotions were not unlike my own – the anticipation of things to come. Whether they feared the future or, like me, looked forward to a great adventure, the one thing I'm sure bound us together was... the unknown.

So there I was on a cool spring morning in 1975, departing from a small mainline station in the heart of South Devon. This journey, which I was sure would lead me into a man's world of excitement and adventure had been planned from the age of seven...

My upbringing had been the very best my loving parents could provide. I spent my childhood in a tiny hamlet on the southern edge of Dartmoor and a real highlight in my life was the annual Mothers' Union trip that our family embarked on. One such outing had been to London, during which I saw the Change of the Guard at Buckingham Palace. From that day I knew that my destiny lay in soldiering.

As I grew up I held this vision in place, and films such as that great epic *Zulu* did nothing but reinforce my belief in the greatness of the British Army. At 13 years of age I started my twice-weekly 5-mile journey to the nearest town to be an Army cadet. After this, my next step would be the regular Army.

The story that follows is a true recollection of my fifteen years in a tank regiment. I have attempted not only to reflect the serious side of the business of 'tanking' but also to emphasise the humour, which has always been such a part of the tankie's life.

Someone once said, "It takes a certain breed of men to live and work on tanks." I can personally vouch for this and am proud to say that without exception I have never worked or lived with such a great group of people as those who upheld the reputation of the Third Royal Tank Regiment.

As you read this story I can assure you that no matter how funny the anecdote, our humour never detracted from the serious business of being a thoroughly professional and combat-ready tank unit.

1. Junior 'Bleeder'

Well then, here I was in May 1975, on a train into the unknown. This journey had begun some time prior to my boarding of the train. I had been through the recruitment process, having stepped through the Army Careers Office door in Plymouth earlier that year. My most vivid memory of that visit was that, due to the large queue of Army volunteers, I had to sit in the waiting area belonging to the RAF, who shared the office with the Army recruiters. A chap with an immense moustache kept peering out of an office door. When his question of "Anyone for the RAF?" was answered with "No" he quickly returned to whatever else occupied him in his office.

Having completed the various selection processes I had to undergo, I was given a list of options from which I could choose the unit I would join. I immediately opted for the Royal Armoured Corps. Let's face it, belting around the countryside at the helm of an awesome metal monster looked like pure joy to a sixteen-year-old whose only prior experience of large machinery was a tractor. Well, I had seen combine harvesters, but my uncle wouldn't allow me behind the wheel of one of those!

To join at my age I would have to become a Junior Leader. From these hallowed ranks, I was informed, would come the regular Army's future Non Commissioned Officers or NCOs. Quite frankly, by this stage I couldn't care less if I had to have extensions sewed onto my ears to make me a better listener.

"When do I get to drive a tank?" came my eager question.

"It'll take about a year before that happens," came the reply from Graham Pearson, the 3rd Royal Tank Regiment's Recruiting Sergeant.

"Bugger!" exclaimed I, little realising that in a very short while my Anglo Saxon swearing vocabulary would expand beyond all known boundaries.

So I 'signed on' as a junior soldier and gave my oath of allegiance to Queen and Country with my hand on a small black book. This book was to become my personal copy of *The Soldier's Bible* and I still have it today.

All these thoughts filled my head as I rattled my way up the railway lines towards Bovington Camp in Dorset, the Royal Armoured Corps training centre and my home-to-be for the next fifteen years... The Army.

Later that day, at the end of a long and at times mentally harrowing journey, I arrived at Wool station in Dorset. As I battled my way off the train along with a crowd of other new recruits, all of us dragging our baggage behind us, I became aware of someone shouting. My days as an Army cadet told me to head towards the verbal onslaught echoing along the platform, which I duly did.

Stood at the platform exit was a towering example of British military might. He looked as if he had jumped straight from the pages of an issue of *The Eagle*, where he had been involved in some heroic action. His eyes were dark, pitiless holes, emphasised by the shadow cast from the peak of his parade hat.

The effect of his shouting was amazing. The throng heading towards him parted before him like some biblical sea before Moses. Having passed him by, the human mass closed again in its hurry to get through the gate leading to the buses waiting to transport us to the barracks.

"Come on you miserable little buggers, move out to the buses! Next stop Bovington Camp! You are now ALL at 'er Majesty's pleasure. You there! Yes you... Spotty! Are you a Junior Bleeder? Yes? Well GET ON THE BLOODY BUS THEN!"

Was this it then? A Junior Bleeder? Someone who strange men in large hats hurled verbal abuse at for no apparent reason? Yup, that seemed to sum it up perfectly!

The rest of the day passed in a rush of military precision as we were herded, cajoled and generally pushed into 'the Army way', firstly at the Quartermasters stores...

"You, name? Right bloody stand there. you're in C Squadron."

"You, name? Stand in bloody line for measuring."

"You, name? That's right lad, YOU were made to fit THIS uniform".

At this point my arms were pulled out in front of me and articles of uniform and equipment, including the biggest damned china mug I'd ever seen, were piled indiscriminately onto my now painfully outstretched arms, like a contestant on the popular BBCtv show *Crackerjack*. A belt adorned with various objects mysteriously attached itself around my waist. A storeman's face appeared before me, he winked, smiled and then, having lulled me into a false sense of security, piled even more gear onto my arms, the strain of which made me feel as though I had sustained some incurable injury in my already bursting shoulder sockets.

"Twat," I thought, making use of a new addition to my vocabulary.

Having been fully 'kitted', the next few days consisted of C1 Troop (as we'd become known) being fully inducted into the 'Army way'. One of the first things we were told was that the Army now owned our souls and that we were now a number. Mine was 24358180, definitely a number I shan't forget!

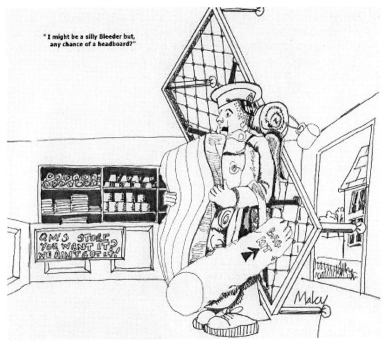

" I might be a silly Bleeder but, any chance of a headboard?"

We were informed that the Army was the only thing we needed, the first proof of this being the haircut. Now the term 'to have one's hair cut' can be viewed in many different ways for a civilian, especially back then in the seventies, when hair length varied between 'slightly effeminate' and 'bloody ludicrous'. However in the Junior Leaders Regiment of The Royal Armoured Corps 'haircut' simply meant you were destined to end up looking like 'the head from hell'. I am sure you could have a skirmish against a hover mower, lose, have most of your hair removed from your head during the fight and still look better than the end result of a 'Sweeny Todd special'. I should, at this juncture, like to point out that J.L.R., as it was known, had a particularly vicious 'Sweeny', who's instructions were quite clear as to how we should look. In a nutshell, bloody bald, or is that as bloody bald as a nutshell? Certainly, after my haircut I couldn't work out which had more hair, my head or my bloody nuts!

As time passed, the great military machine cajoled, manipulated and ground us into professional soldiers, albeit young ones. Our training was a routine, but one that could be changed at any time night or day. All this was (I realise now) carefully constructed to transform our self-motivation from 'I have to do this' to 'I want to do this and give me some more'. Teamwork. A much vaunted but abused term in civilian life. In the Army it has always meant the achieving of a goal by a group of individuals working together to use each other's skills quickly and effectively.

Our first lesson in teamwork was to be 'drilled'. This had nothing to do with dentists, although the pain, at times, could be as intense. Drill is a term is familiar to everyone in the military. Marching; and plenty of it.

How *do* you march? In conceptual terms it's quite simple; its an exaggerated form of walking. Let's face it, as toddlers we learn how to put one foot in front of the other. Well... nobody actually teaches us to walk, we sort of pick it up as we go along. At this stage it is really quite simple. We place our feet down in a happy and timeless manner of coordination. So, why is it so bloody difficult to march? After our first drill lesson we all pondered this problem that evening. I lay on my bed, nursing a blister the size of my head that had manifested itself on my foot and thought that, somehow, walking would never be the same again.

Our 'drill squad' was useless. Our drill sergeant had left us in no doubt of this fact. His terminology was very graphic...

"You useless bunch of fucking scabs!" "You twats! My granny could do better with her fucking formation Zimmer frame team!" "You, that man! Yes you, Lawrence isn't it? Yes I thought so, well you fat bastard, if you go much slower the sun'll melt you like the tub of fucking lard that you are!"

As you can imagine, my vocabulary was expanding at a phenomenal rate. I thank the Lord for the miracle that is the English language. Of course we had plenty of time to digest and practise these expletives as we hobbled around each evening. Our bodies were aching and bruised, somebody had even drawn blood from a blister. My god, that interested us for a whole morbid evening. Also our heads hurt, as we all had to wear the dreaded red and yellow No.2 dress cap – dreadful to look at but a whole lot worse to wear, as the leather sweatband inside pinched your forehead and when you sweated, which was unavoidable, the band seemed to contract and hurt even more. This was, as we called it, a 'twat hat', because that it made you look and feel like a complete twaaaaat.

If at this stage we thought our Drill Sergeant was a shit, we were in for a surprise... Every Saturday morning was a drill morning. On our first Saturday we were introduced to Satan's right hand man. We could hear him long before we could see him. His presence emanated through the entire barracks like a small tactical nuclear bomb. A loud scream echoed across the parade ground announcing his arrival, even though he was some two minutes away from our vicinity. The subject of his tirade was an injured soldier excused duties.

"Get those bloody arms up to your shoulder level! I don't give a flying fuck if it's in plaster you shirker! MOVE! LEFT, RIGHT, LEFT! Get on, move it, move it!"

Our faces must have been a picture. Chins dropped like mechanical shovels, our throats suddenly dry and a general lack of any muscular control.

CRUNCH, CRUNCH, CRUNCH came the sound of hobnailed boots moving along the nearby road in a precise, crisp and strangely menacing manner. Even our Drill Sergeant looked a tad uncomfortable; beads of sweat ran down his neck and darkened his collar. So here it was... Armageddon.

A large guttural clearing of throat and a final crunch of boots and there he was... the personification of evil. The gargantuan creature snapped to a precision halt and flexed his muscular frame. He looked like Blackpool tower with a hat on. Seven feet of man with a head like an artillery shell perched on his shoulders. I can honestly say that I never did see his eyes because, welded to his head, was a Coldstream Guards peaked cap, with the peak slashed so severely that it formed a visor. Under the peak was the tip of his nose and under that a Boer War style moustache, truly magnificent in all its waxed glory.

Tucked into his armpit was a pace stick, and at the base of his immaculately pressed trousers was a pair of 'ammo' boots that had been 'bulled' so much that many a car manufacturer could have learned a great deal about paint finish.

This was Drill Sergeant Major 'B' of the Coldstream Guards. Yes, the Guards. Shit! Drill had really taken a turn for the worse. We never did figure out whether the 'B' was really his name or was to indicate that he was a right proper BASTARD!

Having informed us of his identity and that his sole aim in life was "to make you bastards suffer", he proceeded to watch us in our (suddenly more energetic) demonstrations of drill prowess. It would become second nature to keep our eyes and ears open for any sight or sound of his approach for the duration of our time at J.L.R.

However, it was later said that, when, in our 4th term, our troop became the first drill squad ever to win the drill competition in all four of our terms, that the Sergeant Major had bet a significant amount of cash on our winning. He was seen marching off to the Sergeants Mess bar with a large smirk under his moustache.

Alongside our drill training we were, of course, learning other soldiering skills, such as shooting, camouflage and concealment and other arts of foot soldiering, the emphasis being placed firmly on the fitness of the British soldier. The training was, to say the least, arduous, running for five miles carrying a telegraph pole between four of us was a particular favourite of the PT instructors. At the end of such an exercise our bodies felt as if aliens had snatched us and were just waiting for the opportunity to burst from our chests and leave us for dead. Of course the real catch about the five miles was that this was only the outward leg and we could look forward to the pain of the return to barracks. Well, eventually ... because the PTIs would ensure we saw plenty of sights en route by detouring a few times up and down the notorious 'heartbreak hill', which every British Garrison seems to have in its vicinity. After the first few weeks of this, our bodies and limbs started to swell alarmingly with strange new muscular growths where hitherto only flesh and bone had held sway.

The next favourite form of physical torture was the assault course. This was, to many of my chums and I, quite simply 'something designed by that arsehole Satan and all his little twatting goblins!' Many of us emerged time after time with various levels of injury. It is fair to say that none of us was seriously maimed, but we all had our share of near misses.

The worst days of assault course hammering were, without doubt, in mid-summer, as we launched ourselves across the obstacles fully kitted for action, including wearing full NBC protection and gas masks. NBC, or Nuclear, Biological and Chemical warfare protection, consisted of the 'noddy suit' (so named after our comical appearance when worn): rubber gloves and over-boots teamed with a gas mask (or 'respirator', to give it the technical term). All the articles seemed to be designed to inflict maximum discomfort, although I'm sure that, in the event of a chemical attack, we would have been grateful for its protective qualities.

One thing we never could understand was the inclusion of the word 'nuclear'. Lets face it, if the big bang happened, our earthly remains wouldn't have been substantial enough to fill an ashtray. Hence the saying, 'in the event of a nuclear explosion, remove your respirator, place your head firmly between your knees ... and kiss your arse goodbye!'

"Okay C1 any others amongst you confused over the term 'NODDY SUIT'???!!!"

2.   The Beast

Up to this point I have only spoken about our infantry training or 'grunting', as we called it. The infantry soldier was colloquially known as a 'grunt' (General Recruit, UNTrainable) and therefore participated in the art of 'grunting'.

Now here we were in the Royal Armoured Corps and today would be the first day when we would get to smell, feel and even sit in our first real tank…

The morning started with the obligatory torture of getting run off our feet, then back to the barrack room, a quick shower and change into our overalls. Having got changed, we all formed up for our daily 'first parade', which consisted mainly of our Troop Sergeants inspecting us and informing us of our inadequacies in wearing the Queens uniform.

"What the fuck is that on your head son? A fucking beret? I fucking think not! It looks like you've done a wee in it! Yes, there, look a wee."

With that, the poor unfortunate lad's beret was swiftly plucked from his bonce and the Sergeant 'frisbeed' it across the landscape, while screaming, "WEEEEEEEEEEEEEEEEEEEE!"

The beret came to rest in a suspiciously foul-looking puddle and lay there, looking unwanted and dishevelled.

Having sated himself at the poor chap's expense he then turned to the rest of us and made the long awaited announcement.

"Okay, listen up you crapheads, today is the day, yes the day when you start your transformation from tin to armoured soldiers. I have my doubts whether you'll ever rate as tank men, but the curriculum says we will at least have a crack at training your bloody miserable souls."

With all that cheery repartee we just couldn't wait for this next step in our adventure, so off we marched to a date with destiny, well, with a huge cloud of smoke actually. As we neared the tank hangers all we could hear was a loud wail from an engine as a dense cloud of smoke drifted out from the hanger doors. Then, squeaking, roaring and belching smoke from its exhausts, the beast known as a Chieftain tank loomed into view.

The Chieftain main battle tank had first entered service in the early 1960s, so by the time I first laid my sweaty palms on this one it had already gone through many evolutionary stages to become what stood before us now, the Mark 2. Little did I realise just how many changes were still to happen to Chieftain before its life effectively ended as it handed over the baton to its successor, the Challenger, later in my career. But at this stage, quite frankly, its very presence was awe-inspiring. This leviathan was rated the best MBT in the world... and boy could I sense it.

Our instructor now turned to face us.

"Right lads, it's my dubious honour today to introduce you to the Chieftain Mark 2 MBT, so without further ado... Chieftain Mark 2 this is C1 troop, C1 troop this is Chieftain Mark 2."

He seemed to find this introduction amusing, so we thought it best to politely titter along with him. Having got through this formality he then, amidst much pointing and flailing of limbs, showed us the tank's salient points. He slapped his hand onto the front of the vehicle. "This, my lads, is the glacis plate. No it has got bugger all to do with mints and polar bears. It is, in fact, the thickest piece of armour on the vehicle. It protects the front section of the hull, which is the name for the main body of the tank. Why, I hear you ask is it so important to protect the front? Well it's because we, in British tanks, do not, I repeat DO NOT, show our fucking arses to the enemy at any time. Well, other than if we're doing a moony, but not while we're in a tank! The hole you can see in the glacis plate is the driver's hatch."

Well that sealed it; I would be a driver then. The safest seat in the vehicle, just my cup of tea. I mean, come on, self preservation has to be the greatest natural human instinct, hasn't it?

"Right then, one at a time into the driver's seat and I'll show..."

Stupid bloke, there was no way he was ever going to finish that sentence as we stormed over him as one, all trying to get onto the tank first.

He quickly recouped, "AAAARGH, you bunch of bastards, off the tank NOW and give me fifty pushups!"

Having duly exercised our biceps, we all stood up and cautiously waited our turn to descend into the depths of the drivers cab.

At last it was my turn, I lowered my legs followed by my torso through the opening until I came to rest on the seat. As my eyes became accustomed to the gloom I realised that the drivers cab was in fact fairly cramped. The instructor's hand came in next to my face and began pointing out various features.

"On the left is the control panel for the Generator unit engine which powers the vehicle's electrics. On the right is the control panel for the main engine which gives us our automotive power".

Yes, things were becoming clear, clear as mud anyway!

"Down by your knees", the instructor continued, "That long panel shows you engine revs, speed and a variety of warning lights and gauges".

"Bet you won't be going so bloody fast in a minute while you're each giving me 50 frigging pushups!!!"

This really was becoming confusing.... pushbike to tank was a pretty big jump for a young country lad.

"On the floor you'll see three pedals, right is the accelerator, centre is the brake and on the left the gear change".

"Gear change?" I said.

"Yeah, look, up a bit, in the corner, yes that's it, looks like a motorbike pedal. You hook your toes under it and flick up to change up a gear and put your foot on top of it and push down to change down a gear".

"Oh, I get it", I replied, "But where's the clutch?" My thought was that this snippet of mechanical knowledge would impress him, but of course it didn't.

"What fucking clutch? This is a semi-automatic gearbox, so you don't need a bloody clutch you knobhead!".

How stupid of me, I should have known better. The rest of the troop clustered on the outside of the tank obviously did know better by the way they sniggered loudly at my blatant stupidity.

"Okay, on either side of you is a long stick, these are your steering levers or tillers as we call them. To go left pull the left one and vice versa for right. On the left on the floor is the handbrake".

So far everything seemed fairly straightforward, and of course it was all new and exciting.

"As you are sat now is how the driver sits when driving 'opened up' he explained.

" In battle we close all the hatches of course as we don't want to die, now do we?" Much vigorous shaking of heads from all assembled ensued as the words 'we' and 'dead' sailed through the air.

" The driver has to change his position so that he can close his hatch. He does this by activating these levers on his seat". With that he reached in and pulled on a lever by my side and my backrest shot backwards at the same time as the seat dropped and I smacked the back of my head on the hatch rim as I collapsed with the seat. The result of course (apart from my sore head) was a massive guffaw from the assembled throng.

The instructor regained control of the group and continued relentlessly with his explanations.

"Look behind you monkey face, can you see a headrest flopped down behind you? Good!" Came his reply to his own question.

" Now adjust it upwards until your head is supported by it and you can comfortably see out of the drivers sight above you."

His words had become quite muffled now as I lay in the dark depths of the tank's hull. I fumbled with the headrest and having grazed my head on some protuberance I managed to achieve the required position.

As I peered out of the periscopic sight in front of me, I could clearly see the instructor's head and shoulders as he peered down into the hatch at the area now occupied by my groin.

" Please Sarge, no blow jobs!" Came my witty remark, immediately followed by my witty scream as he punched me straight in my testicles!

" Think you're funny do you lad? Right lets have you out and give me a hundred push ups!"

Having 'nearly' completed the push-ups I climbed up to where the group had clustered around the loaders hatch and the commanders hatch with its surrounding cupola. We all peered in through the open hatches at the instructor who was inside explaining the basics of the 'fighting compartment' as the turret interior was referred to. The Chieftain had a crew of four, we had seen where one lived we could now only wonder as to how the remaining three could fit inside the turrets confines.

" So on the left of the main armament, that's the big gun, is where the radio operator lives. He is also the loader for the guns and also makes the sandwiches and cups of tea. Its fair to say he is the bloke the commander relies on most, so a good operator is worth his weight in gold."

"Bollocks!" I thought, it did seem like a bit of a duff job to me. How the hell was he supposed to load guns, take radio messages and make cups of tea or 'brews' as they were called while buttering bread and all at the same time?"

The plus side to his job was that he had the whole side of the turret to himself (about 3 square feet!), he needed it, my vision was now of some whirling dervish spinning madly in action as he performed these record breaking feats.

The instructor continued with his explanation of the crew positions, "on the right of the main armament sits the gunner." We all peered into the gloom in an attempt to see where the instructors pointing fore digit was aiming. Ah, yes there it was, a seat, well a one-foot square padded bum rest with a none to secure looking collapsible back pad. It had to be collapsible otherwise the gunner simply wouldn't be able to slide down through the turret to get to this position. When the instructor then explained that the tank commander sits above and behind the gunner my mind could only visualise one thing... The gunner would have to be the size of a flaming Pixie! Surely no normal human could fit comfortably into the space the gunner was expected to occupy. Well, as I discovered once I'd struggled down to the depths of that seat, my assessment of the space was indeed correct. Once positioned there I found that the gunner's position was more cramped than I'd imagined. His only view out of the tank was through a one by two inch window placed in the top of his periscopic sight. I think it would be fair to say I've never suffered from claustrophobia but that small space would worry anyone. On the gunner's left, the main armament is basically the only thing he can see and indeed feel as it presses firmly against his left hip and shoulder. On his right are various clusters of controls that project from the turret wall and press into his right side. As I mentioned before, directly in front of his face is the gunner's sight, which, is above his gun controls that in turn protrude on a stanchion into his groin area. Behind him is a gap of about one foot, which, normally would of course house the commanders feet whose knees would then poke into the gunners neck. So that was the gunners lot, sat in a confined space with machinery to his left and front which moves quite alarmingly with the tank's motion. To his right, boxes and controls, which have a dreadful habit of taking chunks of flesh from his limbs and torso if he tries to move. And behind him a commander who the gunner hopes is not of a nervous or indeed athletic disposition. And all this contained in an enforced seating position which makes you look like a garden gnome on a toadstool... sheer luxury! I can hear you all out there (who've not experienced it) just champing at the bit for a go in that seat!

"Shit, ouch, fuck, what the hell!" These exclamations shot from my mouth as someone got in the commanders position behind me, his knees slamming my head into the gunner's sight. Okay, that was it, no way would I be a gunner!

I do not intend to dwell at this stage on the operator or commander's positions, as more will be said in later chapters of my tale.

Having completed our internal tour of the turret we were once more outside. The instructor was now telling us about the chieftain's fire fighting equipment.

"Okay lads, should the enemy be lucky enough to hit your Tonka toy and it brews up... get the fuck out... and run like hell for your lives!"

What? Tonka toy? Brew up.... in the middle of a battle? I was convinced the instructor had been using some trick and somehow got pissed without our knowing. The look of bemusement on our faces triggered an explanation and we learnt 'Tonka toy' was a term of endearment for MBT'S in the same way that 'Dinky toy'' was for the smaller armoured vehicles. 'Brew up' was in fact not only a term for making tea, but also an expression for the vehicle being hit by an enemy shot, catching fire and subsequently burning the crew alive! UUMMM... nice!

The instructor jolted us from our contemplation of death by continuing his explanation.

"Of course the main reason for the fire equipment is so you can put out fires which you start without the help of our enemies!"

Oh shit this didn't sound any better at all, why would we want to set fire to our home? Was the ministry insured for our antics? Slowly, as the lesson continued all became clear.

"Should the engine catch fire as can happen, we have two large foam extinguishers in the drivers cab, these pump foam to the engine compartment and it smothers the fire."

Damned clever all this, thought I, but somehow I had a sneaking suspicion that if the enemy didn't get us, our tank would!

" Also, situated at various points inside and outside the vehicle are 5 small, hand held extinguishers. These are for dealing with small fires such as rag or paper, which ignites on something hot. YOU ARE NOT, I REPEAT, NOT ALLOWED TO SMOKE ON TANKS!" he then bellowed.

Ever onwards we went on our tour of chieftain. Next was the engine compartment. Nestled none too comfortably on the left was the generator unit engine or G.U.E as it was referred to in technical terms. Over the following years we all simply referred to it as the 'Jenny'. So there it sat, covered in black, sticky, congealed oil looking like a malignant growth inside the silver painted hull. This engine supplied electrical power to the tank. If this engine failed all was not lost as the main engine had a generator fitted, the only drawback being that unlike an alternator which operates constantly at any engine rpm, this meant the driver keeping his foot on the accelerator to maintain the engine revs above 1000r.p.m. Not bad when stationary, but engaging first gear from neutral could be a tad tricky, as many whip lashed crews will testify.

Across the back of the compartment was the gearbox. This was painted green unlike the engines, which were 'duck egg blue'. It was a very large gearbox I remember thinking. But it became apparent that its size was required to transmit the engine power to the tracks and move all 56tons from point to point.

Having been shown the engine compartment that would be the last I'd see of it before leaving J.L.R.

The instructor completed our tour and proceeded to quiz our newly found knowledge of chieftain.

"What calibre is the main armament..? Trooper Blythe?"

"Er, um.." Started the reply.

"Too fucking slow, give me fifty pushups you twat!" Barked the Sergeant.

"Tell him... Trooper... Jones!"

"You didn't tell us Sarge".

"Bollocks, down fifty!"

This questioning continued until not only our brains ached but also every sinew in our tortured bodies. Eventually the Sergeant gave up and ran us twice through the nearby assault course in frustration screaming at us all the way.

So ended our first real encounter with the tank.

3. Adventure training

During training at J.L.R each of the 4 terms we went away to a permanent camp near Plymouth on the cliffs just outside the village of Down Thomas. These visits were each of two weeks duration and were centred on adventure training activities to 'build our characters'. What that actually meant was …'let's bugger the boys about until they get really tetchy and pissed off!'

Our camp was simply a cluster of nissen huts huddled together against the weather blowing in off the English Channel. In fact our Troop only spent our first term at 'Renney' as it was known (Renney Lentney) being the full name of the location. The following three terms were spent at other locations.

Adventure training to me was simply another form of physical hell to be endured. Certain aspects were highly enjoyable, some dreadful, but they all contained elements that made your muscles and blisters ache.

We usually had reveille at 05:00 and were leaping naked like merboys from rocks into the sea by 05:30. Boy oh boy, what a fine falsetto choir we made as we screamed from the chill of our morning dip. From there our activities centred on canoeing, rock climbing, pot holing and lots and lots of walking, not to forget lots and lots of running of course.

In our second term we were based at an old Royal Naval site, Pier Cellars in Cornwall near Cawsands. This base during the Second World War had been used to house mini submarines and featured a small

"Seals? Off Devon? Naw, they be they bleddy Junior somats down
from Dorset........behave like bleddy Idiots they do!!!"

walled harbour at the cliff base. Perched high above on the cliff top was our accommodation, a couple of huts (for us) and a house (for instructors). The cliff top and base were joined by a truly awesome flight of stone steps.

Slung around and over the top of the harbour was the inevitable assault course. We would, of course come to hate this object of mans ability to make the hard, even harder.

Every morning at 05:00, foot inspection, but only after you had run top to bottom down the cliff steps, barefoot of course. Dirty feet? Of course! Bad soldier? Of course! Into the fucking sea as punishment? Of course! Naked? Well... of fucking course!

Having completed this ritual, run back up the steps clutching our frozen genitals in case they should fall off and have us chasing them back down the steps, change into full combat gear, run back down the steps and run three times over the assault course.

As I mentioned before, the assault course crossed the harbour waters. On our third lap of the course our Sergeants would stand at opposing ends of the rope across the harbour and try (mostly succeeding) to shake you off into the waters below.

It was during one such foray that I sustained my first injury. While doing a marvellous impression of a springbok in full flight, I fell over and damaged my knee and was taken to a naval hospital for examination. No serious damage done was the verdict, and so with my knee firmly bandaged I was returned to camp. For the rest of that camp I was classed as a light duties case. That is, apart from one day when we went to an abandoned flooded quarry near Gunnislake. The quarry had a huge cliff some 110 feet high. On this cliff we were to practice abseiling down ropes and the famous 'death slide'. Due to my knee I was deemed unfit for abseiling but I was allowed to take the death slide if I felt up to it.

The more aggressive members of our group obviously felt I was fit enough and cajoled me into agreeing. As I stood at the cliff edge, I looked down the length of the rope at the bank opposite some 100 feet below. Positioned there were the 'brakemen'. These colleagues of mine were to hold a length of rope slung over the slide rope taught to slow the descent of the 'slider' when the block and tackle he was grasping came into contact with said rope. If this were not done, the next point of braking would be the tree to which the bottom end of the slide rope was anchored.

As I stared downwards the full horror of my situation hit me. There, gleefully staring back at me were the faces of two bullying ringleaders. I looked around, but the pleading look on my face had no effect on the instructor.

"Off you go lad!" Followed by "Banzai" he screamed as he pushed me off and I hurtled towards my fate. The trees came rushing to greet me as I heard the 'brakemen' laugh, and true to form I whooshed straight through their feeble braking attempt and ended up in the tree, suspended upside down by my injured knee. The two lads responsible for my shouting in agony got 50 push-ups each, but I think they deemed that as worthwhile having seen the agony on my face.

In our third term we spent our two weeks split between Renney and in some tin shacks at Willsworthy Down on Dartmoor near Okehampton. I say tin shacks and that was exactly what they were. Constructed of tin sheeting on concrete slabbed floors. The first couple of days passed fairly uneventfully as we did run after run between various moorland features. However it was bitterly cold, and one evening as dusk drew in, our troop sergeant gazed at the sky murmuring to himself. His murmuring resulted in a loud "fucking snow" and with that we all went to our sleeping bags and thought no more of it. Not until we woke up next morning anyway. Then as I awoke I glanced at the far end of the hut and pondered as to why I could see daylight through the roof. Through the roof? Fucking hell! Where was the fucking roof? I was in fact staring at a gaping hole where that end of the roof had been the previous evening. Beneath the hole lay a massive pile of snow, and surprise, surprise the mound could move of its own volition, fucking hell! it even had two pairs of eyes and could swear most violently!

"Fuck me what's this shit?" it said.

Then it quite violently erupted, and two of my chums appeared still zipped up in their sleeping bags, they proceeded to hop around trying to escape their predicament looking for the entire world like some crazed sack race.

Eventually they escaped their duck down lined prisons and headed, like the rest of us, for the door. This was no panic driven exodus; it was merely our newly awoken bodies expressing the need for early morning bladder release. A need made more desperate by the bitter cold that beset us upon waking.

Shock, dismay, desperation and generally pissed off were the expressions on our faces as we attempted to open the door. 'Piggy' Humphries was trying to open the door unsuccessfully and only when five other lads joined in did the door eventually open, but only then because it was kicked down. We then discovered the reason was that a huge snowdrift was blown up along that entire side of the building.

Having got our ablutions finished, and attired ourselves in more kit than an Eskimo sees in an entire lifetime, we paraded.

As we stood shivering in three ranks our sergeants told us that our situation was... "No gas, water or communications, so we're up shit creek in a leaky canoe with no paddles. We'll just sit tight and wait for help".

We soon found out that 'sit tight' actually meant 'run four miles in full kit with weapons!' I cannot begin to explain how difficult this was in deep snow. Eventually we came to a small hamlet where, to our surprise we found a teashop open. So in we tramped and proceeded to thaw all over the carpets. I don't think the staff minded as sales rocketed, and 'off season' too.

Either way the day ended with a rescue mission which removed us from the wilds of Dartmoor and deposited us back in a snowy but relatively safe Renney Lentney.

" Come on you orrible little oiks - get a bloody move on and let's dig out............................the whole of bloody Dartmoor!!"

My last recollection of adventure training is that one fresh morning we were loaded onto trucks and driven to an outward-bound centre near Ashburton in Devon. There we were thrown across the mother of all assault courses known as the 'Ashburton high ropes'. This 'confidence' course was a cunningly designed course of ropes, which peaked at around fifty feet up in the treetops. Fifty feet? It may as well have been five hundred feet for a lad nervous of heights like me. Never the less, we all completed this trip of terror without incident.

Having just calmed the adrenalin surge I had just experienced, I realised with dismay that there was more fun instore for us. We didn't know what lay ahead as we marched single file off down a lane.

Our destination, it turned out, was Holne Chase Bridge. We were halted out of sight of the bridge and a Sergeant came up the line numbering us. Number fifteen, or me as I was known, received the number and a slap on the shoulder. We were then informed that we were to jump from the bridge into the swirling dark waters of the river below. I glanced nervously around but was met with other eyes all displaying alarm and fear. The questions flashing through my mind were why? What for? And me! Die?

Obviously the concepts of character and confidence building still hadn't penetrated the quivering grey matter in my skull.

Then came the briefing.

"Right chaps, the technique is to jump feet first as if you're standing to attention. If you flap your arms, you won't fly, you'll fucking belly flop! And from about 40 feet that'll hurt!"

Thanks a bloody bunch! Thought I, that's me done for! As I visualised my ungainly entry to the black depths of the river.

"As you touch the water open your legs wide and put your arms out to the sides, this will slow your descent!"

I could imagine this action doing more than slowing my descent, in fact my testicles were already somewhere in my throat as they fought for self preservation.

"When you surface, shout your number and name so we know you're okay".

You bastard, keep talking, I'm not ready yet, I thought. But no, that was it; Number one was escorted from our sight to the bridge.

There followed screams and shouting amidst splashing as the poor soul launched himself into the abyss.

So, here we were, number fifteen was called forward and with trembling legs I walked forward to the bridge parapet.

The instructor slapped me on the shoulder, winked and then shouted, "GO!"

To my amazement I reacted automatically and jumped.

The sensation of flying was great, everything suddenly seemed to slow down and I realised I was actually enjoying myself.

Then... the shock of cold water. The freezing water quite literally suspended my breathing. Cold? That's an understatement! I sank down and, due to the rivers low level in autumn, hit the riverbed. As I pushed off towards the surface my only thought was AIR.

As my head appeared out of the bubbling torrent all thoughts of "fifteen" and "Okay sir" were long gone.

"Fuck me, that's fucking freezing" shot from my mouth.

"I take it you're okay then number fifteen?" Came a shout from the riverbank.

One man of course had to do it wrong. Trooper Mason flew like a bird but entered the water head first damaging his teeth in the process. This resulted in false teeth and earned him the nickname of 'chopper'. So then are military nicknames born?

4. Pass off or piss off

So here we were, Fourth termers, the senior troop ready for one final term and then off to our Regiments. This term was known as 'Pass off' or more colloquially as 'Piss off' term. At the end of term we would endure one last 'Pass off' parade and that was it, J.L.R. over and done with. I and three of my pals had opted for The Third Royal Tank Regiment. This was due to our Westcountry heritage and 3R.T.R.'s name as 'The West Country's Own Armoured Regiment". We soon found that other members of our troop also knew it as either, 'The Armoured farmers' or 'The Third Rusty Tractor Regiment'.

I should at this juncture like to take the opportunity to explain a little about the Royal Armoured Corps.

The Corps consisted of a mix of cavalry units, which had swapped their 'nags' for armour prior to World War Two and The Royal Tank Regiment. The RTR was split into 4 Regiments numbered one to four (the number of R.T.R's had once peaked in the high sixties), the RTR had been formed during the First World War to man the new secret weapon, the Tank. The title The Royal Tank Regiment was the collective title for all four Regiments as they were, in certain respects, a Corps within a Corps. Headquarters R.A.C. was shadowed by Headquarters The R.T.R. The R.T.R. has over its relatively short history by Cavalry standards evolved in line with tanks themselves. This was initially due to a marked lack of interest in armour shown by sceptical Cavalry traditionalists who regarded tanks as a non-starter in the early 20th century.

However, at Horse Guards one day when an esteemed Cavalry General was heard to say "Bloody Tanks! Scrap the bally lot of them, that's what I say!" Unfortunately for him it was the visiting King who heard the comment as he exited a nearby toilet buttoning his uniform. The King promptly wiped his hands down his trousers, squared up in front of the General and loudly shouted in his face... "You know what Rodney? I'm just about totally pissed off with all this twatting cavalry this and cavalry that so... from now on the tank Corps is bally mine and it's earned the name Royal tank Corps!" The Cavalry had inevitably lost their cause and by the end of 1939 had traded their trusty steeds for a more modern method of conducting warfare. This has always been the source of mainly good-humoured rivalry between 'Tankies' and the

'Donkey wallopers'. The 'Tankies' always maintained they were the true tank soldiers.

Anyway, back to J.L.R. and term four.

It was a great feeling, here we were, the senior 'Bleeders' on camp, the new recruits looking at us already as if we were adults.

This was also the term of confirmation; all our training would be tested. We had all by now, been trained as Radio operators, and Gunner/Loaders.

Through Gunnery training I had also begun smoking, purely peer pressure I can assure you.

During firing days on the range at Lulworth in Dorset the three tanks that we used for training were grossly over manned by the thirty of us. Obviously we couldn't all fire the guns at the same time so we did a substantial amount of waiting around. During one such period I was given a cigarette and WAS accepted into the club. Comradeship for us was simply sharing a fag and a 'yarn' or two.

The Gunnery training itself was actually very stimulating. From the first minute you are encouraged to shout as loudly as possible. This is not as strange as it may sound, the 'drills' involved in Gunnery have to be as automated as possible. All your actions are 'drills' which have been formed so that the crew become part of the machine for efficiency and for safety. At this point it became apparent as to why we had endured so much marching.

We were now to operate as part of a tank crew, a team in the true meaning of the word.

The gunnery instructors were the commanders and we juniors made up the gunners and loaders. This was now 'it' we had arrived on 'ranges'. Up until this point all our training had consisted of practising drills in a 'mock up' turret using dummy or 'drill' ammunition. This gunnery simulator allowed us to do everything except fire real ammunition at a target. Now though was the time for big bangs and the rattle of machine gun fire.

At this time Chieftain's armament consisted of three machine guns (Mg's) and the 120mm main armament. The MGs were firstly a.50 calibre browning, which was used as a ranging gun to find the range to a target without wasting main armament ammo. The other two MGs were 7.62mm general-purpose machine guns (GPMG) or 'jimpies' as we knew them. One of these was in the turret and the other was situated on the commander's cupola for his use. The use for both being, the destruction of Infantry forces.

Chieftain's 120mm ammunition was ground breaking; it was a separate charge (bagged charge) and projectile (proj). The bagged charge is ignited by a brass cartridge (vent tube). When the bagged charge is ignited it creates pressure, which forces the projectile on its way to the target.

The art of loading the main armament is a skill which when viewed in full flow is a most impressive sight. There is a rhythm and efficiency, which actually belies the weight of the objects being handled.

Projectiles, as I mentioned these are the objects, which fly out the end of the main armament and smash the target into eternal damnation! The 'proj' came in two main forms, firstly the A.P.D.S or as we knew it 'sabot'. This armour defeating nature of ammo flew through the air at upwards of a gut wrenching 1400 meters per second, flew in a straight line and basically went straight through the enemy tank and out the other side. The mess left between the enemy tank's walls would have kept police scenes of crime officers picking up pieces of human remains for months.

British tanks traditionally have always had rifled barrels. It was always said they were more accurate, I believe the real reason was more like 'you can fire a fucking long way more accurately'. This brings me to the next proj, the H.E.S.H round or simply 'hesh' as we called it. The hesh round is a 'chemical energy' nature of ammunition. Where sabot engagements would be expected in Europe to be at a typical distance no greater than 2400 metres which involved direct sight, one shot, quickly with a guarantee of 'first time hit', hesh was a different beast altogether. Hesh was a fairly languid proj; it flew at around 600 metres per second with a burning trace element in its tail for spotting fall on target. So with a forward spotting facility Chieftain could in fact engage targets at around 8 Kilometres.

At shorter distances the gunner could see his own tracer and correct his own fall of shot. Sabot was very much 'fire and forget' too quick for the human eye, but it did have a magnesium tip which flashed as it hit a solid object such as the enemy tank. This could be seen even through the obscuration that firing it created. The hesh however could be seen as it adopted its 'looping' trajectory, created by the copper 'driving band' wrapped around its shell, driving the shell through the barrels rifling setting it spinning. The hesh round is probably the only reason British tank guns have remained rifled. For accurate long-range gunnery a traditional trajectory is required and hesh fits the bill. It is however an armour defeating round, as the name implies it works by coming down on armour plate, the explosive head squashes against the armour and in the tail is a fuse which, as the last thing to make contact, sets off the squashed explosive head. This does not penetrate the armour but sets up a massive shock wave through the armour. Inside the target, an effect called 'scabbing' takes place. This basically means that anything bolted to the turret interior flies off and proceeds to 'eat' the tank's crew. The actual 'scabs' are large flakes of armour of considerable weight, which break from the tanks structure with edges as sharp as the average razor blade and proceed to dissect the already mutilated crew.

I've no doubt that the uninitiated among you, having realised that there is no painless or quick death in a tank would have no intention of manning such a machine. The truth is it only ever made us more determined to 'get the other bastard first'.

To enable us to get that other bastard first, we needed a brilliant loader to keep loading ammunition as quickly as possible.

As the loader strives to increase his pals survival rate he gets a 'loaders rash'. This is the term for all the lacerations and bruises he receives from hurriedly smashing his limbs into the extremities of the guns. The loader's activities are, if he's good, carried out at breathtaking speed. As he punches round after round of ammo into the breech he smashes his hands into the surrounding metalwork. The forces exerted in loading I have always likened to punching a moving truck. Yes, okay, so nobody punches moving trucks, but at least I can imagine what it would be like. The loader is the man that is relied on most heavily in the heat of battle, no matter what happens it comes down to whoever loads and fires fastest, survives the longest. So teamwork really does matter in this kind of environment. As training progresses it becomes more and more apparent how every member of the crew is vital in the achievement of the common goal, survival. As for the loader? I can never forget when my gunnery instructor told me that, "A good loader is measured by how much blood is left on the breech!"

I shall probably never be told how good a loader I was, but I did leave, what seemed like a few gallons of blood on every breech that was in my charge.

As I mentioned earlier, our other trade training had been as radio operators. This was definitely NOT the most interesting facet of training. In fact it was, mostly, quite boring. We spent a great deal of time in classrooms learning about radio frequency theory, basic electricity and voice procedure (signals jargon for speaking drills). These voice procedures are the means by which soldiers converse with each other on the airwaves in a laid down, security conscious method.

All this, combined with practical training on the radio sets themselves taught us how to be proficient operators. We proved this by embarking on numerous exercises. Up and down hills we went on these occasions, either sat in speeding Landrovers as they whizzed through the narrow winding lanes of Dorset, or more commonly on our poor feet. An A41 'man-pack' radio leaves huge dents in your back we quickly discovered after 10 miles lugging it round. Coupled with the fact that radio waves communicate better from the top of large hills and there you have it,

"Nothing heard........out!!"

pure misery. Sod being a 'Grunt'. During our exercise period if anyone had wanted to see a soldier, all he had to do was find a high enough hill. Having climbed said hill he would have found a pile of bodies with a long antenna stuck out of the middle. Sounds would be emanating from the gaggle that sounded like a piglet being turned alive on a spit. The sounds of course would be coming from the radio in our midst as we unsuccessfully attempted to tune it in.

The old 'Larkspur' range of radio equipment was designed specifically to improve the average soldiers use of expletives. Abuse flew everywhere as our best attempts at using the set were continually thwarted.

As we huddled around this object of our frustration, one of us would come up with a fresh idea on how to facilitate speech between 'control' and us. This would be taken in, digested, cast to one side and we would all resume kicking the hell out of the radio. Then, as if by magic, through the atmospheric mush, which was such a trade mark of 'Larkspur' sets, a faint message could be heard.

"H..llo....three four...this..is....radio ch...ck, over".

A swift kick to fine tune reception, then there it was again.

"Hello three four this is zero, radio check, over".

Hoo.. fucking..ray, success, we scrambled to grab the microphone and reply.

"Three four okay over!" God we were chuffed with ourselves.

"Zero, where have you been, over?" Came the response.

"Three four, er, er, we had trouble with our, er, er, means, over". This was the only thing we could think to say.

"Zero, roger, get a grip, out!" Came controls terse reply.

To clarify, 'means' is jargon for the radio set itself. You never mention the radio set itself over the air. This apparently would let the enemy know you're communicating with a radio! This is of course if, in their vodka induced stupor, they haven't already fathomed out what you're using to speak to each other.

Either way we had communicated for around ten seconds, covered up our ineptitude with the radio and proven what a good kick on transistors could achieve. All we had to do now was, walk all the way back to camp.

We were however not alone in our radio problems. The 'Larkspur' range of equipment we had at that time were antiquities of a bygone era, and were anything but efficient. All of the sets, C42,B47,C13 and our loathed A41 man pack needed constant molly coddling. Their tendency to 'wander' off frequency was a constant source of frustration.

More about radios later, suffice it to say that we youngsters were confronted with a bewildering array of technology, terminology and secret codes.

This then has covered most of the training we 'Bleeders' received at J.L.R. R.A.C. We were now nearing the end of our stay. We took all the trade tests required for our immediate 'adult' career as either a gunner or radio operator. Alongside these we took tests on so-called ancillary subjects such as the aforementioned N.B.C. warfare, the test consisted of being thrown into a large tent full of tear gas. We then had to carry out certain drills. You would think having completed the drills that would be it? Wrong, the instructor would now loom out of the gas cloud at you, his wild staring eyes leering out of his respirator eyepieces. A muffled instruction would come to you and you would have to unmask, shout your name, rank and army number and then leave the tent.

My turn came, I unmasked, shouted the required information and then, opened my bloody eyes to find the exit, what a mistake! Searing pain, agony, it was all there in an instant. I fell through the exit, collapsing on the ground outside in a heap and an urge to vomit my lungs out overtook my body. I had you see, managed to take a breath of tear gas. I was, of course, not alone, those that had preceded me were already in their death throes. Another instructor walked around telling us to stand up, walk around, take deep breaths and try to stand in a breeze to clear any residual gas from our bodies. Tried it, tried it again, failed. It didn't help for some time. Later that day we jumped in the showers and the heat from the water set off residual gas caught on our skin. Off we went again, writhing in agony until the vapours cleared! We also had N.B.C. theory tests. These lessons had scared us out of our skins. Would we ever find a pleasant, quick death? Still, at sixteen or seventeen who really cares?

Either way, this was all behind us now, only two words had our attention from here on in.... 'Pass off!'

All our training was now complete and our endless drill parades would soon culminate in the pass off parade. All our families and friends were invited to this ceremony and it would be our chance to preen and strut in front of our loved ones. Parade over we would share tea with them all and then disperse for a spot of 'leave' and then on to our adult life. Of course, if we had thought that we had done enough drill we were sadly mistaken. Our last term started with a vengeance on the parade square. We had already paraded on three pass offs as previous Junior Leaders had come of age and duly left Bovington. But this was special, whereas previously we had only served as 'background extras', this time we would be centre stage. Consequently our standard of marching had to be special.

Our parade would be in the summer of 1976 and I remember so well that it was a damned hot summer. We not only had to contend with aching feet and leg muscles, but also with the fact that our brains were bloody boiling! The 'twat hats' took on a new vengeance as our very heads swelled in the intense heat. Luckily we future 'Tankies' could look forward to our dress headgear becoming The R.T.R black beret No.1. A whole lot more comfortable than the J.L.R twat hats. We knew this as we had already been measured and fitted for our smart new Regimental uniforms. Boy what pride we felt at the Quartermasters as we tried on our regalia, comparing the various traditions displayed on ours, and our colleagues different uniforms. I thought that although the plainest, the R.T.R uniform with its traditional 'Tank arm badge' sewn on the right arm and the lanyard in regimental colour was the smartest. The colour of lanyard as I've mentioned was in the colour associated with each of the four Regiments, 1st R.T.R, red, 2nd, yellow, 3rd Brunswick green and the 4th, Navy blue. The 'Tank arm badge' was in the shape of a First World War tank and had originally been awarded to crewmen who had qualified in tank training. But by now had become simply a symbol of tradition although it was, and no doubt still is, worn with pride.

Our dress beret looked particularly smart. It was firstly, as with the R.T.R 'working' beret, true black, a distinction of the R.T.R originating once again from shortly after the regiments inception. All other 'black' berets you see in the British army are in fact dark blue. Secondly it was raised high on the left to accommodate the wearing of a 'hackle' behind the cap badge. The hackle was a spray of feathers being vertically banded in the three colours of the R.T.R flag, brown, red and green, signifying 'from the mud, through the blood to the green fields beyond. Not of course the official motto of 'Fear naught' on our cap badge, but somehow it sums up the 'Tankies' life. We were also to receive our first issue of the tank Regiments other unique item of uniform, the famous black overalls. God, the anticipation fair took my breath away.

But, back to the last term. We spent hour after hour on the drill square tramping around to the beat of a single bass drummer hammering out the pace of the marching. We were practising carrying the armoured soldiers personal weapon, the Sterling sub machine gun. Not a particularly heavy or bulky weapon but when marching it was carried one handed across the chest. It felt like a dumbbell after just a half hour of drill practise.

During these lengthy sessions we also perfected the art of standing still. 'Still', yes it means precisely what it says. Sounds easy? Well try it for an hour or two in blazing sunlight! Bollocks to easy, it hurts like hell. As we stood there films such as 'Beau Geste' sprang to mind. Many was the man who simply fainted from the prolonged effects of standing still in that awful heat. We were told that the oldest trick was to wiggle our toes inside our boots! Wiggle? We couldn't even feel our bloody toes! But we tried and achieved limited success. The other 'lack of circulation beater' was to very gently rock on the balls of your feet. But we couldn't move? Well apparently we had to perfect this without looking like we were moving. Yeah, okay, no fucking chance!

Most of us who rocked were simply on the first move in the act of falling flat on our faces from heat exposure! But fainting as we quickly learnt, was not a good idea. The first chap we saw faint did manage to stay at attention as instructed and fall flat on his face. We then heard the crunch of running boots as two orderlies ran across the square to remove this offending object. They arrived, grabbed him each hooking their hands in one of his armpits, lifted and dragged him face down from the square. We could hear the scrape of his toecaps as he was dragged away. I could almost hear all of us thinking "Fuck, he'll have to re-bull his boots now!" This was for us, probably the biggest deterrent from fainting. Suddenly we became as rocks baking in the sun. Pity the poor bastards in the cavalry units who would have the extra pain of their individual units' 'twat hats'.

It was worth it though to be able each evening to swagger around barracks in our regimental regalia. We suddenly became objects of wonder, the younger 'bleeders' gawking at us in much the same way as we had looked at our predecessors before. We knew how much they must have already longed for their own pass off term.

Honesty permits me to say that from that time until my last day of service, I was always proud to wear my uniform. Even the mentality of any 'bullies' seemed to mellow as if suddenly we had matured and become united in one aim. Our one thought had become Regimental pride and our bearing reflected this.

I refuse to slur the reputation of the modern Army as it is still full of fine men and women doing a superb job. However as with all professions, I am prepared to say that during my career I saw a vast change in the reasons for joining and the attitudes of youngsters in the service. I saw everything from the great 'dole queue escapes' of the late seventies to the 'seemed like a good idea at the time' attitudes of the eighties. Unfortunately quite a high proportion of these people fell by the way. I say unfortunately as many who left had very promising futures before them. Had they made more of a 'go of it' they may have found a more rewarding future.

Anyway, the great morning of the pass off had arrived and with it the bloody sun. A certain amount of trepidation showed on our faces as we went to breakfast. Silent prayers were heading heavenward "please god, don't let me fucking faint!" being the favourite. As we entered the cookhouse our Troop Sergeant greeted us. He stood there like a priest offering Holy Communion. Before him his altar was a table with saucers of salt tablets and plastic cups of water. "Take, eat, drink" he intoned. At this point the Holiness ended, as we swallowed the foul mixture he spoke again.

"Fucking faint and I'll poke my drill stick up your arse and march you round like a lollipop on a stick!" Came the threat.

Having digested both the 'anti fainting' tablets and our breakfast, we returned to our rooms. There we put the finishing touches to our uniforms. My 'hackle' was really giving me problems. It had taken on the characteristics of a flightless bird with ruffled plumage. Try as I might I couldn't get the three colours of the feathers to form clear borders between the colours. I'm sure this was more due to my nerves than anything, but with perseverance I got them to behave.

Having adjusted ourselves to our Troop Sergeants satisfaction, we 'shouldered arms' and swaggered off to the parade.

The main act of the parade was when the pass off Troops from each Squadron split off and marched out to form squads in their new Regimental Groups. I proudly marched out to join my colleagues in the 3 R.T.R squad. Once assembled, we all marched in order of Regimental seniority past the saluting dais. Having completed the last of our duties on the square we 'marched off' to be with our families for tea and the obligatory group photos.

This had been it then, four terms of hardship, madness and fun. With mixed feelings I exited Stanley barracks, I glanced back to see that barrack life was already returning to normal.

My only thought was, no longer was I a 'Bleeder' or a 'Tin soldier, now I was a 'Tankie' and proud of it.

5. 'Tankie'

Having completed my embarkation leave at home, I once again waved farewell to my family from a train and started my journey to 3 R.T.R in Germany as part of The British Army of The Rhine.

My first station with the Third tanks was Fallingbostel in Northwestern Germany. To get there involved my first flight from Luton to Hanover. The mere idea of flying didn't exactly fill me with joy. But the flight passed uneventfully, well until we approached the landing anyway. As we descended the Captain announced that the engine noise would increase and we shouldn't be alarmed as it was simply the reverse thrust as we braked.

The wheels had touched down and it was then that my world fell apart. I was seated behind the wing looking at the back of an engine when suddenly a huge section of the engine seemed to fall down. I stared stupefied at this catastrophe while shaking the passenger next to me and gesticulating at the disaster outside. My neighbour glanced out the window and started to laugh at my predicament. He then explained that the engines rear section had in fact folded downwards to angle the thrust downwards to help the reverse thrust take effect. This information digested, I relaxed and removed my fingers from where they had embedded themselves in my seats armrests.

Once we had left the plane and entered the arrivals terminal, Army transport staff ushered us to buses departing to our respective stations.

My first impressions of Fallingbostel station in 1976 were of a cosy, warm, comfortable, casually paced lifestyle. It certainly was a very pleasant place to be stationed in. This was due to the relatively small amount of British troops in the garrison.

Upon arrival at the barracks we were sorted into which Squadrons would be our new families. The Regiments organisation at that time consisted of five Squadrons. Firstly there was Headquarters Squadron (HQ Sqn) which was colloquially known as 'Stone dead Squadron', this was due to the somewhat senior ages of Squadron Members. The Squadron housed all the support functions such as the two Quartermasters departments, Technical stores, which looked after the vehicular side of the Regiment and, the Regimental Quartermaster Sergeant (RQMS) stores or 'QM boots and socks' as it was affectionately known. Also in this squadron was the supporting staff such as cooks from the Army Catering Corps. As well as these departments, it also contained Motor transport troop (MT), which consisted of HGVs and ancillary support vehicles.

Next came Command and Support Squadron (C& S Sqn), this as the name implies was the command cell of the Regiment. This Squadron contained the tanks of the Regiment's Commanding Officer and his Second in command and a third 'spare' Tank. Also in C&S were the Regimental support troops such as the Reconnaissance (Recce) Troop of Scimitar CVRTs (Combat vehicle Reconnaissance, Tracked), Guided weapons (GW) or 'Gobbly Wobbly' Troop with their FV438 Swingfire vehicles. RHQ Troop apart from the 3 tanks already mentioned also had Ferret scout cars with extra radio equipment and personnel carriers converted for command vehicle use.

Next came the three remaining Squadrons, A, B and C Squadrons. These were collectively referred to as Sabre Squadrons as they were the M.B.T Squadrons expected obviously to be in the thick of the fighting.

Each Sabre Squadron was sub divided into five Troops. Top of the pile was Squadron Headquarters (SHQ); which contained not only the Sqn Leader and his 2i/c's tank but also a further tank with a dozer blade attachment, a tracked Ambulance and his Squadron Quartermaster's (SQMS) group or 'packet' as it was known.

The remaining troops were once more referred to as Sabre Troops. In 3 RTR the Troop numbering system began with 1 to 4 troops in A Squadron, 5 to 8 troops in B Squadron and then 9 to 12 troops in C Squadron. This was unique in each Regiment of the RTR. The accepted practice elsewhere was 1 to 4 troop in each Squadron. 2 RTR for example did and still have unique names for Squadrons i.e. A Squadron is Ajax, B Squadron is Badger and C Squadron is Cyclops, interestingly their HQ Squadron is known as Nero – we all know what that emperor did don't we? Fiddled while Rome burnt the fuck down... eh?

Each sabre troop consisted of 3 chieftain mark 2s. SHQ had the latest, modified vehicles making them mark 2xy's.

Finally each Squadron had a Light Aid Detachment (LAD) of Royal Electrical & Mechanical Engineers (REME) attached for first line recovery and repair of vehicles. These erstwhile chaps were always accepted and treated as integrated members of our family.

This then was the organisation (in a nutshell) of 3 RTR in 1976. I found myself placed as a Gunner.... (Gunner? Oh shit, thought I) in SHQ Troop, C Squadron. I had discovered that 'Nigs' (new in greens) were automatically placed as gunners. 'Nigs' were the lowest of the low, new boys as yet not accepted due to their lack of experience. If ever a nasty duty or fatigue was coming up " put the fucking nig on it" could be heard for miles.

Those first few weeks in my new home confused me somewhat. Gone were the tight-lipped instructors who had tormented me during training. Here NCOs talked to people properly. There was definitely a feeling of 'family' in 3 R.T.R. I believe this was, and probably still is, due to the need for working in such close proximity with each other. I am certain that this is apparent in all armoured regiments. Rank in most aspects was not a matter of social barrier building. Officers were obviously addressed as 'Sir'. The Regimental Sergeant Major was always spoken to as 'Your Worshipfulness', normally whilst on bended knee.

The squadron rank structure was, the O.C. a Major, the 2ic a Captain, and then came the Senior NCOs. Firstly the Squadron Sergeant Major (SSM). then came the S.Q.M.S a Staff Sergeant. The Sabre troops each had a Troop Leader who was normally a Lieutenant, but my experience was that each of 3rd tanks squadrons had one sabre troop whose troop leaders was a senior Staff Sergeant. This was blamed on a shortage of recruits into the officer ranks. It was perhaps that the R.T.R. was regarded as not having the history and glamour of the cavalry regiments. Certainly a nickname of the R.T.R. was 'the poor mans cavalry'. This was because a fair amount of our officers joined as 'university entrants' fresh from further education. However that was not a bad thing as they mucked in on exercise with their crews to a far greater degree than their cavalry counterparts who were regarded as snobs. Sure, we had our share of snobs, but they were mainly senior officers who, having served their time were, in my opinion entitled to snobbishness as befitted their rank and experience.

So, after the Troop Leaders each troop had a Troop Sergeant and thirdly a Troop Corporal. The ranks involved in the last two jobs could get confusing, it was common that Troop Sergeants were in fact Senior Corporals and Troop Corporals were Senior Lance Corporals. This was due to ranks going away for prolonged periods on posting. Even though they were absent from station, their ranks could not be replaced, in other words nobody could be promoted to replace them. Instead the more junior ranks were elevated to cover their jobs without the pay of the higher ranks. Each one of these three personalities commanded one of the troop's three Chieftains.

I have only explained the rank structure to emphasise the family aspect of life in a tank regiment. Whilst on exercise or 'scheme' as we called it, the formal rank structure normally became a more relaxed affair. The Troop Leaders sometimes became known and addressed as

'Boss'. Sergeants and below were all known by their first names. In no way did any 'familiarity breeds contempt' become evident. Everybody respected each other's ability to carry out their duties. After all it is the man not his rank which earns the respect of his colleagues. All this finery did not of course apply to we 'nigs'. It took weeks for us to gain the honour of first name terms with full corporals and months to be able to speak with familiarity to Sergeants.

Or at least on the tank park this was the case. Now the Squadron Bar, that was a different matter.

Each of our Squadrons in Fallingbostel had its own squadron bar contained within the squadron's barrack block. Its primary function was to allow all ranks within the squadron to socialise at an informal level once again reinforcing the family. Profits from the bar were used to help support the 'squadron fund' which was used at the OC's' discretion to benefit the 'lot' of the squadrons members. The bar was a marvellous institution, personal differences, problems and as I mentioned, even the rank structure disappeared inside its walls. We were able to sit and moan, whine and generally say what we liked without fear of retribution. It was also a 'think tank', it was a wise OC who spent time in the bar listening to the views and ideas expressed over a beer.

My first evening in C Squadron started with a couple of chaps appearing in my room and announcing it was time to be initiated. My thoughts flashed through the nightmares ahead. Would it be strange secret handshakes? Dancing naked through the barracks? No, none of the above. I was directed through the door just in time to be greeted by the sight of a drunken body flying through a pyramid of empty beer cans on a table. That body hurtling through the air crashed to the floor amid much laughter and cheering from the assembled throng. The hero lurched to his feet howling and one of my escorts told me that was Chris 'Switches' Lock. Everybody seemed to have some form of nickname. 'Switches' had earned his whilst driving and leaving the safety switch on in his cab. This meant that the turret and gun control equipment couldn't be operated, to the frustration of the turret crew, their shouts of 'switches!' earning him his nickname.

The can pyramid was only one of many party pieces taking place around the bar. Two men were having a beer can eating competition while three men were on the bar top attempting a form of wild can-can dance. One common factor was that everyone was blind drunk. Scared? Me? Fucking right I was. My immediate thought, faced with this vision for the first time was 'fuck me, I'm dead'. No, wrong, I was in fact marched to the bar. When I arrived there I was presented with a huge glass. In this glass was a double measure of every spirit behind the bar topped off with beer to make the glass full. Or at least that was the recipe explained to me. I try, even today, not to dwell on the contents of that glass. The initiation task was quite simple... drink the contents... in one go! Well, drink it I did, suddenly everything seemed to gain a rosy glow. As I drained the last drop a huge cheer arose from the assembled throng. Much backslapping and "well dones" later I decided I was a happy chap. Even better, my drinks were free for the rest of the night. But, most importantly, I was now officially 'adopted' as a member of the squadron albeit as a 'nig'.

That night I also met Staff Sergeant Jack Moreton. I was stood at the bar when a hand clapped me on the shoulder and he introduced himself. I was then subjected to about an hours worth of 'war stories'. These were however real war stories. Jack was a veteran, during an exchange period with an Australian unit he had even served in Vietnam. Within ten minutes his stories of napalm-injured children nearly had me in tears. But Jack had really been there, when he had parade dress on, his medals were an awesome sight. It would be true to say that Jack, Troop Leader 12 Troop was the last of a breed. And his party piece for all new recruits was to inform them of the horrors of warfare.

Many more nights of happiness would be spent under the hospitable eaves of our squadron bar.

Another watering hole I frequented with new chum, Lance Corporal 'Charlie' Chaplin, was a quiet pub in town called 'The Friendship'. This was owned by Sid (a British ex-Artilleryman) and his German wife Rita; they served the most wonderful food when we wanted a change from our cockroach-infested cookhouse.

The Regiment at this time was preparing to move station back to England and Tidworth in Hampshire. This meant that all our vehicles were to be handed to our 'swap' regiment the $4^{th}/7^{th}$ Royal Dragoon Guards. Therefore I was quickly exposed to the joys of vehicle servicing and painting… lots of painting. One afternoon in SHQ's vehicle hangars we were told to paint the Squadron Landrover. In fact the troop corporal Terry Ackrell told us "if it don't fucking move, paint it green and black". That was it, Trooper 'plod' that evening in the bar, was still sporting the remnants of a unique green and black paint job. He was, quote 'not fucking amused' unquote.

Our Squadron Leader at this time was Major 'Bruce of the galloping teeth'. His nickname was earned one morning as we paraded outside the squadron block. As the SSM gathered us together the OC came running out the block door waving his stick frantically while shouting to the

SSM. He opened his mouth exposing his magnificent teeth and shouted "S'arnt Major' this was followed by a surprised howl as he left the top step. He then did a marvellous mid air running demonstration as if in a cartoon. As the realisation of his inability to fly dawned on him, he nose-dived like a gooney bird into the pavement.

"Bollocks!" Came his muffled retort as he picked himself up. He then wiped as much blood as he could from his chin and surprised us with a sheepish grin. Needless to say, our immediate reaction was to howl with laughter at his misfortune.

First parade as it is still known is the morning ritual to gather the squadron together, check everybody's present and correct, and then any special tasks are doled out and any announcements are made which will affect individuals, Troops or in fact the whole squadron.

Quite quickly in Fallingbostel I came to realise that first parades were in fact sometimes a source of amusement. One morning on parade 10 Troop's sergeant reported one man absent. When the SSM asked who was missing the answer "Trooper Brown Sir!" was barked out in reply. SSM 'Taff' promptly spun on his heel to face the squadron block and began a monstrous shouting bout aimed at the building to his front.

" Trooper Brown you bastard, get your lazy fuckin arse out here on parade!"

This tirade lasted some five minutes as we all stood tittering awaiting the arrival of the miscreant. Eventually a loud " Fuck off!" emanated from a large bush in front of the block. "What's all the fucking fuss?" followed accompanied by the bush collapsing as Brown fell, naked out of the bush at the SSM's feet. I say naked, but in fact Terry was wearing one sock, his tattoos and a party fez from the squadron bars festivities the night before. He was still clutching a can of beer in his hand, evidence that he was still 'pissed as a cricket'. As the naked vision before us attempted to stand up the SSM exploded in rage, "Corporal Berwick, get this fucking idiot to the jail, NOW! I'll see him at 18:00 tonight in best dress AND, HE'D BETTER BE FUCKING SOBER!" With that Brown was quick marched (wobbled is a better description) off to the guardroom to spend the day behind bars. That evening having paraded for the SSM and received 14 extra guard duties, he was back in the bar getting drunk with the rest of us. But discipline of this art worked very well in 3 RTR of the seventies because in a strange way we were being treated as adults. However had this event happened while on exercise or active duty the outcome would have been far removed from a 'cooling' period in the jail.

First parade completed, we would 'fall out to our duties' and head for the tank park. Quite a feat of endurance in its own right as it involved a lengthy walk across scrubland to reach the hangars.

The tank parks were laid out, each squadron's hangars running parallel to each other with a concrete yard between them for working on. The hangars started with A sqn at the top, B sqn in the middle and ours at the bottom. The respective hangars did not face each other, so we could not watch the activity in front of B squadrons sheds and likewise they couldn't watch us at work. The same obviously applied for A sqn.

As the warm summer days drew on to be replaced by the cooler pre-autumnal climate our preparations for 'handover' and our move to Tidworth became more hectic. Each day brought us a fresh batch of problems to play with. Somehow through the mayhem our sense of humour prevailed.

One day as we toiled on the tank park we suddenly heard muffled explosions echoing from the far side of B sqns hangars. Then, three steel helmets came falling from the sky crashing and rattling across the concrete. One however, made no noise whatsoever, this was because it hit Jack on the shoulder and knocked him from the top of a turret where he was working, to the ground. The cursing that ensued was surpassed only by the speed with which Jack disappeared off towards B Sqns Park. We could hear him ranting about how he'd "Stick my fucking boot so far up some bastards arse he'll be able to undo my fucking laces with his fucking teeth!" for some time.

Meanwhile, with a shout of 'mortar attack' we were all galvanised into action. From nowhere bricks appeared, these were laid out in pairs across our park, about thirty helmets were produced from the hangar and placed with the rim of the helmet balanced on the bricks so that the helmet was effectively 'aimed' towards B sqn over the top of their hangar. Then loads of 'thunderflashes' (oversize bangers) were mysteriously produced and bound together in threes. A count down was then bawled across to us, as "one" was shouted we all simultaneously ignited our explosives and thrust them under the helmet in our charge. Suddenly the tank park erupted as a ragged volley of explosions thundered out and the helmets all took off and flew through the air and disappeared beyond B sqns roof. There followed an angry roar as a hail of steel helmets swamped B sqns men. Shortly after, Jack appeared at the end of our park looking pretty dishevelled as of course his own sqn had now also had a go at prematurely ending his career. The helmet salvoes continued until we all ran out of 'thunderflashes'. B sqn came off worse of course because A sqn joined in the melee and B got caught in the middle of two barrages.

That night, naturally we had to celebrate our victory in the squadron bar amid much laughter, even Jack was seen enjoying himself. We worked out that he had in fact found the 'helmet culprit' and attempted to rearrange the wretched individuals internal organs. A strange man indeed our Jack, as hard as nails but not as hard as the helmet, which had hurled him from the tank. He found the next day that he'd fractured his arm during the fall.

The handover drew ever nearer, but not for me. I suddenly found myself having to wait a further three years for a handover.

This was because I, along with numerous others was returned to England and Tidworth early to prepare for a 'Quarter guard'. The guard was to be provided in London at the M.O.D to mark the retirement of an ex-Tankie in the form of Field Marshall Carver.

" Whoa guys, that's not the last can of cleaneasy, Joe the spiv will be back with some more!!"

All the recent arrivals from Junior Leaders were included along with other 'selected' ranks as the ability to march in step was still fresh in our minds. But in the week before the parade our RSM ensured we got plenty of practice 'just in case we'd forgotten'. A strange phenomenon occurs in Tankies once basic training has faded over the years in service. Marching in particular becomes something 'the infantry do'. Infantry seem to do quite a lot of marching. But Tankies? "No! We bloody drive everywhere!" This would be the stock answer to any enquiry as to our prowess at drill. The Quarter guard was to be a one off.

Once the RSM or 'grot' as he was affectionately known was happy that our drill was to the accepted standard, he 'square bashed us for one last time and pronounced us ready. The only thing left to do was finish bulling our boots, oh dear, did I say finish bulling our boots? Ah, well, in reality we hadn't actually started bulling our boots! The $4^{th}/7^{th}$ to the rescue!

" Not a problem announced one of my colleagues. I know one of the Dragoons here and he's got contacts!" So in due course a chap appeared with a suitcase looking for the entire world like the 'spiv' Joe Walker off 'Dads Army'. He opened the case and informed us what an Aladdin's cave it was. We peered in side to find spray cans with plain brown labels and the word 'cleaneasy' on them.

He explained that in these cans was..

"Instant bull lads, not even the oldest Guards Sergeant Major would be able to tell the fucking difference!"

We looked on sceptically, in training we had all experimented with false bull. The best results had been with 'Klear' floor polish, until it rained that is. Then we could all be seen with a bright blue haze on our feet. It also cracked and flaked in the creased leather under the pressure of our stamping of feet. Needless to say, the result had been pain as our instructors meted out the merciless punishments. So instant bull? Yeah, yeah we'd heard it all before. But, undeterred this bloke asked for a pair of ordinary working boots to demonstrate. These were duly provided and he went to work. Firstly he brush polished the boots and then with a flourish produced a spray can and covered the boots with its contents. A smell of plastic filled the air, but lo, the boots looked like mirrors! Bloody bright mirrors at that.

He then got us to follow him to the washroom where he bounced the boots off the floor a few times and then held them under running water in a bath.

"Jesus H Christ, flaming wonderful!" We exclaimed in chorus as the boots were placed before us for inspection. They looked great and were not disrupted by the test they had just undergone. That was it; we couldn't get our grubby paws on enough cans of this miracle. The guy was back another two days running demand was so great.

Of course when we next did a 'best boots' parade the RSM was mightily impressed. Strangely enough his boots looked like ours too. The only drawback to this discovery was for the poor soul who had provided his working boots for the demonstration. You see, once the parade was over he had two pairs of high gloss boots. One of which were for tank park use. The amount of piss taking on first parade was phenomenal and try as he might he couldn't get the damn stuff off.

Anyway, duly polished and drilled we set off for London. There was to be no practice run, marching through the capital is a one-chance wonder. But the night before we walked the route to see where we would be performing. Just seeing Horse Guards and the arch we had to march under en – route to the Ministry of Defence made the hair on the back of my neck stand on end. Outside the MOD we were shown a manhole cover on which the leading men would halt, and then 'left dress' our ranks. Right, that done it was back to Cavalry Barracks, Hounslow where we were accommodated. Once there we embarked that evening on a massive drinking competition in Traditional Tankie style. We were undoubtedly a novelty that night in the NAAFI. The girls of the WRAC thought Tankies were wonderful, especially ones with West Country accents and seemingly limitless supplies of beer. They even competed against us in a game of 'Pass it on'. This dubious pastime involved a very large glass of beer, which is passed once round the assembled group who each take a drink. On the second pass around having taken a drink, that person is allowed to deposit just what he or she wants in the glass. The first person that can't or won't drink from the glass buys a round of spirits. I can assure you that dead spiders and cigarette ends were the least of our worries that night.

Next morning having filled our bellies with a hearty cookhouse breakfast we nursed our aching heads and paraded for transportation to the city. The RSM having got wind of our exploits the previous night decided on an impromptu bout of marching to shake up any vomit which might have later proved embarrassing. But, steadfast as ever we held on to our stomach contents and marched with vigour around barracks, amid much whistling from the WRAC block.

Off we went then, into the city, dismounted from the buses and got 'formed up' ready to march off on our route.

I explained earlier what we had to do, it sounded simple didn't it? Ha Ha, nothing could be that simple for us Tankies.

The first error came as we marched through Admiralty Arch, we were to salute the Lifeguards Officer of the day mounted on horseback to our left, this we duly did except we should have been told right and ended up saluting a fucking Trooper on his steed, a huge grin under the peak of his gleaming helmet. We corrected this on our return but later discovered we had saluted the Trooper again as the Officer had changed sides to try and compensate for our error. The mirth in their bars that evening could probably be heard for miles!

We marched bravely on as tourist cameras clicked as the spectacle of Black berets with Hackles swaying in the breeze, Sub machine guns and tank Arm Badges passed them by. Tourist London has many wonderful sights including of course, the Guards resplendent in scarlet and bearskins. But that day I felt about ten feet tall, we were so different to the Guards, children ran beside us pointing at our tank insignia.

"They're tank men dad". Shouted a young lad.

"Too fuckin' right" I thought as I increased my swagger to an alarming degree.

Then we arrived outside the MOD. We halted at the manhole cover as prearranged, but then had to 'left dress' some fifty feet to our right as it had been the wrong bloody manhole. We muttered about "Crap Guards S'arnt Majors" and their "crap instructions" under our breath. This was all made worse as many staff were peering from their office windows to witness this 'unusual' event.

I suspect the Field Marshall was just superbly tactful as opposed to blind not to have noticed our lengthy shuffle. Never the less he didn't bat an eyelid, and proceeded through our ranks to inspect us, stopping to chat with relish to some of our number. My mind switched to thoughts of him, what had he witnessed in his military career? Did he remember our regalia with fondness? Did he see similarities between previous Tankies and us? I suppose I will never know the answers to those questions, but he certainly seemed to enjoy the experience of meeting us.

The parade over, we returned to Hounslow, got changed, trooped onto the buses and waved a fond farewell to the girls of the WRAC and departed.

Next stop, Bhurtpore Barracks, Tidworth in Hampshire.

6. 'TIDDY'

The first weeks at Tidworth or 'Tiddy' as we came to know it, seemed to rush by in a semi controlled form of mayhem. As part of C Sqns takeover team for SHQ, I was tasked with sorting out one of the Troops 'new' tanks.

That morning as I walked from our accommodation uphill towards our tank parks I was quite excited at the prospect of seeing our 'new' hangars. Between the blocks and the tank park stood 'Coronation Street'. This was the name given to an estate of ancient Victorian terraced married quarters for our married couples or 'pads' to live in. These quarters stretched in a long line right across the back of the neighbouring barracks and ours. Having crossed the road and circumnavigated the last house I found myself in front of the tank Park. Until now I have constantly referred to our 'new' this and 'new' that. I can now reveal that in late 1976 our facilities in Tidworth were anything but new.

As I crossed the fuelling (POL) point I realised that the Hangars were exactly that, two huge sheds, the lower hangar to my front was to house B Sqn's vehicles and the hangar further up the hill to its rear was C Sqn's. A Sqn were not to be housed at Tidworth but instead at Warminster in the role of 'Demonstration Squadron' for the School of Infantry there. Their role would be to demonstrate all aspects of armoured warfare to various training establishments.

Command and Support Squadron were spread out in various buildings around our barracks. I walked on towards our hangar, as I entered, a grim sight met my gaze. As I had left 'Fally' I had seen our Chieftains drawn up on the parks immaculately painted and bulled for handover. A truly inspiring sight it had been too! Okay so I'd been party to a few 'bodges' to get them looking that way, for example mixing green and yellow paint to look like AL3 Anti freeze!

The sight that now greeted me bore no comparison whatsoever.

Inside the hangars cavernous space I could only count five tanks. Each of these 'panzers' was caked in a thick layer of mud. One vehicle was even missing a track!

"Well, fuck me with a Nagasaki ditch diggers left flip flop!" came an exclamation from behind me. I looked around and there was Terry my Troop Corporal his mouth agape and a look of horror in his eyes.

"What the fuck have the 4th/7th been doing? The twats must have been on leave for the last two years!" Having got these preliminaries out the way, he strode into the hangar. In one of the Troop offices or 'cages' we found a lonely looking Sergeant from the 4th/7th who, to be fair, looked more than a little embarrassed as we approached. We regarded him as if he were some sacrificial lamb left as rear party to face our wrath and offer explanations to our questions.

The explanations were not long in coming. The poor chap blurted and burbled about "lack of spares", "fucking Labour Party and their defence cuts", "the drought this summer... couldn't wash the wagons... hosepipe ban" and "fucking Labour... no fuel" seemed to fly over the top of Terry's head. The obscenities that flew from his mouth as any sense of decorum he had was promptly thrown out of the nearest window, did nothing for any inter unit detente which may have previously existed.

Later, to our cost, we discovered that there had been a hosepipe ban due to a drought that summer and there were only five vehicles in situ as the rest were parked at the workshops broken down. This was partly due to the Chieftain engine's uncanny knack of breaking down due to unreliability and because of the heavy exercise commitments for the Tidworth armoured units. We did in due course find the balance of our vehicles at the workshops 'awaiting' repair due to the shortage of spares initiated by the Labour government's 'spending rationalisation' on defence.

Having got over our initial shock, we proceeded to 'takeover' our vehicles and equipment. Our first tank to inspect was radio callsign 'Three Charlie' this was SHQ's 'dozer Tank'. In 'Fally' we had left a chieftain with its modern 'dozer blade'. Each SHQ had a 'dozer' converted MBT to provide a 'scrape' digging facility in the field. Theses scrapes were dug for the Sabre Troop tanks to drive into, providing extra protection from mother earth in their firing positions during battle. The British Armoured tactical doctrine was always to stand and fight a delaying battle against any communist horde, which would stream through Western Europe. Thereby allowing the politicians time to work their 'magic'.

The Germans on the other hand see attack and mobility as the best form of defence, we were always convinced that, had the Eastern block invaded, the German armoured divisions would have been in Moscow the next day. These doctrines are apparent in the way that our nations have combined the tanks main characteristics of Firepower, protection and mobility. The German Leopard tanks are fairly lightly armoured, very fast and agile with adequate firepower. British MBTs since World

War 2 have tended to be Heavy, well armoured but underpowered vehicles with immense firepower. It is fair to say though that with the advent of Challenger the power to weight ratio problem has been addressed more satisfactorily. Chieftain was, undoubtedly the most technically advanced MBT in the world. But rapidly as the Eighties progressed it became outpaced by foreign rivals, irregardless of the amount of upgrading it received as a cheap option against development costs for a replacement. But I do admit, as do many of my old chums that Chieftain held a very special place in my heart and it will always stay there.

"Oi, You've not even told me what the hell this thing is, much less what the hell I'm meant to do with it!!!!"

But, back to Tidworth. As Terry and I walked towards our 'dozer' Terry started to laugh, I looked at the tank and realised that this was no Chieftain, oh no, it was a Centurion! Centurion?

"Fucking hell, I thought they were all gone?" I exclaimed.

"Gun tanks have" replied Terry. He continued, "The REME still have Centurion ARVs (Recovery Vehicles) and the Engineers have AVREs with 'Dustbin chuckers' (a gun for demolitions), but Gun tanks with 105mm guns are long gone". He paused, "Well I thought they had anyway!"

"Obviously not". I ventured.

The next two hours were an achievement in anyone's book as we puzzled over which tool was which as described in the vehicles equipment schedule. And why did we sign our names for 'Hammocks sleeping', all four of them?

The 'Cent' would stay with SHQ for some time completing both exercises and a range firing period with aplomb. This artefact of British engineering did earn our respect and a place in our hearts, especially when on scheme we discovered you could fry eggs on its hot 'jenny' exhaust thereby negating the need to light the dreaded petrol cooker. It was also more reliable than its Chieftain replacement; the quiet hum of its Rolls Royce Meteor engine was somehow relentlessly reassuring. However, driving it was a challenge and I remember well the driver's knuckles bleeding from poorly timed battles with clutch and gear lever. A testament to Centurion is that even today in some far off land you will find a 'Cent' serving in someone's army.

So, the rest of the settling in period at Tidworth passed fairly uneventfully and we got into a more normal routine.

7.   'Mad Dogs and Westcountrymen'

By the middle of November 1976 the whole of 3 RTR had become UK based and we had settled into the normal routines associated with barrack life.

The first routine, which was new to me, was Cambrai day.

Within the RTR Cambrai day is a name synonymous with November 20th. On this day in 1917 the first successful and significant tank action in history took place at Cambrai on the then Western Front. Our regimental ancestors in what was then the tank Corps had sallied forth against the might of the Imperial German army and given them a damn good thrashing. To us, each year on that date we celebrated the great day when tanks and their crews came of age. It has always been an opportunity as I say, to celebrate this battle honour but also to remember the fallen members of our ranks who had paid the supreme sacrifice in an attempt to secure the future generations.

I will now relate my first Cambrai day experience by the clock. Chronological occurrences vary little year to year but obviously the various stunts and pranks in between do!

First thing in the morning at 'worm fart' (it was he who beat the early bird!) we were rudely awoken in bed by our Sqn's Officers and senior

NCOs who were banging dustbin lids, blowing bugles and generally screaming the block down. This was the announcement of the days start known as 'Gunfire', lets face it however, all that noise was no substitute for the roar of guns. So as our room door was thrown open, a lit thunderflash careened across the floor and as it exploded our beds and bodies rocked with the shock of percussion! In came the culprits who included 'Taff' the SSM, between them they pushed a trolley with an urn of tea wobbling precariously on top. Around the urn were stacked full and empty rum bottles. The previous night we had each placed a mug on our bedside lockers ready for the tea. But it would be fair to say that I was not prepared for my head being pulled backwards and an over generous gush of rum being poured down my exposed throat. I then received a pat on the head and the praise "good lad" during which time my mug had been filled with tea from the urn and placed in my hand. I eagerly gulped the tea to wash the acrid taste of rum from my mouth, then I discovered that the tea was in fact more rum than tea. Faced with this fresh onslaught to my taste buds I simply gave up and drank heartily.

I should like at this juncture to explain the rum. When the tank Corps was formed by our forefathers, the fledgling corps was held under the auspices of the Admiralty and not the Army. So if you see pictures of the first tanks you may see them with the initials HMLS painted on followed by the tanks name. These initials stand for His Majesties Land Ship echoing the nautical origins of the Corps. Our cap badge motto of 'Fear Naught' was nearly 'Dread Naught' until someone thought this Naval connection was 'beyond the pale'. Indeed as the first guns found suitable for tank use were designed for ships a number of recruits were taken from the ranks of Matelots. So our Naval origins stuck, and some traditions such as the 'tot' before action. Certainly each of our SQMS' stores had wax sealed bottles of rum 'For war issue' locked away while I served.

All this tradition served to make a rousing start to Cambrai day.

After 'Gunfire' we went to breakfast, returned to our room where our chum 'Rabbit' was dishing out bottles of beer. It was still not 8 o'clock and here we were drinking like fish. As we sat talking, a loud roar from outside grabbed our attention. We rushed outside onto the veranda walkway to see what was causing all the shouting. There before us we saw, on the grass outside B Sqn block, a white wooden horse with three 'nigs', naked, tied to its back. Other members of the Sqn were running from the block and throwing the contents of some buckets over the poor captives, I won't describe the contents of the buckets, but leave it to your imagination.

The horse, it transpired, was the result of a 'raiding party' on the wire hut containing the Garrison's Polo training equipment. The hut now lay on its side and the wooden horse was gone. The poor horse ended up dismembered in various locations around our barracks. This was another Cambrai tradition, raiding parties were despatched to all the neighbouring barracks, their mission being to steal as much paraphernalia from other units as possible. This caused much consternation among the various owners as absolutely nothing was sacred.

In fact when we had been in Fallingbostel a neighbouring Cavalry regiment had celebrated their battle honour day by sending in a raid overnight to carry out a prank. The following morning when our RHQ Troop opened their hangars they found two scout cars painted shocking pink. Well it was only natural that on the next Cambrai day a party had raided their barracks to repay the favour, the upshot of this escapade was that two days later the Cavalry units CO had his horse put down as it was suffering from lead poisoning due to the fact it had been painted silver. What didn't help were the words 'Hi Ho silver away' splashed in red on its rump! Relations between our units were never the same again. But more on Cambrai raids later.

After we had stopped laughing over the now filthy 'nigs' below, we returned to our rooms to prepare for the mornings church service. This was our regiments personal act of remembrance and was a solemn affair albeit we were often still quite under the influence of 'Gunfire'. The service over, we returned to drinking and got ready for lunch. Lunch was a quite fraught affair on Cambrai day, we Junior ranks would get to the cookhouse and await the arrival of the Officers and Senior NCOs who would serve us our lunch washed down with beer. The Officers and Senior NCOs would have also been drinking together in the Mess, so by now they too were in 'high spirits'. Either way, served we were and during the meal the Commanding Officer would make a speech about the Third tanks and what a crack unit we were and other morale boosting comments amid much banging on tables and cheering from us. God it was good being a Tankie.

After the speech we sat cheering and generally being very vocal. That afternoon we were to see the final of the 'Tommy cup'. This was an inter squadron football competition the final of which was always reserved for Cambrai day. The final was between C and A squadron and we were fully prepared and let A squadron, who had bussed over from

Warminster for the day, know all about it. Our shouting match soon erupted into the inevitable food fight. It started with a lonely 'flicked' pea. The pea didn't stay lonely for long as it was quickly being followed by food including complete meals on plates hurtling through the air. The seventies were known for football hooliganism after all! The Officers quickly vacated the cookhouse leaving the NCOs to try and stop the fracas. The NCOs however, could plainly be seen searching for slit trenches in the tiled floor as they attempted to dodge the gastronomic missiles screaming overhead. The RSM turned purple and screaming, attempted to rally the NCOs into resistance. He didn't meet with any success but eventually, due to a lack of ammunition and a fresh delivery of beer, a truce was called.

That afternoon the Tommy cup was won by the narrowest of margins by A sqn. The day then rolled on fairly uneventfully and was rounded off by the all ranks party that evening.

Before I finish this chapter I would like to mention the 'Old comrades' weekends we used to occasionally host at Tidworth. This was an opportunity for us to invite previous members of the regiment to visit us as our guests to witness the modern RTR and allow them to share their memories of 'Tanking' with us. These guys were great. I did wonder however, when one veteran of WW2 commented on his accommodation as 'being little better than in 1944'. We met chaps who had even served in WW1, and my lasting memory will always be that whatever hardships they had suffered during their time, we were all linked by one passion, Tanks. The other thing that became apparent was the sparkle in their eyes and the wonderful sense of humour that only Tankies have. Everyone who met these men commented on what a great occasion it had been to share all their experiences good and bad.

8. To tank or not to Tank

With Cambrai day behind us we once again settled into our normal routine. Our days started of course, with squadron parade. I feel we always looked smart on parade, this was mainly due to our 'baggy black skin' as we referred to our overalls. Whoever had thought of black as our working colours had been very clever as it disguised the oil and grease which was so synonymous with our daily tasks. We were all undoubtedly proud of our unique black garb especially when we were near other Cavalry or Infantry units clad in green. I and many of my mates were often approached for 'swaps' for our overalls but never a pair left our hands. The REME fitters attached to us thought it great as they also got issued with black overalls for tank park use.

First parade having finished, we all dispersed up the hill to the tank Park. Once there we would have a Troop meeting to allocate any special tasks to individuals. Then on with first parade for our vehicles. This first parade was always our first task. It consisted of individual crewmembers carrying out checks on the systems associated with their crew job to ensure serviceability.

The driver would, for example, check all of his oil levels, and carry out other maintenance tasks laid down in the Chieftains servicing schedule finishing off by starting his engines to check for leaks in the lubrication system. Having finished the first parade tasks the crew would then carry out any scheduled servicing tasks, which required completion. This could range from cleaning the gun to changing the vehicle's tracks. All these servicing tasks at times amounted to 'over servicing' as tank usage can be somewhat spasmodic. At Tidworth however we soon found ourselves trundling around Salisbury Plain on a weekly basis.

This was because B squadron and ourselves were the only MBT units available for training exercises in the UK. Even our A squadron was not available due to their commitments at the school of Infantry. So if any non-Tank units needed to train with Armour support, we were it!

So whereas normally a tank can sit for maybe 3 months on a tank Park without moving anywhere other than around barracks, Tidworth meant that both the vehicles and crews were continually on the training area. Now this should not have worried us in the slightest but with Chieftains uncanny knack for mechanical breakdown it could rapidly become a major nightmare for all.

As I mentioned earlier the Chieftain's power pack was not the most reliable of objects.

Many rumours abound on how Chieftain ended up to be dogged by this engine; my favourite story is as follows.

When Chieftain was designed in the very late 50s and early 60s it was decided that it should follow on from its successful ancestor Centurion. "Fantastic!" said someone. Then somebody else said, "ah, but, we could do with a different kind of engine, one that will run on multi fuels, so anything from diesel to 'the morning afters' urine". "Oh fucking Yes, yes, yes!" The assembled study group agreed and this idea was included in the tender document for the engine design. When the tenders were returned, two main contenders appeared, the military divisions of Rolls Royce and that great icon of the era, British Leyland. One slight problem was that when Rolls Royce came to put their engine into the Chieftain hull it was about six inches too long for the available space. "Fuck it... but not a problem!" said the boffins; "we'll go back, revamp the design and be ready in six months!"

The clever lads from BL however had a design adapted from either a marine or train engine, which filled all the relevant criteria and was half the price of the Roll Royce unit. "Fuck it! See if it'll fit?" Came the shout from the MOD. And fit it did. And what's more the Chieftain could move when it started up, albeit at a less than impressive speed. The tests for tank reliability at this stage usually consist of absolutely hammering the hell out of the vehicle 24 hours a day to see if it will break down. Lo, it didn't break down under this pressure. "Fucking great!" Came the resounding shout from the MOD. "We'll buy fucking loads of them!" they continued, and from that moment on BLs L60 multi fuel (but ran on diesel) power pack became an integral part of the Chieftains bowel. I say bowel as the only thing that came out the back end of our tanks was shit.

You see what the boffins had forgotten during testing was that tanks don't actually run for 24/7, they actually sit in barracks for long periods of time. A big feature of the L60s design was the amount of rubber hoses on the outside of the engine to enable the oil to circulate. The engine oils used by the British Army were all a number prefixed by the letters OMD. Now these letters were not a reference to some pop group, they actually stood for Oil Mineral Detergent. So this meant that we were continually pouring gallons of oil in the engine containing a quite caustic cleaning agent to keep the engines interior clean. The main problem being that when the tank sat with little activity, these detergents settled and started to eat the rubber hoses. This caused weak spots in the hoses, so within a short time of putting the engine under real stress such as exercise the lubrication system would blow. At that moment the only oil to be found in the engine would in fact be on its exterior!

We tried many remedies to counter this unfortunate characteristic, the most successful being the German trick of starting the engine each morning and running it for 30 minutes or so to circulate the oil. Which was great except that, at one stage the Labour governments spending cuts bit home so hard that we were only allowed to start the engines with a written approval from the Regimental CO. This was due to a chronic fuel shortage within the Army, meaning at one point the only fuel we had was that which was in the vehicle fuel Tanks. The 'up' side to this was that we couldn't go on exercise, so more drinking times at our favourite hostelries!

In defence of the L60 power pack it is fair to say that matters did improve later when it was uprated from 750 to 850 Brake Horsepower in later marks of Chieftain. But it never did really achieve the blistering performance of the nearest of its competitors, Germanys Leopard 1 which contained a Maybach engine in a vehicle some ten to fifteen tons lighter than Chieftain.

I believe another important factor that somehow got lost in the halls of MOD was that no matter how cheap each unit was, they didn't realise how much money would in fact be spent on Chieftain in spares for the engine. This to any financial genius would have been a major concern when trying to set an annual budget cost. Especially when the first budget to be slashed annually at that time was the MoD's. We certainly had reason for concern over safety at the time. Certain items of equipment used on the vehicle were single use only, this meant that, for example the locking nuts used to keep the heavy roadwheels in place should be thrown away if we changed wheels and replaced by new ones. But we found ourselves re-using these nuts three or four times. We found ourselves continually tightening these wheel nuts as the nylon lock washer inside each nut was so worn down that the nuts themselves became loose at an alarming rate.

My only word of warning to any government would be that no matter how you change the Armed Forces structure, maintain what equipment you have, well. Don't play with budgets on a hidden political agenda, the men and women that serve you have an often dangerous and very hard job as it is without you tampering with the money available for them to complete the tasks you set. The really odd thing about the Armed Forces is that we just simply don't know when they'll be needed. Unlike most historical wars, modern wars generally happen in a relatively short timespan. Even civil or industrial problems, which require military intervention, happen 'out of the blue!'

Tank Park life rolled from day to day punctuated by incidents which were so out of the ordinary that they stood out a mile. I explained that our hangars were huge caverns. To explain more clearly picture a huge shed in your mind, then picture tanks entering this shed from one end, each one reversing down the middle of its length. In front of each tank a man would stand as 'guider' giving the driver hand signals to control his reversing. As the tank reached its Troop parking spot it would be directed and parked in a 'herringbone' fashion on the hangar wall. This was great when yours was the only tank in the hangar but when the entire squadron was already parked; it was a little 'snug' to say the least. The other problem for the guider was that the tanks gun would invariably be clamped into the 'gun crutch' at the rear of the engine decks. This 'crutch' was used when the guns stabiliser equipment was switched off so that the vehicles movement wouldn't damage the gun and turret. But in Fallingbostel the hangars had been constructed in bays for individual vehicles with plenty of room. Tidworth then caught many guiders off guard, they would forget to watch the tip of the gun barrel and before they knew it, crash; the gun barrel would be stuck through a hole in the wall. Oops... Extra guard duties dished out as punishment.

Even better than this was the day I acted as guider to one of SHQs Chieftains with 'Ollie' at the helm. It seemed simple enough as tasks go,

"Malc, take Ollie and 3B down the POL point and fill up with diesel said my pal 'Lucy' one of the other drivers in SHQ. So off we duly went with me walking in front. It would be fair to say that at this point I was still inexperienced at guiding as I had still to pass my driving course. The POL point in 'Fally' had been a fairly simple drive in, drive out affair, but Tidworth's diesel pump was situated on the kerb of a sort of lay-by which involved steering into it. All went well until we came to pull out the other end. Ollie was becoming impatient at my 'over careful' approach, as he pulled forward I signalled for him to steer right, this he did, very enthusiastically. In fact he was so enthusiastic that when I dropped my hand so he would let go of the steering and come straight forward, he fucking didn't! The consequence was a disaster, the rear of the tank clipped the kerb dislodging the entire fucking diesel pump and sending a yellow gush of diesel straight up in the air. As if we didn't have enough problems with fuel shortages! When we got back to the hangar 'Lucy' was beside himself as 'Ollie' and I blamed each other. However later that evening in the bar Ollie, Lucy and myself saw the funny side. Lucy and I were to become firm friends which has lasted to this day.

One day S/Sgt George Thomas, who was Troop Leader of a Sabre Troop, was stood on the engine decks leaning on the gun barrel while a 'nig', Trooper 'GH', was in the turret carrying out some gun control equipment checks. The next thing, George found himself being whizzed through the air still hanging on to the gun. 'GH' had proceeded with a turret traverse test without checking the exterior of the Tank.

"GH YOU FUCKING LITTLE SHIT!" bellowed George as the turret speed picked up. "STOP YOU TWAT" continued George, 'GH's face appeared out of the Commanders hatch but the turret continued to spin, the look of horror on his face was a picture but still the turret spun on. Quite obviously 'GH' couldn't decide what to do; keep George on the move thereby delaying the punishment that would follow or, stop the turret and accept George's wrath. The decision was taken from him by someone leaping onto the turret and throwing the safety switch in the loaders hatch to halt the turrets movement. The sudden cessation of movement dislodged George from his grip, and he fell to the ground with a dusty thump. As he picked himself up 'GH' was already imitating a human bullet as he raced down the hangar. George duly gave chase and caught 'GH', who though built like a 'racing snake' was incredibly unfit, in a vice like grip and dragged him behind the nearest tank to 'discipline' him. 'Tank park discipline' was commonplace at this time. It meant giving an offender a short sharp physical shock to bring him back into line. It should never be misconstrued as bullying, that is a persistent persecution of an individual. In a tank each crewmember is totally reliant on his comrades and their ability to co-exist as a team. Quite simply if one member of the crew is failing it could cost the lives of everyone, therefore unorthodox methods of team building were adopted. I am aware however that this form of punishment has now been stamped out due to the changing attitudes of modern society. Is it better now? I don't have the answer to that conundrum; it's better to let you decide on your own.

Another incident that comes to mind is the day we had a runaway Tank.

As I explained earlier our hangars were built on the side of a hill. One day a 9 Troop vehicle had been to the POL point to refuel. On its return the driver, 'Swilly' (named after an old area of Plymouth from which he came) Winsor had to park outside the hangar as the entrance was blocked by another vehicle. 'Swilly' although qualified as a driver was relatively inexperienced, his main trade having been gunner. He parked the tank facing uphill and applied the handbrake. The handbrake had to be 'winched' on by a ratchet mechanism in the driver's cab. Because the tank was facing uphill 'Swilly' had to maintain pressure on the footbrake to stop the tank rolling backwards. But 'Swilly' forgot to release the footbrake gently to compensate as the handbrake pressure was applied. Thus it was that when 'Swilly' thought the handbrake was on, it in fact was only partially on. His colleague, 'Woody senior' Woodcraft had, meanwhile, jumped up into the turret to switch off the gun control equipment (gun kit). As the whirring of the gun kit subsided, 'Woody' heard the engines die as 'Swilly' switched them off. But then, surprise-surprise, he felt the tank lurch. 'Swilly', having turned off the engines, had caused the brake system's hydraulic pressure to drop. Because the handbrake wasn't properly applied, it failed under the vehicle's weight. As 'Woody' stuck his head out of the turret, he saw 'Swilly' running up the hill, away from the tank, at a high rate of knots. 'Swilly' had obviously decided he didn't want to play anymore. 'Woody', realising his predicament on a runaway tank, quickly ducked back down inside, slamming the hatch shut above him. As the tank ran back down the hill it had, of course, attracted our attention and the rest of the squadron quickly gathered at the hangar entrance to observe the events unfolding before us. 'Swilly' was by now crouched with his head in his hands, suffering from nervous exhaustion, getting ready for the wrath of Pete 'The Mad Bastard' Joyce, 9 Troop's sergeant.

Callsign 31A was by now picking up speed. Its first target was the B squadron workers outside their hangar, who beat a hasty retreat amid much shouting in alarm. This shouting served as a warning to the next obstacle, which was the NAAFI van and its waiting queue of Royal Anglians from the neighbouring barracks. The queue dissolved in panic and the NAAFI van disappeared in a cloud of dust, its serving hatch still open with paper cups and food flying out into the air.

The tank was now through the obstacle course and had gained a fairly good turn of speed; the only obstacle left in its path now was the vehicle hangar belonging to the Anglians. The impending collision did not, however happen as, before it could reach the wall, the tank came up against a very high kerb, over which, without any engine power, it could not climb. The tank came to a halt, rocking on its suspension. 'Woody', realising that it could just possibly now be safe to exit the turret, appeared, looking a little shaken, to be greeted by our howls of laughter and jeering. In due course 'Mad Pete' dished out 'Swilly's' punishment; he was on extra guard duties for weeks.

One of our more onerous tasks on the tank Park was the weekly sweeping of the large concrete 'standing' area situated on the hill above our hangar. In fact sweeping was a really big part of our lives in general. The saying was, "Join the Army and see the world, join the Third tanks and sweep the fucking world!"

The best thing about sweeping the world was that once finished we could, if not on duty that weekend, depart to be with our families. As we were all Westcountrymen Tidworth as a posting was ideal for the trip home. On our earnings at that time, few of us had our own cars, so we all used to 'chip in' with the car owners to share the petrol cost on our journeys home. This worked out to be very beneficial to all concerned as it was cheaper than bus or train for us (and quicker), and the car owner always ended up not having to pay a penny for the petrol. We even had one guy, Kenny Spurr, who came from Cornwall and (as we all were) was keen to return home at any available weekend. To do this he had a Morris 1100, complete with that marvellous 'ultra springy' suspension! However, what was incomplete was any form of legal documentation other than his driving licence – and there was a fair chance he'd printed that himself!

So, every Friday afternoon that we could, we'd be off in our vintage motors towards home. The only stop on the A303 was near Sparkford at what was a truck stop called 'The Frying Pan'. No longer there, I fear but, what a place. We even qualified for trucker's prices, as we always wore our blackened overalls!

9. Salisbury Plain 'Scheming'

I told you earlier how we referred to a field training exercise as a 'scheme'. These schemes come in a variety of forms; the first exercise of each year is Troop Training. This is a 'shakedown' exercise to allow any 'nigs' who joined at the end of the previous scheme season to learn specific tank tasks and to give the crews and vehicles a chance to once again, come to terms with each other. During these schemes training on all aspects of Tanking is given. From how to hide a tank in a wood to Battle tactics is practised over and over, ensuring that each crew member knows the part he is to play in the event of hostilities. Individual skills such as cooking, putting up a tank shelter or 'bivvie', putting up the infamous camouflage netting and making a cup of tea to name but a few are imparted on the youngsters by the more experienced crew members.

At this time in early 1977 I was still in SHQ and on my first Troop training scheme I was to carry the title of 'spare crewman'. This was not uncommon as, if for example, vehicle breakdowns prevented vehicles from taking to the field the squadron personnel would all be shuffled to fill the remaining Tanks. Unfortunately this meant that in SHQ I failed to get on a crew. It more importantly meant that I would travel around Salisbury in the back of the squadron ambulance. Anyone who has had to suffer this will tell you how uncomfortable this is. My biggest memory of this is the feeling of seasickness I had. It wasn't too bad though because I had recently passed my driving test on the FV432 to get my tracked vehicle licence so once in a while the regular driver 'Ginge' would let me have a drive.

Troop training was quite literally a crash course in Tanking. It normally lasted two weeks, during this time Tanking would become second nature to us. Well, if I could get on a tank that is. The Troop training period would culminate in 'Troop tests'; these were a series of tests set by our Colonel to see if we had learnt our tasks well. These tests would last for two to three days and consisted of a series of 'stands' set up around the training area to test us on all aspects of tank warfare as both Troops and individual tank crews. Each stand would be manned by staff from RHQ who specialised in the subject to be tested there. The tester would award marks to both Troop and tank level, the combined marks for each Troop would be totalled and the Troop with most points became 'Cock Troop' for the year.

Cock Troop was quite an honour as each tank in the Troop was awarded a pennant in their squadron colour to be flown from an antenna. This was an honour on the grounds that such flourishes of independence were generally frowned on in the British Army on security grounds, namely all vehicles should look alike to the enemy as it prevents individuals being identified and singled out for special attention. On a tank the only identification marks visible at that time were the radio Callsign on the back of the turret painted in white on black. As the radio Callsign system changed in later years the Callsign had to be still white on black but contained inside a white painted squadron symbol. In our case a circle. But in 1977 the squadron symbol was displayed in either green or black (according to the background colour) on either side of the turret. The symbol was also painted as for the turret sides, on each side of the tank at the front so that at night should someone wish to verify a vehicle's squadron he needed only to shine a torch at this small position on the vehicles front wing.

The only other identification mark on the tank (and then not always at this time) could be the vehicles name. Each vehicle in each of the tank regiments had a name designated by RHQ The Royal Tank Regiment. Vehicles in 1st RTR had names beginning with the letter A and so on for the other Regiments. So the Third had names beginning with C. Well, that is except for D. Squadron, which was formed from the C&S Squadron in later years, and was given names beginning with F, this harked back to the beginnings of the Corps and the F Battalion in WW1. This history lesson also brought us into conflict with 4th RTR who had the tradition of painting what were known as 'Chinese eyes' on each side of their turrets. After WW1 a Chinese Emperor funded a Tank, but, before he would part with any cash he insisted its 'spirit' must be able to see. The tank Corps unit receiving this tank was... F Battalion. So a verbal war broke out as we maintained that our newly formed D Squadron should wear these 'eyes'. As can be imagined 4 RTR were not amused and a stalemate prevailed as no decision could be reached. The most memorable names I retain from C. Squadron are Charlemagne, Chivalrous, Commando, Cavalier and Crockbrack to name but a few.

But, to return to Troop Training, I was to be 'spare' for only the first four days of scheme. This was because 11 Troop Sergeant's crew sustained an injury when it's radio operator got his foot trapped in the turret while it was traversing. My chance had come, a real crew of my own. Now it has to be said that 11 Troop didn't have the best of reputations for attitude. When I arrived I reported to my crew who were Frank, the Troop Sergeant, 'Jud', the driver and 'Pep' the gunner. My first task was to prepare a meal so I went to the storage bin where all crews keep their rations known as the 'compo bin' as the tinned composite rations were simply known as 'compo', it was only logical to name this storage space as the 'compo bin'. Every individual tank has a common storage plan so that when, as in my case a fresh crewman joins the crew he can easily identify where everything is stowed. Having opened the bin I was dismayed to find nothing in it except an opened fucking packet of mashed potato powder. Apparently Frank's crew weren't very good at regulating their eating habits. An empty bin and we wouldn't be replenished (replened) until the next evening. I did however breathe a sigh of relief as quite frankly I didn't yet know if I could cook for a crew. I returned to where the crew were seated and reported to Frank that we had no rations.

"Fucking what" he seethed. His beady eyes glared from behind his spectacles, he looked at 'Jud', then 'pep' and then proceeded to shout at them.

"Bugger me, I thought we'd been eating well, what have you two been doing with the bloody rations?" Silence was all he received in return to this question. Luckily next day we managed to beg some extra rations from the SQMS.

I quickly found out about my new crew. Frank it seemed, was a bit inept at most of the tasks that a tank Commander should find simple. 'Jud' was a large chap who while loving driving, found it quite difficult to accept orders from Frank. 'Pep' was a quiet lad who befriended me but had an almost schizophrenic tendency to violence when provoked. So this then was my crew and I was their buttie and brew maker, loader and radio operator.

And so it was that 11 Troop with us in Callsign 33A sallied forth into the actual Troop Tests. As we started the tests we found that each test would, this year be marked only by individual crew. The results would be totalled by Troop, but each crew would be tested on its own merits. I vividly remember the tactics stand that year. We were required to advance up a hill and adopt a 'hull down' position which meant that the 'enemy' on the far side of said hill would only be able to see top of our turret above the crest. The 'enemy' in this case was the Regimental 2ic in his Landrover. As we neared the top of the hill Frank announced on the intercom (IC) that control of 'Jud' was now in 'Peps' hands. The idea of this was that when the gunner, looking through his sight, could observe the target he would tell the driver to halt, the tank now being in the perfect 'hull down' firing position.

As I sat in the gloom of the operator's position I could clearly hear 'Pep' passing instructions to 'Jud' over the IC.

"OK Jud just a bit more, slow down or we'll go too far" the tank continued its advance not seeming to slow down at all. Suddenly 'Pep' started bellowing.

"Jud you fat fucking twat, where the fuck are you going?" There was still no reply from the cab or automotive systems and suddenly I could sense that we had gone over the top of the hill and were if anything, picking up speed. So here we were like the Light Brigade at Balaclava running headlong into the muzzles of the enemy guns.

Frank now stopped studying his map and attempted to take control of the situation.

" Shit, fuck, bugger" crackled in my headset, followed rapidly by,

" Jud you fucking goon, what the fuck are you doing?" these words were becoming drowned now by the wail of the engine as the vehicles tempo increased. Still nothing from the cab, Frank shouted "traverse left" to 'Pep' who duly started to turn the turret to the left. As the turret rotated Frank pointed and waved to me, indicating that I should look down into the back of the cab as it appeared below the turret. We were now quite literally hammering down towards the 2ic who could be seen frantically trying to move his Landrover out of the way.

Then, below us, the back of 'Jud's' head came into view. Two burning questions were immediately answered. Firstly the reason we'd received no response was that 'Jud' had shoved his bloody headset on to the back of his head. Secondly this was because he was wrestling with a can opener and a can of 'compo chocolate and sweets' which he had stashed in his cab along with other various supplies of food. No wonder we had nothing to eat, he had it all in his fucking cab! Frank on seeing this, grabbed his signal flare pistol and launched it at the back of 'Jud's' bonce. The result being that the tank suddenly lurched to a halt accompanied by a chorus of abuse from the crew. As we sat arguing inside our tank Frank decided in his excitement to kick 'Pep' neatly in his kidneys. Although this was unintentional, 'Pep's' reaction was devastating. A '2 pound hammer hand barstard' appeared as if by magic in his hand and he turned as best he could in the gunners seat and smacked Frank on the knee with the hammer. I then sat back in stunned silence and watched the resulting maelstrom as chaos ensued on that side of the turret. Here I was locked in a steel box with a bunch of fucking certifiable nuts!

Eventually calm prevailed, we received no points for this stand and we waited for a radio message to give us our next instructions. The next instruction was not long in coming across the airwaves encoded using the code of the era known as 'Mapco'. As operator I dutifully sat and wrote down the message and then decoded the content. Frank was getting impatient by now. Never the less, once I'd finished it I passed the message to Frank. He read it, transferred the map reference to his map, studied the map and then said; "This is utter fucking bollocks! It doesn't make sense, I know where we're meant to be going and it isn't here!" He then got 'Pep' to try and confirm my decoding as I was a 'nig' and when 'Pep' agreed with my decode Frank continued; "I've got inside information, this is a fucking red herring, so we'll go where we should be going and not where this piece of crap says!" I never did really find out whether the piece of crap was me or the message because Frank ordered 'Jud' to move off, which of course 'Jud' did with great aplomb nearly causing us all to sustain whiplash injuries.

So off we trundled in search of Franks 'inside information'. It obviously didn't occur to Frank that the person who had so 'generously' given him the info was actually misleading him. Eleven miles later we had not found the stand, and we were now late on the time given to us. This was bad, very bad. This stage of the test was strictly timed to test Franks map reading ability. The stand we were seeking was the replen stand, during replens timings are critical because during the time taken to refuel, grab fresh supplies of ammo, water, rations and mail etc. our vehicles were at there most vulnerable. Therefore an SQMS would be at a certain place at a certain time and stay there only for a limited duration. During this period his vehicles are laid out nose to tail (making a perfect target) so that as each tank in turn 'rolls' through the replen it takes the minimum amount of time for each crew to gather what it needs. This then was what was known as a 'rolling replen', at this time replens where the SQMS dragged his vehicles through 'hides' in woods to each individual tank were not favoured. Therefore when our tank eventually arrived at the replen the SQMS in charge was very much less than amused.

"Frank you fucker, where the fuck have you been you twaaaaaat?" He loudly enquired. "Don't you ever come the fuck through one of my replens for real will you?" He continued. Frank's only reaction to this tirade was an inane grin sat on top of a large shrug of his shoulders.

Needless to say, 11 Troop didn't win Troop Tests that year. But, on the last night, Frank mysteriously came down with the 'shits'. Did it have anything to do with laxative laced food? Who knows? But, it would be fair to say that, unbeknown to me, both pep and Jud had laced various food and liquids for Frank, with laxatives! Unbeknown to them… so had fucking I… to the tune of 4 tablets in his cup of tea. That long wet night, we made sure Frank slept on the gearbox decks so as not to disturb us each time he felt the 'call'. He was on and off the engine decks every 30 minutes or so throughout the night. We'd hear his sleeping bag zip go down amid grumbles and moans such as "Fucking hell, have I got the bloody squits or what? Christ that hurts!" Then would come a splash as he jumped from our engine decks. Then there would be the tortured squeak of a bin opening as he grabbed a shovel and toilet roll. 'Splat, splat, splosh' fading into the night as he trekked off through the mud into the wood. Then 10 minutes later he'd be back.

We gallant three, of course, were lying in our bags laughing like drains each time he disappeared! Next morning we discovered he'd actually worn his own track into the ground where he kept disappearing into the trees! Laugh? I nearly wet myself I laughed that much.

10. UNFICYP

Our seemingly endless trail of schemes continued through the beginning of 1977 during which time we had received a new Squadron Leader in the form of Major 'Billy' B. One morning on Squadron parade he announced that we were to become the independent armoured car Squadron for the UN Forces in Cyprus (UNFICYP). This would last for six months at the end of this year, and would involve us all training on Ferret scout cars. Once SSM 'Taff' had quietened our excited tittering with choice words like "Shut the fuck up you choice cunts!", the OC went on to explain a little more detail. And then we all broke off to the tank Park. The next few weeks passed in a blur. We had an extensive period of over servicing our tanks to prepare them for our absence, so that during the six months B Squadron would be left in charge and needed only to carry out minimum maintenance on them.

So began an intensive training period on the Ferrets. These vehicles were first designed in the late 40s early 50s as a replacement for the Dingo scout cars. Powered by a petrol Rolls Royce engine these 'cars' were good fun to drive and could reach a good turn of speed compared to an MBT. The version we were to use was the Mark 2 with a small turret mounting the.30 calibre Browning Machine gun, which in fact was a smaller version of the.50 which Chieftain used as the ranging gun I mentioned earlier.

As the Troop restructure was announced to reflect the Cyprus Squadrons organisation, I realised that I would be staying in SHQ. Not only that but I was doomed to be an Officers Mess barman. WHAT? It just couldn't get any crueller than this. But never the less I would receive Ferret training as on my days off I could drive on patrol! DAYS OFF? Christ, what was I being let in for? All will, I promise become clear.

Another course I had to complete was a Stewards and cellar management course with the Army Catering Corps at Aldershot. I can't say I particularly enjoyed the experience as it wasn't what I'd joined up for, however it was quite interesting to see how the other half lived. Also our black 'Barrack dress' pullovers were quite a novelty for the girls there as they'd never met a Tankie. But I won't dwell on that! So having completed that little episode it was back to 'Tiddy' and Ferret driving lessons.

At this point I would like to introduce you to 'Beans', no, not the baked variety but a Trooper. 'Beans' Kirrage was a real character, a bit of a comedian. His nickname apparently stemmed from his rotundness and his tendency to flatulence, which at times could make the surrounding atmosphere somewhat colourful to say the bloody least.

'Beans' was that man who while learning to drive a Ferret came badly unstuck. One day while descending a steep hill with a bend at the bottom, his Ferret's brakes failed. This cataclysmic event caused 'Beans' to lose any control passed from his nerve centre to his hands controlling the steering wheel. Consequently instead of turning through the bend his Ferret careered straight on 'Beans, loudly screaming "FFFFFUUUUUUUUCCCCCCCKKKKKKKK!" as they bounced over the grass verge. Now, given fields, that would have not been so bad but given a house it was of course, a disaster. The Ferret entered this house by the side entrance namely a wall and came to rest in the living room.

The Commander/Instructor later described the scene;

" We was in this fucking living room. Well, fucked if we weren't just sat staring at the fucking mess we'd made when suddenly the room door opened like! Then this pair of eyes looks at us through the dust and I could see this little old 'dear'. She gives a little squeak and fucks off again! Five minutes later she's back again with a cup of 'char' for us and some 'biccies'! All I could say to her was sorry and ta very much!"

I hope this gives you a picture of the chaos as it still brings a smile to my face today. That evening 'Beans' recovered with us at the NAAFI over a couple of beers but was strangely silent over the whole affair. His Ferret was parked outside the workshop for many months with a mountain of house bricks pointing skywards out the top as testament to that day.

In September that year, all our training completed we flew off to Cyprus for six months of sun tan lotion splashing and peace keeping. I remember as we descended the steps from the aircraft onto the runway at RAF Akrotiri we were met by a colossal wave of heat. It was something that we were totally unprepared for as English summer temperatures never reached these heights. We were then put on coaches and driven from Akrotiri to Nicosia where we were to be based in the UN camp area which was a collection of smaller camps ours being titled Force Reserve. As we drove across this island I was taken in by it's sometimes, desert like appearance. This was my first adventure into a Mediterranean climate and so far I wasn't that impressed. Then we saw our first result of a Cypriot traffic accident. On one side of the road was the front of a tractor, on the other, the back wheels and seat of the same bloody tractor. A little further up the road was the crumpled remains of a motorcycle which had obviously been the reason for the two severed halves of the tractor. We surmised that the tractor must have been crossing the road when the motorcycle zoomed straight through the middle. We couldn't comprehend this, as we hadn't seen any speed limit signs over 50mph. Come to that though we hadn't seen many road signs of any description. We would soon realise that driving in Cyprus, though I can't' speak for today, certainly then involved quite literally taking your life in your own hands. For example, in towns if they had traffic lights, a red light simply meant 'drive a fuck load faster than when a green light is showing!'

Our barracks consisted of small bungalow type structures with the toilet and shower facilities being in a separate building, in my case, some way from the sleeping blocks. The camp also had the normal Squadron Admin offices along with an operations room full of maps and radio equipment to control our patrol cycle. There were of course the usual Officers and Sergeants Messes and for we low lifes a cookhouse. For recreational purposes we had a NAAFI bar and canteen, but also a small shop and canteen run by Cypriots which we referred to as the 'choggy shop'. The name 'choggy' was how we referred to the Greek Cypriot inhabitants of the island. The Turks when we referred to them were simply Turks! But the majority of Greeks in whose half of the island we were living seemed to generally resent us (but not our cash!) hence a less than affectionate nickname.

The 'choggy shop' could and would try to sell us anything our hearts desired as long as it was obtainable and wasn't alcoholic (due to a trade agreement with the nearby NAAFI bar). A feature of the 'choggy shop' was that inside was a vast array of one-armed bandits. Many a lad could be seen throwing coins with wild abandon into these machines while attempting to rip the arm off in frenzied combat.

Once we had acclimatised to the fierce temperatures and some of the more quirky aspects of camp life, such as long tailed lizards sleeping on rafters above our beds at night, we settled into what was to be a different daily routine. For example we were used to parading for fitness training in Europe at 8am twice weekly. This was normally for our Squadron run as it was called, but in Cyprus this occurred as regularly, but at bloody 5am in the morning before it got too hot. Our normal working day started with Squadron parade, but at 6am or earlier. This only applied however to Troops not involved on patrols. We 'base' Troops tended to only work until 1 or maybe 2pm, as the temperatures became too hot at that time. Of course I was in the Officers mess so my hours of work were all day and well into the night or until the last Officer had finished drinking. But the upside to my job was that I only had duty every other day, so on my days off I would drive Ferrets on patrol as a 'break' from my subservient existence.

What an obvious target!

Even to this day I feel uncomfortable if someone serves me anything as I remember too well how 'put down' I felt at my task. I will however say on the positive side that it gave me an insight into the life of an Officer which on the outside seems quite glamorous but, I know now that Officers often 'copped' for jobs which to them seemed dreadful. It could have been worse, I could have been in a Cavalry Officers mess. Their traditions and history promoted snobbery of the worst kind and each Regiments Officers Mess was measured on its monetary wealth both of property and the private incomes of its members. At least RTR Officers were more human and able to communicate at the soldiers level. This was at this time because to join some of the Cavalry units it was not unheard of for the applicants to be able to display a private income to support their social standing within the Mess. Who said that 'buying' your commission died out in the 19th century? This was 1977 not, 1877. However, once again I cannot comment on modern commission or indeed Mess standards. Talking about inter Cavalry/RTR rivalries brings an RTR Officers Mess joke to mind that I once heard;

There was an RTR Officer who, having finished a training course in the UK, was waiting to return to his unit in Germany. He was at Luton airport when a delay was announced. He was then told to stay overnight in the London barracks of the Household Cavalry. So he reported to the Officers Mess at these barracks and was duly given a room for the night.

The next morning he went down to the dining room and a steward showed him to a place right at the end of an immaculately polished, absolutely massive dining table which had once belonged to Napoleon Bonaparte and which had been seized as bounty by this Cavalry unit. The young RTR Subaltern glanced around the room taking in the paraphernalia associated with this illustrious Regiments history. Looking down he saw that a place had been set and that he had a bowl of cornflakes before him, to one side was a bowl of sugar but, nowhere was there any milk. As he looked around he could only spy one other Officer in the room and he was up at the opposite end of the table, clad in Household uniform and wearing a cap. Next to this Officer was a jug of milk but the chap had his head down obviously ignoring the Subaltern who by now just wanted to finish breakfast and escape. The RTR chap then asked the distant figure;

" Excuse me, please can you pass the milk?"

The Cavalry type just carried on chomping, head down".

Again our chap asks, only louder;

"Hello there, please can I have the milk?"

Still no answer or acknowledgement, our guy is now becoming quite upset and bawls out;

"Oi mush, pass the bloody milk!"

At last the Cavalry chap lifts his head and speaks in an extremely posh tone; "In the Household Cavalry we have a long lasting tradition that, when a brother Officer attends breakfast wearing his cap, he wishes not to be spoken to nor does he wish to converse with anyone!" With that he continues to solemnly eat his bowl of cereal.

Well, this is beyond a joke to our chap, who jumps up onto the tabletop and proceeds to smartly march along its length to the far end. Having arrived, he comes to a stomping halt with his brogue-clad feet slap in the Cavalry Officers cereal bowl. He then bends down so that his mouth is next to the guys face and bellows, "We in the fucking RTR Mess also have a tradition; when a fucking brother officer is found standing in your cereal... he wants the fucking milk pronto!"

This joke still makes me smile.

Hells teeth! In the C Squadron Officer's Mess there was 'Flora' the Mess everything. When I worked the Bar in the mess alternating patrol days with drinking - the mess bills I have to admit charging scotch but drinking Campari (Well, apart from the 15 crates of Carlsberg export which I passed out the back door to my pals switches, Dai and co on Cambrai day) with Chris 'The Animal' Trevers as mess caterer. The woman was about 80 and totally indomitable – she'd (apparently) been raped by Turkish Paras during the invasion. Her achievements during our 6 months included:

Beating another choggie member of mess staff senseless with a mop when CT sacked him for nicking meat out the kitchen and being discovered hiding it under his moped seat.

Beating (repeatedly) Paul 'the black whale' the mess waiter over the head with a broom while chasing him twice round the mess exterior perimeter after he'd hidden a chameleon under a pan on the drainer which, when she lifted the pan to dry it, puffed up, hissed and scared the crap out of her sending her screaming to the bar where CT and I were plastered and showed her no sympathy resulting in her beating us with a towel before setting about Paul with the broom.

She also hit 'Murphy' the mess cat with a saucepan which resulted in multiple fractures and a twist of the neck by us followed by ritual burial. I believe that was actually Murphy mk 2, mk1's fate being unknown?

She was also responsible for the merciless beating of my shirts to bleached extinction in her DIY laundrette consisting of a nearby stream and some stones with soap.

We believed that she was also the Amazon warrior queen responsible for, but not proven, of mixing of the 2i/c (Chris Patey's) contact lens solution on his dresser resulting in him running, screaming "Help me, my fucking eyes are on fire!" early one morning as he bounced off the corridor walls from his room. CT and I really pissed ourselves at witnessing that one.

The incessant screaming of "Pezevengi, pezevengi!" at everyone until we got the translation which was "motherfucker" and CT gave her such a bollocking that she cried!

We also believed that it was 'Admiral Flora' smashing and sinking (with a broom of course) the Subalterns flotilla of wind up boats in the pond with which they played each evening over cocktails.

Yes indeed, she was pretty amazing!

The other occasion of maritime destruction was at Cambrai when the new fleet got scuppered by 'all the lads' drunkenly trying to float a trestle table in the pond while wearing pirate hats and shouting into the mess "wankers!" very loudly. 'Billy' B really saw his backside over that one, me copping for most of the blame over 15 crates of beer which were seen being consumed in the pond with me drunkenly besporting myself at the helm of the HMS trestle wearing nothing but barrack dress trousers. The 'crew' was busy ripping branches from the overhanging tree while led in a chorus of "BEEEDEEEB" by Switches!

But, once my duties in the Mess were over, it would be a rush to the NAAFI for a beer and chat with my mates. They were always eager to hear of any gossip I'd picked up from the Officers, who once they'd had a drink or two were sometimes less than politically correct. Normally as I'd sit chatting one of the NCOs would ask me if I fancied a drive on patrol next day. Invariably I would answer yes, and then head for bed as the patrols always started really early. I seemed to be quite popular among the lads as if they wanted time off I was only too willing to help.

The Sabre troops at this time were still 9, 10, 11 and 12 troops but they had also given themselves 'names'. 9 Troop were known as 'Penguin Troop'(all flap and no fly), 10 Troop were 'Wings Troop' as the Troop Leader was known as a bit of a 'Flapper'. 11 Troop were 'Shelly's Heroes' after Pete 'Shelly' Sheldrake, who was an NCO of the same ilk as 'Oddball' the tank Commander in the film Kelly's Heroes which was a cult film of ours. 12 Troop was 'The flying fish-slice' after their aptitude for fried cookery. As a bit of an artist I had the task of designing the small Troop cartoon emblems and painting them on the Ferrets. So, 9 Troops vehicles received a small black and white penguin, 10's a pair of wings, 11's a steel helmet with eyes and a pair of boots wearing it and 12 Troop got a Frying spatula with a pair of wings. I seem to remember the Troops getting the emblems transferred onto T shirts aswell.

On the subject of clothing, the UN protocol demanded that while on service and out in the public eye of Cypriots we could only wear UN uniform. This meant that our civilian attire in camp consisted mainly of shorts, T shirts and 'flip flops' on our feet. This took some getting used to as we were unaccustomed to leaving barracks for 'drinking duties' while still in uniform. More on drinking later.

The Sabre Troop patrol routine involved them rotating through 'outstations', I can't remember now how long each Troop stayed at an outstation for but they were glad to get back to base. The outstations were basically old disused buildings, one notably the 'carton factory', an old packaging plant. We at base camp could look forward to the amenities of base camp on return from patrol, but at the outstations it was on a self help basis for most things. Also, while serving with the UN you have to go to the nearest UN medical services that may not be British. We were not allowed near any of the Sovereign base areas on

Cyprus, as we were officially detached from their jurisdiction. So on outstation you had to go to a doctor belonging to whichever UN nation was responsible for the area you were operating in. In Cyprus at the time there were contingents of Swedish, Finnish, Canadian, Austrian and British operating. They were known as Swedcon, Finncon, Cancon, Austcon and we were Britcon.

One poor bloke of ours, Timmy, fell foul of the medics ruling. While on outstation he discovered he had contracted Gonorrhoea (he was warned about the pleasures of the flesh in the climate) so he duly reported sick. The nearest medics were Austrian and it appeared that their attitude to VD was less than sympathetic. There was no chance of penicillin and a pat on the head for a naughty boy, nor was there any chance of escape as they forced a tool known as the 'umbrella' into the tip of his manhood (and on three further occasions too!). He howled in pain "Fuuucccckkkking OUCCCHHHH!", I know this because his pals were all stood outside watching through a window, as they'd stopped during a patrol while the poor chap went to the doctor. The worst thing for the lad was that they were all laughing loudly like twats as the deed was done. So there was no sympathy from either the medical staff or his mates.

From base camp our patrol routes always started with a mad dash through Nicosia centre, dodging buses, pedestrians, animals and school parades (a strange phenomena) and if not the leading Ferret, hammering with gusto through red lights so that the patrol did not get split up. Anyway the Cypriots ignored traffic lights so why shouldn't we? The buses we saw were antique flat bed trucks with what looked like old railway carriages attached to them. They were inevitably filled with people and strapped to the open boot lid would be livestock in or out of containers. The roofs always seemed to have baskets of chickens on them. Please don't tell me it's still like that, it was truly dreadful. As I've said, traffic was a catastrophe, one day 'Shelly' drove a brand new Landrover, freshly delivered with only 4 miles on the Speedo into town. Two hours later it returned with him, but in pieces on the back of a truck. He'd driven quite normally through a green light only to find a bus bearing down on him as it shot through a red light. The resulting crash sent the Landrover and 'Shelly' rolling over and over down the street.

Anyway, having got safely through the city centre our patrol would either head to 'bomb alley, or to one of the other patrol routes South of Nicosia.

11. Buffer Zone Patrolling

It has to be said that I thoroughly enjoyed going on patrol as it broke the monotony of Officers mess duty. My pals though, probably thought patrolling every day was monotonous, but who am I to judge? All I know is that I had a great time. I've just explained the Nicosia dash so lets continue down a route. I mentioned 'bomb alley' and this was a patrol route through the suburbs of Nicosia. As you will have no doubt learnt, Cyprus is divided into North and South by a line known as the Buffer zone. This zone is a no mans land kept to separate the Turkish held North from the Greeks in the South. 'Bomb Alley' was an extension of this zone running through Nicosia's suburbs. In parts it was simply a street with buildings so close to each other across this street, that the weapon muzzles of the opposing armies poking from the windows almost touched each other above our heads. Tensions were still very high between the two nations, and they would continually 'play chicken' with each other to see if someone would shoot first. This game could at times be quite alarming for us as we were sat in white vehicles with reflective UN signs on the side, a better target would never be found. Our instructions were strictly no shooting unless in self-protection, scary because we knew that before we would be able to fire we'd actually be fucking dead. Every building lining the street had its doorways and windows blocked with sandbags or bricks as a defensive measure. Midnight patrol was the worst as the opponents would all be shouting at each other with loudspeakers and shining spotlights across at each other. Also at night you could hear them continually cocking their guns as if ready to fire just to see if the enemy would react.

Once we had passed out the far end of the street we broke into more open countryside only to find it was dotted with Turkish tanks sat continually in readiness. It would be true to say that the tanks were old by NATO standards as they were only modernised Russian post WW2 T34's. But still there were quite a few of them about. One day we came across an example of the Greek armies answer to this threat, a Marmon-Herrington armoured car which looked as if it had come straight from battle in the 1930's Khyber pass. It was truly ancient with both its rear wheels moving on flat tyres. It was hardly surprising that the relatively modern Turkish army had rolled up half the island in a short period of time.

Another patrol route, which brought us into regular contact, was when we had to travel from Nicosia towards Larnaca on the then main road to patrol the south-eastern end of the zone. This involved us travelling through what was called the Louroujina salient. This was a thin Southwards bulge of Turkish held land in the southern tip of which was the small town of Louroujina. When the Turks had invaded they decided that this Turkish inhabited town would be taken and protected by them. This they did and it remains today a Turkish town in the Greek part of the island connected only by this thin strip of land or salient. As we neared the salient we would firstly pass a Greek army checkpoint. I say passed as we swept past the Troops who were invariably asleep inside, with their Thompson machine guns neatly stacked outside the hut. Then onwards until we came to the Turkish checkpoint marked by a large arch extolling the virtues of Agar Turk and the Republic. Beneath the arch, across the road was a large metal barrier with a wheel and rail affair to allow it to be opened. Marching behind the gate back and forth would be two Turkish sentries clad in battle gear. Before we even reached the barrier our Ferrets would be attacked by what appeared to be wild dogs that jumped on board and attempted to bite any limb we left protruding from the 'car'.

We would now produce our UN identity cards and having satisfied themselves to our validity we would be allowed through. During one such stop we found ourselves chatting to a Turkish guard who was in fact English born and bred. We gathered he was an adventurer who had joined the Turkish army before the Cypriot war for a laugh! He told us a little about the way the conscripts with him were treated. They were fed once a day from a tractor and trailer on which was a large urn full of gruel. The troops would have to run, jump on, help themselves and jump down again, whatever remained in their cups was for them to digest. If they failed to meet the tractor (which never stopped), that was it until next day. We found a new respect for the Turkish soldiers that day, as they weren't our enemy, just fellow soldiers doing their job. He also told us about the orange groves found on their land. It seemed the Greeks had strewn them with anti personnel mines, no Turk soldiers were allowed in and infringement could actually be punished by death. So when we passed through on Christmas day that year, giving the Turks cigarettes and chocolate, and on the return journey that they gave us an orange each, we were quite touched as we knew what they had risked to give us this fruit. We had no such respect for the Greeks, as they just weren't professional.

Once we left the Turk checkpoint we were on a stop watch, they monitored how long we took to pass through the salient and were given an amount of time to present ourselves at the other end. Once there we passed out through another Turk checkpoint then a Greek one and on to our start point for the patrol. When we were in the salient it never ceased to amaze me how bomb scarred and derelict everything looked. There were fenced areas full of rotting cars and minefield signs dotted everywhere. Cars in Cyprus at that time were all very old British marques, which looked as if they come from a museum but somehow due to the climate looked like new with not a spot of rust.

I have not dwelt on the Turkish-Greek conflict, as this book is in no way intended to be a political statement. I will leave political history to the professionals. From a soldiers point of view Cyprus was not a pretty place at that time. We saw all the non-tourist highlights such as refugee villages with children and adults defecating in open drainage gutters. This left us all in wonderment how politicians can be willing to put their populations into such poverty. We were not even allowed as troops to stop and offer sweets to the children. But we did manage to throw some goodies out when the occasion arose.

Anyway upon return to Nicosia we finished work for the day and headed for the nearby outdoor swimming pool reserved for our use, along with the few RAF helicopter detachment's staff with who we shared our camp. Life at the pool could be quite hazardous as Timmy found to his cost one day. We were sat at the poolside enjoying the sun when we heard a humming sound loudly heading towards us. It sounded like a flight of WW2 bombers as it droned on, then a large black cloud appeared and swarmed around us. The cloud consisted of Hornets, BIG 'fuck off'hornets with fucking red arses and a yellow tip to them. Poor Tim managed to get stung and his neck swelled up to the size of a large tennis ball. It took days and loads of anti-biotics before his neck regained its normal appearance. Once bitten, twice shy? Too bloody right, after that if, at poolside we heard that drone, two seconds later we were all imitating bricks at the bottom of the pool.

We were fortunate during our 'tour' not to have any shooting incidents, well, we did have two. The first was when an irate farmer loosed off both barrels of his shotgun at a passing Ferret. The salvo was caused as a Troop whizzed down a patrol route onto which the farmers goat herd had strayed. The approaching scout cars scared the goats so badly that it would definitely take the farmer ages to gather his herd back into some semblance of order. So he vented his spleen by venting both barrels of his 12 bore. Strangely enough it was a herd of goats that caused the second incident. I was driving Corporal John Berwick on patrol down part of a route along an ancient Roman road. Suddenly from the Turkish positions on our left a man came running towards us firing his pistol in the air.

"Fuck me, I'll have this bastard, see if I don't!" shouted John as he spun our turret towards the Turk. A mechanical crunch signified that 'JB' had cocked the.30. A loud giggle escaped his lips as he prepared for action. Suddenly the Turk, who by now could be identified as an officer, stopped and started to wave at us. 'JB' now cursed "what the fucking hell does he want?" 'JB' and our other vehicle commander both dismounted and, clutching their loaded SMGs went to investigate. Shortly, all three men climbed up to the positions and disappeared. Five minutes later a herd of goats came scampering down the hill towards us followed by our commanders. The entire herd ran across our front with 'JB' and the other chap in hot pursuit puffing loudly in the heat as they disappeared from view around a hill. After about twenty minutes they reappeared without the goats. It turned out that the Turks were 'mildly pissed off' as a Greek goatherd had allowed his charges to get into the Turk positions and then promptly buggered off leaving the Turks to it. So ended an interesting diversion.

12. Spare time

Back in Nicosia, life seemed to be a roller coaster of drinking. One evening in the NAAFI bar we had a riot, at least to an outsider it would have seemed like a riot. To us though it was simply a game of 'bar rugby'. This game is definitely not one I would recommend to anyone on the grounds that it can only ever lead to disaster.

It had started courtesy of 'Switches' who had, some time previously decided he was a bloody diesel locomotive. He had been heard for days as he went around camp sounding his vocal horn; "BEEEEEEE DEEEEEB' he would bellow. On the night in question we were all sat comfortably having a nice calm drink when in through the french window came the echo of his signature horn. Having arrived and got his drink we were treated to more Beee Deeebs than we could stomach. Some of us though must have thought it hilarious as they encouraged 'Switches' to continue. 'Switches' was as usual willing to oblige. In the end a prolonged example of his prowess resulted in someone frisbeeing a metal ashtray at 'Switches'' head. It narrowly missed and bounced off a wall. Amongst shouts of 'bar rugby' the squadron members assembled rapidly formed into two roughly equal sides.

The first group named themselves 'the Bee-Deebs and appointed 'switches', who was by now wearing a metal litter bin on his head for protection, as captain. The other group had no captain but announced themselves as 'the Anti Bee-Deebs'. Both teams adopted 'altars' at opposing ends of the bar and prepared to defend them, potentially to the death. At this point the poor Greek barman decided it may be prudent to close the bar. Wrong, nothing could be so imprudent, two men launched themselves across the bar and kept it open for 'replen' purposes. With an almighty roar the match began, the tin ashtray screaming through the air at a frightening speed. I seem to remember the object of the game being to score points by touching the 'ball' down on your opponents 'altar', but it was hazy then as it is now. There didn't seem to be any more rules judging by the amount of flailing arms and legs appearing from the resulting 'scrum'. The game continued, stopping only for the participants to take on more beer in a vain attempt to keep cool. During one such break the Orderly Officer entered through the now demolished french windows. That night the duty was being covered by a Staff

Sergeant who's name I'll once more withhold out of respect. This poor man tried to halt proceedings and close the bar. A mistake indeed, as he suddenly found himself well fucking totempoled by a right to the chin, prone and on the floor semi conscious.

A favourite saying at the time, taken from the film 'Monty Python and the Holy Grail', was "Burn him". This shout went up and before we knew it someone had fetched a five gallon can of petrol and was pouring it over the Orderly Officer. However when this idiot tried lighting a match with which to light the fire, his matches were sopping wet. Suddenly the room hushed, what the fuck was this idiot doing? You simply don't burn Tankie comrades, knob head or not. Someone quickly wrested the matches from the fool and along with a couple of other willing helpers helped the 'witch' to his feet and the bar quietly and quickly emptied as we decided that enough was enough. The next day the search was on for a member of SHQ 'Stumpy' as he was known. He had last been seen somewhat the worse for wear the previous night. The search was on, high and low everybody looked, then, when we thought we'd lost him for good, from up on higher than we'd looked we heard a loud bawling noise. All glanced up and, there was 'Stumpy' tied into a wicker chair but, balanced somewhat precariously on top of the cookhouse chimney. Some japesters had managed to imprison him in the chair and get up to his new perch. God knows how they'd achieved this because it took ages to get the poor screaming sod down. When we had all finished laughing, we were all chastised severely by both the OC and 'Taff'. The punishment was bar closure for a couple of nights and we were all confined to barracks.

Please don't misunderstand this event, it was only ever intended as a game it should not detract from our excellent character and devotion to duty. Such games normally result in good morale and team building. In this case it simply got too boisterous. No harm was done and discipline was maintained. The old saying that Tankies work hard and play even harder certainly applied that night. A Tankies ability to carry out his duty in a professional manner was never jeopardised by his foolishness in his 'spare' time.

It is well known that servicemen have a tarnished reputation when it comes to free time fun and games. We were as mischievous as anyone when we were drinking. In Nicosia there was a street called Regina Street which we lovingly called 'Vagina' Street. This street was lined wall to wall with bars. Each bar had the letters UN somewhere in the name, for example; Sweet Carolyn's UN bar. Each of these bars displayed insignia from every UN contingent past and present which had served in Cyprus. We 'Brits' were never hugely popular in the bars as we were noted for not having as much cash to spend as the other nations' troops. But, undeterred we sallied forth on some occasions to drink 'downtown'. Most of these bars were populated by 'whisky dollies' who's job it was to entice us into buying them drinks at extortionate prices so that the bar owner split the profits with the girls. They went to extraordinary lengths to get us to buy these drinks. We could expect to walk into these bars and within seconds have a small hand thrust down our trousers to grab our 'privates' followed by the exclamation; "oh! you a big boy Johnny, you buy me whisky, I show you a good time ficky, ficky, jig a jig!" this always made us laugh because there was no way we were going to fall for this. Possibly it was because of our wise rebuffs of these antics that we became so unpopular. That being the case it was no wonder that the medics of other nations frowned so heavily on soldiers with VD as was the case with the Austrians on outstation.

One bar of note was Helen's bar which was and, judging by the amount of people I've since met who've heard of it, still is, totally notorious. Helen herself was a woman who was blessed by many men's standards with a pair of magnificent breasts. She would guarantee that anyone could give her a key ring, regardless of the amount of keys on it and hang, then twirl it on one of her nipples, which she regularly did.

A favourite prank of C squadron at the time was to hunt the Military Police. This started after we celebrated Cambrai day in Nicosia. The day had started in the traditional fashion. But the raiding parties got completely out of hand and, before we knew it our NAAFI bar was festooned with all the various nations signs which had been at the entrances to their respective camps. At around lunchtime two UN military policemen appeared in the NAAFI to enquire where their sign had gone. It had in fact been unbolted from the wall next to their duty room hatch under their very noses. What an achievement! When they tried to retrieve it these two poor guys were despatched from our camp in their 'birthday suits!' From that moment on 'pig baiting' became our favourite sport 'downtown'.

A casual observer on any given night would have seen an MP vehicle park in Regina street and the occupants get out and enter a bar to check if everything was okay. As soon as the policemen disappeared in through the door, furtive, uniformed figures would appear from the gloom of the nearest alleyway, proceed to strip the vehicle of anything removable(including blue flashing lights, distributor caps and spare wheels) let down the tyres and then disappear back into the dark. These figures were of course members of C squadron. Upon returning the MPs would find their vehicle immobilised and have to phone for help.

One night a chum 'Kim' Telfer was drinking with others at the '22 Steps' bar which, strangely, was atop 22 steps! 'Kim' was bursting for the toilet but it was already overloaded and awash with drunken soldiers! 'Kim' promptly stepped drunkenly out onto the balcony overlooking the street, loosed the last turkey in the shop from it's prison and stared to urinate. This was quickly followed by the sound of liquid splashing on metal and a loud shout from below. Kim was actually pissing on the helmets of 2 patrolling MP's below. As they ran up the 22 steps Kim was shinning rapidly down a drain pipe in an attempt to evade having his collar felt by the 'fucking rozzers!"

As the end of our stay in Cyprus approached the Troops found themselves preparing for a mounted parade on the abandoned Nicosia Airport within the UN base area. When the parade day arrived the 'selected few' were presented with their UN Peacekeeping medals during the parade by the UNFICYP residing British commanding officer. During his farewell speech to us the Brigadier praised us for our professional approach to soldiering in helping maintain the peace. Back at our barracks that afternoon, those of us who had not been chosen to receive our medals had ours thrown at us in small blue boxes in the SQMS' stores, it did take the edge off our egos. That evening as we got out of a taxi in Regina street I saw Kev House swimming in flooded road works still wearing full uniform and 'Sam' Boundy was down a dark alley having the crap knocked out of him by two hairy Greeks, professionally of course, and yes, we did intervene to stop the assault. Well that was it, Cyprus finished and, back to 'Blighty'.

Before I leave Cyprus behind I should just like to say a farewell to SSM 'Taff'. I feel it right to do so.

During our time in Cyprus, 'Taff' decided it was time to retire. This he did, and the night before his departure we all gathered in the NAAFI bar to say our farewells. It was a good night with many emotions vented. 'Taff' was undoubtedly sad to be leaving and even though he put on a brave face until, after our stirring rendition of an Adge Cutler and the Wurzels song he felt he had to sing a reply. Amid much cheering 'Taff' climbed atop a table and let loose with a wonderful deep tenor voice in the song 'Goodbye'. He truly had a wonderful voice and by the time he'd finished there wasn't a dry eye in the place. With that we bade him farewell and he departed. Some two weeks later as we got up one morning and went for breakfast we noticed that our flags were at half mast. As we entered the cookhouse we found to our dismay that 'Taff' had indeed returned to his family but had died in tragic circumstances. The official announcement was made later on Squadron parade. This moved us all deeply as 'Taff' had been a real character, from riding in his Ferret across Salisbury Plain wildly dispatching rabbits and other wildlife with his trademark shotguns, to screaming at naked Troopers on Squadron parade. I personally owed him much as through him as a Queens Testing Officer I had passed all my driving tests.

Life of course went on. We had our new SSM for our return to the UK in 'Bernie' Foster and a fine one he would be too. But, somewhere deep down we missed 'Taff' who now I suspect will be chastising somebody on that Great tank park in the sky.

13. "How bloody much?"

As we returned from Cyprus, our plane landed at RAF Brize Norton and as we clumped down the steps we were met by a huge wave of... Brrrrrrr it was flaming freezing. Or at least compared to Cyprus!

We milled about for a while as heated discussions were going on over by a telephone. Apparently while we'd been away, our barracks at 'Tiddy' had been swapped around and we were going to be housed in a different block. That in itself wasn't a great issue except that the block wasn't ready for our arrival. To us it was no issue whatsoever because, there on the spot, we were issued with leave passes for ten days along with train tickets and told to return to barracks at the end of that period.

With these instructions ringing in our ears, we boarded buses and sped to the nearest railway station at Swindon and away we went. Those of us heading towards Devon had the inevitable changes at Taunton, Bristol and then at Exeter St Davids. While at Bristol we dived into the buffet for a drink. Without even thinking we ordered a round of brandy sours which we had discovered in Cyprus. First problem? Explaining to the BR staff how to make a bloody brandy sour. Second problem? Once successfully made, the price that was announced made us all chorus..."how bloody much? How bloody fucking much?" Of course everything in Cyprus was so cheap we had obviously lost touch with what the Chancellor of the Exchequer had been up to at home. Anyway we dutifully chipped in to pay for the round. Third problem? "What the fuck is this supposed to be?" we exclaimed as we were handed some one pound notes as change. "Don't try slipping us your scabby Monopoly money mate!" We continued little realising that these were indeed new currency and in fact perfectly legal. At that point we were ejected from the buffet with a flea in our ear about language and its correct usage. Oh joy to be home!

It was a joy to be home and after six months away there was so much catching up to do. So after I had handed over all the souvenirs I'd brought back for my family, it was off to the pub. AAAAAH! What a lovely cool pint of Devon Scrumpy can do for the soul. Of course, there were many admiring comments about my wonderful tan, and as I was something of a novelty (Soldiers, tiny Hamlets, and South Devon were not words that fitted well together at that time), many drinks were bought for me. So, little surprise then, that I was helped home at a thoroughly ungodly hour.

I found it strange going on leave because when I arrived the first question my mother Jean always asked was "Malc, when are you going back?" Strange in as much as when some lost traveller would stop in the village, see my father Gordon and ask him for directions, my fathers first question would invariably be, "well, where 'ave 'e just come from?" At this point the poor soul would look worriedly at my father and say, "Birmingham!" The conversation from that point on could become quite confusing. But, as usual leave always came to its inevitable end too soon.

Back at Tidworth we found that, other than where we were now sleeping not much had changed. The food in the cookhouse was steadily improving under the control of a new 'Master Chef'. And the tanks were still there, at least, still there in body or what was left of them. While we had been away the B Squadron 'mice' had been at play. Obviously while we'd been away 'Bumbles' exercise commitment had escalated not helped by the governments ever increasing spending cuts. Quite apart from a Fireman's Strike having got in the way, most of our guys found themselves in Edinburgh for a while. So it should have been no surprise to find our Tanks, instead of serviced, cannibalised.

The spending cuts had become so heavy-handed that it really was now, almost impossible to acquire spare parts. Our uniform too, was now suffering, as we couldn't even get fucking new socks. I don't pretend to understand what the Labour party were trying to achieve, other than to appease any other malcontents that came under their nationalised scheme of things. But they certainly didn't make any friends in the forces. Either way my only concern at this stage was that on returning to Tidworth, I found that at last I'd received my wish and was now a Crewman in a Sabre Troop. Namely 9 Troop, as Operator on the Troop Corporals Tank, Callsign Three One Bravo (31B). Oh what joy! My commander was to be Corporal Pete 'Stan Janner' Davis ('Janner' being a colloquialism for a Bristolian). The driver was Gordon 'Rabbit' Menhennit (now sadly passed on, RIP) and the gunner, a new recruit from Yorkshire, 'Cooperman'. I'll now take the time to give you a brief rundown on these personalities.

'Stan'… how or where do I begin… well, he was a towering chap well over 6 feet in height with a personality to match. His trade marks were firstly, a magnificent handlebar moustache, which various senior ranks were continually telling him to "fucking shave it off Corporal!"(It was to do with respirators and their face seals not working properly with such a growth on the face) but 'Stan' always just smiled. Having seen 'Stan' at a couple of reunions I can tell you that even today it is still, safely ensconced under his nose. Secondly 'Stan' had a propensity for wearing non-regulation uniform. He always wore an old style British camouflage 'para' smock that he'd acquired instead of our issued DPM 'cam' jackets. But to be fair we all adapted the way we dressed when on 'scheme'. He was undoubtedly one of the best commanders we had at that time in C. Squadron. If anyone was to leave a mark on me during my career it was 'Stan'. He was always in control, nothing seemed to 'phase' him. No matter what the situation he always had control of both his own and our senses. He treated his crew in a firm but fair manner and was the original 'old sweat' tank Commander. When I became a Commander in my later years I attempted to remember everything I'd learnt from 'Stan', was I successful? Only my crews would be able to answer that one.

'Rabbit' just the name makes you wonder doesn't it? Apparently as I remember it his name sprung from a liking for the fairer sex. I was never sure whether it was because he was successful with girls or whether he would have liked to 'go at it like a rabbit' given the chance with a girl. His motto was certainly, "If it has tits and stands still long enough, bonk it!" Either way, a damned good bloke and a cracking tank driver, always up to his elbows in grease and shit. No task seemed to great or difficult, well other than walking, he always walked like John Wayne without a horse as he was slightly bow legged. Sadly Rabbit is no more, he too has passed up to the 'great tank park in the sky' he is also sadly missed.

Brian 'Cooperman', now, a strange one this as at this time he was an unknown quantity. We did know however that he had a knack for trouble. On one of his first nights with us, we were sat in the NAAFI having a few beers. Brian went to buy the next round having told us how hard Yorkshiremen were, and there sat on a bar stool was Jack. Jack had taken to drinking in the NAAFI periodically to escape the Sergeants Mess. Now, Brian approached the bar and in his own cocksure way acknowledged Jack as 'mate'. As I've previously explained, Jack then treated Brian to Thirty minutes of war experience. Brian stood and listened, occasionally glancing and winking at us over his shoulder. When Jack finally wiped a tear from his eye having finished, Brian smirked at him and thinking it clever, said to Jack... "Fuck, that must have been some fucking scheme mate?" At that point we all ducked for cover, Jack stood up, grabbed Brian by his throat and then punched him clean across the bar, his only comment being "Fucking nigs, and DON'T CALL ME FUCKING MATE!" Unfortunately Brian was never to learn his lesson.

So that, in a nutshell was our crew. The rest of the Troop? Our Troop Leader was S/Sgt Brian 'Scouse' Lindores; 'Staff' to his chums. Our Troop Sergeant was Chris 'The Animal' T. Other personalities included drivers, 'Ribbo' and, oh god, 'Switches', Gunner 'Swilly' (by now sometimes called 'Twinkletoes' after the runaway tank incident), and a good friend of mine Nick 'The Spot' Allen. This then was the backbone of 9 'Penguin' Troop which sallied forth together for its shakedown exercise on Salisbury plain. We had retained 'Penguin' from Cyprus as had all our Troops kept their 'identities'. I had of course, dutifully painted our penguins onto the Tanks. Just a small black and white bird inside the C. Squadron circles on each side of our turrets.

This first exercise got off to a less than an auspicious start. Within the first fifteen miles of the Squadron's journey all of our vehicles lay broken down with various mechanical failures. Radio calls for REME assistance scattered through the airwaves like confetti. Our tanks had obviously missed us during our Mediterranean absence, and boy were they being vengeful now! Our Panzer was one of the last to go, its demise being announced by 'rabbit' over the IC as, "Stan, the fucking engines hot!" Both 'Stan' and I automatically glanced over our shoulders at the back of the Tank, only to see a massive, dense white cloud of smoke billowing out behind us. 'Fuck, the liners have blown' 'Stan' cursed. The 'liners' being the coolant jackets around each cylinder which had a tendency to wear out allowing coolant to pour into the engine and 'burn' off through the intense heat. "Keep going Rabbit, well make it to the wood" 'Stan' told 'Rabbit'. And make it to the wood we did. Having sent a radio message asking for assistance we sat back to await repair.

On the way 'Stan' had made sure I'd switched on the 'BV' this was the boiling vessel. Any crew will tell you how valuable the BV is, it is simply a square box sealed with a lid, inside the turret and connected to the electric's. Once filled with water and heated it becomes the most important piece of kit on the Tank. You can put tins of 'compo' in it to heat for your meal and use the water for making a brew. So the food was heated as I'd thrown the cans in before departure and now all I had to do was make the tea. Cans in the BV is, I'm sure a sore subject with many crews, as many a can of baked beans or rice pudding has exploded due to over-cooking, leaving a pebble-dash effect on the turret roof as evidence. The BV was so important that a standing joke was that no tank should pass any mechanical examination unless the BV was fully functional. In fact a BV ceasing to function was enough to bring on a mild seizure for the REME electricians, as they knew they would be hounded remorselessly by the owners until it was fixed.

So as we tucked into steak & kidney pudding, peas and mash and a cup of tea, we sat and waited, and waited and fucking waited for the REME. Once we had finished our tea and Cooperman and I had washed up we gave 'Rabbit' a hand in preparing the tank and in particular the main engine, for a 'pack change'. Yes, the only answer to our predicament was to replace the engine. "New?" I hear you ask, no, just an overhauled unit from the field workshops in Tidworth.

Crew 31B watching the record 'pack change'.

We heard the FV434 (REME workshop vehicle) trundling towards us for some time. This was because they were having trouble finding us. But, in due course they did find us and three and a half-hours later (quite a record of speed in those days) we had our new, throbbing mechanical heart. Believe it or not that engine lasted us another two years with only minor running repairs. The Squadron received eight pack changes that night and the other seven ended in disaster as the new 'packs' had not, apparently' been 'prepped' correctly at the workshops. The upshot being that some poor REME Officer had his 'Arse right royally chewed' for causing the debacle that caused all seven of those engines to expire within a collective distance of about one mile. To be fair, this was not the usual way of things, major failures of this nature were relatively rare. British tank crews have always been taught how to effect 'battlefield repairs' or 'bodges' to keep the tank on the go. So running repairs were fairly common for we Brits, unlike our continental and American allies who, having simply dropped a spanner into the engine decks would simply radio for mechanical assistance and wait.

We did break down again that exercise, but not through engine failure. One wet and stormy afternoon we were motoring down a track when suddenly we veered off the track to the right down a small bank. 'Rabbits' only acknowledgement being "Fuck, aaaaaargh, fuck". We climbed out to investigate the cause of our steering problem. In due course we found that we had lost a quillshaft. A quillshaft is a removable drive shaft or steel rod, one found on each side of the Tank. They are shaped effectively like a key and connect the vehicles' Gearbox to the tracks by being inserted from outside into the final drive thereby connecting said final drive with its sprocket wheel to the power transmitted from the gearbox. In short no quillshaft, no motion. The quillshaft was kept in position by a screwed in end cap which; itself was kept secure by a screw to stop it undoing accidentally. However our tank had lost all the bits for one side which was previously unheard of. And of course as it was such a rare occurrence nobody carried spare parts. So we had to sit and wait for the ARV (REME Armoured Recovery Vehicle) to come and tow us to a wood where we could await a spare quillshaft. All four of us squeezed in the turret in attempt to stay out of the rain, while I made the obligatory 'cup o' char'. 'Stan' had elevated the gun barrel to lower the height of the breech so, sat in the commanders seat he could stretch his legs out onto the top of the gun. This meant that 'rabbit', Brian and I were cramped into the operators side of the turret. 'Snug' would be one word to describe it, 'fucking cramped' would be two more words you could use.

Suddenly the comic element in our situation hit all of us except 'Stan' who remained resolute in his sadness at breaking down. He always took breakdowns as a personal reflection on his adequacy as a commander. So as the three of us giggled inanely, 'Stan' sat in silence pondering the world and how it had come to this. Suddenly he lashed out at us with his foot exclaiming, "think its fucking funny, do we? Well the next fucker who laughs will double to the end of the track and back with a spare track link under each arm!" This had the desired effect and we duly shut up. But, as is the way I looked at Brian and saw him smirking. At that point we both had the urge to guffaw, but fought it off, the problem being the more we fought, the more we wanted to laugh until suddenly the turret rang with our combined laughter. 'Rabbit' managed to remain composed knowing 'Stan' of old. The next thing we knew Brian and I were perched on the engine decks in the rain. Later 'Stan' packed us onto the Troop Leaders tank and despatched us with the 'Bivvie' and a crate of beer to set up camp for 'Stan' and 'Rabbit's' arrival later that day. At one o'clock the next morning Brian and I, having consumed the beer, were lying in our sleeping bags under the shelter of our leaky 'Tank bivvie'. We were sure we could hear a Chieftain's distinctive engine wail but it appeared to be circling the wood at some distance. "Ha, that'll be Stan and Rabbit doing a big right hand circle trying to get to us!" cracked Brian. Sure enough early next morning 31B appeared, towed in by our REME's Centurion ARV, and bugger me, Brian had been right. When the ARV didn't show up the night before 'Stan and Rabbit' had attempted to reach us in ever decreasing right hand circles. Well we didn't labour the point as 'Stan' looked less than pleased with both the situation and Brian's and my alcohol ringed eyes. Later, when he discovered we'd, in fact, supped the entire beer supply we were chased around the wood!

Stan and me, 1978.

14. 'Boos... ' where?

9 Troop at Boostedt!

1978 became a whirlwind of schemes, nights out drinking (when we had the time) and continually keeping the tanks as prepared as we could for the next scheme. When we were 'on scheme' life still presented us with adventures. Top of the list of social events were evenings where, when we weren't tactical, we could park up and light a small fire, have a couple of beers and pass the evening away fondly remembering previous adventures. Sometimes when the whole Squadron was assembled in the same wood we would have what was termed a 'Squadron Smoker'. These were great fun and involved lighting a 'rather' larger fire and having 'rather' larger amounts of beer. We could then sit as a Squadron and enjoy each other's company and, if the occasion arose, a bloody good singsong. Apart from the usual soldiers chants we, as Westcountrymen, rather liked a fucking good rendition of 'Adge Cutler and the Wurzels' songs. A couple of these spring to mind, namely, 'When the Charlton Mackrell jug band hit the charts' and the 'Wurp di diddle I doe' songs. These singsongs were invariably led by our 'Swilly' who had an uncanny knack of remembering the words to 'Wurzel' songs. I don't want to give you the impression that schemes were just a big piss up. That is simply not true, 'smokers' were normally set up at the end of scheme and were simply designed for us to 'let off steam' and to bond once again in the 'family atmosphere'. Unfortunately as the Eighties progressed we were to find that 'smokers' became quite rare.

But, these were still the Seventies and 'smokers' were still fun. One night as we sat behind our vehicles in 9 Troop in a copse, 'Switches' disappeared from our midst. We just assumed he was going on a walk with shovel and toilet roll. But no, unbeknown to us he had 'borrowed' a tin of thunderflashes and was busy breaking them open in front of his Tank. He was attempting to build the biggest 'Genie' possible from the contents of the thunderflashes. We in the meantime were sat blissfully unaware around our small fire laughing and chatting away. Suddenly, WHOOSH! And a huge flash illuminated the wood for yards around. "Fuck me, what was... " the exclamation didn't finish as from round the front of his tank 'Switches' rushed into view clutching his arm and running like the wind. "OOOOOOOOOOOOWWWWWWWWWFFUUUUCCCCKKK-KIIIINNNNGGGGG OUCH" He howled in pain as he ran straight through our small fire and off into the dark through the trees. I quickly found myself caught up in the chase to catch and control 'Switches'. Once caught it transpired that, having made his mountain of gunpowder, 'Switches', using a box of matches had attempted to ignite the 'Genie'. A major setback to the task was the breeze, which kept blowing out the match. Without thinking 'Switches' had used his hand to shield the flame and had inserted the match in the pile. Bad move because he had left his hand still attached to the match. So when the explosive ignited so did the best part of 'Switches' forearm, result? Oh yes, he was evacuated to Tidworth Military hospital where he became the nurses' worst nightmare.

There were many more adventures to be had such as when one of SHQ's drivers 'Bugsy' turned awkwardly while exiting the drivers cab twisting and trapping a testicle which promptly swelled up like a balloon and had the Squadron laughing raucously for hours. Or the exercise where 'Stan' and CT decided every meal we ate would be curried. It was their job to cook every meal for each other's crew and for them to be the hottest curry possible. The objective being to make a curry that their rival's crew couldn't eat. Our crew won, albeit CT's 'curried egg butties' for breakfast, or his 'curried, puddings-sweet mixed fruit' (like Christmas cake in a tin) were definitely vile to put it mildly. But we didn't let 'Stan' down and ate everything that CT put in front of us. As a victory celebration 'Stan' treated us to a meal in Marlborough one evening in... A curry house of course. A good story was when the Royal

Engineers came to test their ability to dig an anti-Tank ditch. 'Ribbo' and his tank were volunteered for this as the test tank although 'Switches' and CT put up a damn good argument that it should have been them. Each day his tank returned from the test with less binwork but with a larger grin on 'Ribbo's' face. At the end of the week the Engineers virtually gave up because, "they dug the fucker, and I crossed the fucker!" as 'Ribbo' later informed us. The only problem was repairing the tank as, of course there were no spare parts to be had.

We found out one morning that yet another exercise was heading our way. To be more precise we were heading its way. Exercise Bold Guard was to be a massive NATO exercise in Germany that was to involve mobilising both UK regulars and Territorial units and getting them to the 'front line'. In due course we found ourselves transported to Marchwood near Southampton where we and our steel mounts were loaded into the bowels of Sir Lancelot. This ship was an LSL or Landing Ship Logistical, which strangely belonged to the Army not the Navy. Apart from the British military crew it was teeming with small Chinese fellows who made up the bulk of the crew. Once loaded, off we went on our journey to Esjberg in Denmark, hampered only for four hours in the middle of a rather choppy North Sea when the ships bloody engines broke down! We did ask whether they'd been built by British Leyland!

This breakdown had us vomiting over the interior and exterior of the ship in short order. That much of our stomach contents ended up in the sea that, I wouldn't have been surprised if the 'slick' had made the national news headlines. But in due course we arrived at our destination and we disembarked to await the unloading of our tanks.

Before I go on, I should like to point out that this was probably the first time that Sir Lancelot's crew had dealt with MBTs. This had no doubt caused the calamity which follows. When the tanks had loaded on in the UK they had been driven on from the stern and been tightly parked to the bows ready to drive out in Denmark. The problem was that the people in charge of loading had no comprehension of what a tank can or can't do manoeuvrability wise. The consequence was that once Sir Lancelot 'beached' on the Esjberg slipway and opened its bow doors, we stood for over an hour with the many spectators that had assembled to see such an unusual sight. There followed an hour, during which time all that could be heard was the howl of tortured engines and squeaks of steel tracks and great clouds of fumes belched out through the open bow doors. Then slowly the first tank emerged and clambered up the slipway. 'Stan' could be clearly heard screaming at people over their inability to load vehicles correctly.

Soon they were all out of their prison and making their way with us to a railway siding. There we were loaded onto flatbed rail carriages ready for what would become a two-day journey to Germany, north of Hamburg near the town of Neumunster.

Stan and 31B exiting Sir Lancelot at Esjberg... eventually!

In fact we found ourselves near a village named Boostedt in Schleswig-Holstein camped with a German tank Training Battalion. I use the word with; in fact we were camped just outside their barracks perimeter fence in a bog. Camped being the operative word as we had erected 140 pounder canvas tents, two tents housing one Troop. We were to be fed by the German cooks in their barracks cookhouse, but only for lunch and the evening meal. Breakfast was served at our tented wonderland. Its arrival each morning was heralded by the sound of a jeeps engine not dissimilar to a sowing machine. Once arrived, the Germans would give us generous portions of a continental style breakfast of bread rolls, cold meat, cheese, jam or chocolate paste all to be washed down with strong, sweet but very black coffee. During breakfast, activity on the German tank park, out of sight behind some trees, would begin. A cacophony of deep roars from powerful Maybach engines would pollute the air as the Leopard 1's would exit their hangars. The next thing would be the shrill noise of a whistle being blown followed by, the roar of engines as the Leopard's engines were revved up for some twenty minutes, their deep engine note setting up such a resonance that it hurt our ears.

Ablutions! A polite way of describing shaving and shitting! One of our dubious honours was to dig the toilet 'glory hole', this was a 10 foot deep by about 15 foot long hole with a wooden trestle above it holding a telegraph pole. The manner of 'taking a crap' was to drop one's clothing to the ankles and lean back across the hole below using the pole to support you. A somewhat precarious position… if you were to slip? Well, let's not even go there! Back to normal daily routine.

Breakfast out of the way, we would start by having our usual Squadron parade, then first parade the tanks and into the normal routine. Then would come lunch. What an adventure, we would walk through the German camp in our black overalls getting some strange looks from the (predominantly) conscript German trainees. Then into their cookhouse where we queued with Germans for lunch. The delicacies on offer varied daily from pickled herrings (cold) to pickled herrings(cold) served with bread and (it always seemed) a stream of chocolate flavoured milk. I pitied the poor German Army marching on its stomach. The evening meal wasn't much better but at least it was warm fish with mashed potato. We sat at tables marked for us while the Germans sat and stared at us and our looks of outright horror at the fare served to us. Our dislike of the German diet became a standing joke to the conscripts. I can speak German and could make out words like 'fat English bastards' and 'they aren't tough'. Which made my blood boil. Anyway the tables turned after a fortnight as our OC 'Billy' B complained so bitterly to RHQ that we had two cooks shipped in specially, once the Germans gave them permission to use their facilities.

Suddenly we found ourselves looking forward to meal times. And now of course we turned up at the cookhouse for breakfast as well. The looks on the German conscripts faces became the subject of our mirth now. We no longer looked like we might die of malnutrition fended off by the morning visit of a local fast food van, the van who's sales of sausages and chips had escalated madly as we spent vast sums of money to supplement our meagre rations. As we presented our plates to our cooks we nearly buckled under the weight of the steak and chips with all the trimmings which was slapped onto the crockery. As we paraded to our tables the conscripts were drooling like cartoon characters, their noses lifted to drag in the full impact of the aromas wafting from our plates. I can imagine that the British Army looked infinitely like the better bet to these poor creatures. But to be fair they did try their best to keep up the stoical German air of coolness.

Crew 31B having been on camp crapper digging duty

In the evenings we did find ourselves in a strange situation. We often found our way up to the village hostelry, where we found that we were such a novelty that we quickly made friends. That is of course apart from with any conscripts that may have been allowed out. We had to assert our authority quite quickly with the little buggers on a number of occasions. Having said that, the German regular soldiers with who we often shared a beer were a fine bunch of blokes. In fact they seemed to hate the conscripts more than us.

The thing that really pissed us off was the way the Germans insisted in showing off their Leopard tanks. Many was the time one of our commanders was returning from road testing his vehicle, having been overtaken at speed by a Leopard Bergpanzer (ARV) which was towing a Leopard MBT at the time. "Cocky fuckers!" would be loudly announced upon the return of one embarrassed commander after another, this meant only one thing, shown up by Leopards again!

Then one day the Germans had an open day in their camp. Just to add insult to injury we weren't invited, the German commandant obviously didn't want British Tankies about because he went so far as to organise buses to take us on a day trip. To where? Well fucking Kiel of course, to look at a restored WW2 U Boat on a beach, stood on a platform. The trip was well planned by our German hosts as the return bus trip would take most of the day on its own. Especially as we all got lost in pubs in a town on the way. It took our Senior ranks some considerable time to catch and re-bus the lot of us.

Having looked suitably impressed as we gawked at the U Boat we all jumped back on the buses and headed back to our swamp. Swamp was actually quite a fitting name as one morning we awoke to find 10 Troop's suitcases floating through the tents. In fact due to heavy rain during the night most of everyone's belongings were floating across the campsite. That just about summed it up for us, apart from the fact that we then had water borne insects such as mosquitoes to worry about. Still, we grinned and bore it, simply opening more cans of beer.

Admittedly the Germans weren't that bad and a few days later they gave us a couple of Leopards to play with and we got to drive these impressive beasts. We of course for our part, allowed them to inspect Chieftain but wouldn't let them drive it in case of breakdown (and a lack of fuel) but the OC later relented and allowed them a ride. But driven by one of us! So after this interesting interlude at Boostedt we were now ready for the FTX (Field Training Exercise) cunningly named Bold Guard. Don't ask me who thinks up the names!

15. Boldly Guarding

Just before 31B rolled forward, nearly killing Charlie and me.

Off we went then, having packed up camp we said our farewells, and once more were loaded onto trains to move Southwards to Exercise Bold Guard area.

This took about two days, as the German railways seemed to treat our train at a lower priority than cattle trains. We knew this when, after five hours sat in a siding we saw a train full of cows swish by on the mainline. All that waiting wouldn't have been that bad if we had been given a reasonable amount of carriages, but no we were all squashed into two carriages. Never mind we got there in the end.

As we were about to disembark from the train at the exercise area, Nick was sat in the cab while I chatted in front of the tank with our pal Charlie. Nick neglected to tell us that, due to his inexperience he'd already released the handbrake even though the engine was not switched on to power the footbrake.

Suddenly while shunting, the train lurched to a stop and lo, with a clank, the tank started to roll forwards. With a loud exclamation of "fuck me!" both Charlie and I leapt from the flat, narrowly avoiding a premature appointment with the grim reaper and his smelly little pals.

Little did I realise the adventures that were about to unfold. Blimey you could write a book about them, oh yes, I already am. The couple of adventures that follow are true even though it would be easy for you to dismiss them as 'something you only read in books!' Firstly we had had some changes in 9 troop, due to a manning problem, 'Rabbit' had moved to driving the Troop Leader otherwise our crew remained unchanged. My chum Nick ' The Spot' was now our 'cab rat'.

The only other change happened on the day of our first adventure. 'Stan' was seconded to command another tank and 'Charlie' Chaplin who had been commanding the Squadron's ambulance appeared to take over. 'Cooperman' had gone with 'Stan' so we were left as a crew of three. I quickly learned that 'Charlie' had a fairly 'relaxed' command style. Early this fateful morning we drove forth as a Squadron convoy heading for battle elsewhere. As we motored down the road I sensed that Nick was having problems with the steering. This was easy to sense as every time we approached a bend the tank started to jolt and lurch in an alarming manner. This was caused by nick 'pumping' the steering tillers in an attempt to get a response from the steering. 'Charlie' had adopted his 'usual' commanders position of pumping the commanders seat into the fully raised position, effectively jamming him into the commanders 'head out' position. So all you could see was 'Charlie's' head and shoulders with his arms outside the hatch. This combined with his heavy parka to ward off the early morning cold meant that he was immobilised from the armpits upwards. He could move his head and put his microphone to his mouth, and just about read his map but nothing more. I thought this strange, as we had no gunner to control the turret with the gun over the front of the tank as we motored along. Still he was the commander so who was I to question the sanity of this?

Realising that Nick was having problems I spoke to him on the IC;

"What the fuck's up Nick?" I inquired.

A muffled crackling reply came back;

"Fuc...... stee...ng's fuck.... gone!"

Right, okay the steering's up the creek I surmised from the broken message I'd received. I then said to Nick;

"Pull over mate, I'll have a look in the decks and see what's up." 'Charlie' was nodding in agreement. By the way the tank stopped suddenly I assumed that Nick had understood. I released the 'snap' connector on my radio gear and clambered onto the engine decks, joined shortly after by Nick. We opened the decks covering the gearbox and, using a torch (it was still four in the morning) inspected the gearbox for damage. It was immediately clear what our problem was, everything was covered in a thick coating of gearbox oil. The steering was achieved by the tillers, when pulled applying hydraulic pressure to brake pads which pushed onto a large disc each side of the gearbox. This braked the disc forcing the sprocket wheel driving the track on that side to slow down, the other side going faster effectively made the tank corner. I can't really explain it any simpler than that. Now, as everything was covered in oil, the pads weren't able to bring enough pressure to bear on either steering disc, hence Nick's problem. By now the rest of the Squadron had long overtaken us, so we would have to catch them up! My last advice to Nick as a relatively inexperienced driver was;

"Right mate, seen it before, if you stay in a lower gear and keep your revs up then pump like fuck on the tiller the pads will apply more pressure, and 'burn' themselves into the disc!"

"Righty fucking ho!" Came Nick's reply.

I wasn't unduly worried as I clambered back in the turret and plugged myself into the radio system. I lifted a headset on 'Charlie's' head and bellowed the result of our investigation in his ear. 'Charlie' nodded and gave me the thumbs up.

"Okay Nick clear to pull out," I said into my mic' and promptly nearly fell down into the turret with the force of Nicks lightning acceleration. I listened with horror as the tank burbled, clanked and roared its way up through the gearbox into sixth(top) gear. Had Nick understood my advice I wondered, or did he have some sort of death wish? No, Nick was just an enthusiastic, mad, speed demon in a tank who thought he knew better than everyone else. So here we were at four thirty in the morning, hammering down a quiet main road through the German countryside. Little did the poor village before us suspect of the carnage that was about to befall it.

As we entered the outskirts of the village I could see a long sweeping bend to the right, my immediate thought being one of fear. Nick was still in sixth gear bearing down hard on the street before him. I looked across at 'Charlie' and noticed in the light from the passing street lamps that his eyebrows were raised way above the rims of his spectacles. By now I was screaming down my mic';

"Stop Nick, you fucking Looney!" But to no avail, Nick quite obviously had the bit between his teeth.

We then hit the bend which by now had taken on its true form which was considerably sharper than it had at first seemed.

As we entered the bend a whole myriad of things happened at once.

I could see that we weren't going to corner, as our gun was looming towards the houses on the opposite side of the street. I looked at 'Charlie' to find he had obviously identified the danger because his head and shoulders were frantically bobbing about as he tried, unsuccessfully to un-jam himself from the hatch so he could operate his turret controls. Had he achieved this, or had we a gunner, he could have traversed the turret, thereby turning the gun barrel down the street. I could hear Nick screaming; "OOOOOHHHHHH FUUUUUUUUUUCK!" as he realised his steering wouldn't work. Then with a final look at 'Charlie's' terror stricken face I tensed against the loaders hatch as with a terrific smack we drove across the road and with a terrific crunch buried both our main armament and front left wing straight into a house! It could have been worse, but Nick had placed both feet on the main brake pedal and luckily we stopped just before the rest of our tank disappeared into the house. That was that then, we simply sat there atop our throbbing, motionless tank looking up the length of the gun to where it had buried itself through the upstairs wall next to a window. A window in which a light suddenly came on, followed by a gentleman wearing an amazed look on a face below a Wee Willy Winkie style sleep cap. I looked up at him, then at 'charlie' who stared back having extricated himself from his predicament and stood up in the cupola. We then heard Nick in the cab uttering "Fucking hell, Sorry, I didn't mean to do it!"

With a final look at the chap in the window 'Charlie' and I realising how ludicrous the whole situation was, burst into uncontrolled laughter. At this, the now irate German disappeared from view and returned brandishing a shotgun. 'Charlie' now made a command decision, "Okay Nick, reverse" he said over the IC, Nick did this task with gusto, ramming his foot firmly to the floor. The resulting shockwave of 56 tons reversing out of the wall created more damage. The window in which the occupant was stood, plus a large section of wall, came tumbling down in front of us. 'Charlie', once satisfied we were clear ordered Nick to pull off down the road 'full speed ahead'. So we exited the village as house lights were coming on everywhere as people woke up realising that something had happened.

"OOOOP'S"

Later that morning we had arrived at where the rest of our Squadron was assembled. 'Charlie' would have dearly liked to keep the affair secret. But, it was not to be as 'Stan' returned and ordered an impromptu gun inspection. When he peered in the muzzle having noticed how dusty it was, he found to his surprise, two house bricks. That was it, game up, 'Charlie' was left in no doubt by the OC that he would never command an MBT again. The OC was also left to ensure that the proper authorities handled the house owners insurance claim.

Our next adventure that scheme was towards it's end. It was announced one evening that the exercise plan the next day was that C Squadron 3RTR was to spearhead a major 'friendly forces' armoured thrust into enemy territory. Early the next morning we found ourselves busily thrusting away! We were motoring down a main road with our Troop in the forefront, 'Scouse' the Troop Leader leading the entire Divisional 'push' (he wanted the honour), behind him came our tank with 'Stan' looking particularly warlike as he posed in the commanders hatch, CT's tank bringing up the rear. Now if 'Scouse' had put some thought into his decision, he would have realised that as lead Tank, he was not likely to have a long 'battle'. But no, he sailed along the road without a care in the world. So, as we approached a railway level crossing, he must have been very surprised when two enemy Leopards suddenly emerged from neighbouring fields and ambushed him. An umpire wearing a white armband, promptly appeared as if by magic, jumped on the now stationary tank and declared 'Scouse' and his crew as dead!

The rest of the Squadron had by now come clattering to a halt some way behind us, the OC being stuck in the middle of the traffic jam. We on 31B were now, under 'Stan's' guidance, manoeuvring like crazy, traversing the turret and simulating firing at the enemy by launching thunderflashes in every direction. The umpire was dodging these explosions, hopping around the road like a scared rabbit. He was in fact trying to tell us that we too were knocked out, 'Stan' however was having none of it. "Fuck right off out of it!" he shouted at the umpire as a radio message from the OC came through telling us that, "31B, you are to take the lead, push on, push on!" in very excited tones, this was having a strange effect on 'Stan' who, having digested the message, launched a new and vicious attack on both the umpire and the offending Leopards. But having temporarily run out of thunderflashes, he now started using signal flares fired from his pistol. He then ordered Nick to " Fuck the lot of them, push past them and don't stop till I tell you!" With that our Tank, followed by CT with 'Switches' in his plastic police helmet in 31A fairly zoomed across a field where the Leopards tried desperately to block our advance, but failed as we avoided them and slewed back onto the road. Now began a chase that can only be described as mammoth when you consider the size of the vehicles involved.

Safely back on the road with 31A still at our back we broke out into open countryside, we then saw that the two Leopards which had so brutally 'killed' our Troop Leader, were in fact the vanguard of a Company which we now spied parked in a nearby field. 'Stan' immediately ordered Cooperman to "traverse left", and the turret swung round to the left the gun now effectively blocking the road to any oncoming traffic should there be any. 'Stan' and I now began a frenzied 'attack' on the Germans by throwing smoke grenades and thunderflashes in the direction of the enemy. 'Stan' then started firing blank ammunition from his commanders machine gun the spent cartridges flying everywhere, especially as the position of the turret now meant that down in the cab, Nick got a liberal shower of hot brass on the back of his head and neck. At the same time as this was happening on top, Brian was loosing off 'flash bang' gunfire simulators housed above the gun on the turret, by using his normal firing switch. When I looked back at 31A behind us, they too were covered in a thick cloud of smoke as CT and his crew 'let rip' with everything they'd got. This scene must have looked dead impressive to the Germans, the first of whom had their Leopards fired up and were setting off in pursuit of us. Two launched themselves onto the road behind our two vehicles, their acceleration being superior, in no time the first German driver was inhaling pure diesel exhaust from 31A's rear. Luckily for us the road we were on was not wide enough to permit overtaking. A third Leopard was now at top speed running parallel to us, but cutting across the adjacent fields. Its aim was obviously to try and get ahead, then block our advance down the road. "Come on Nick, give this fucking bitch some stick!" ranted 'Stan' into his mic'. "We'll show these fuckers what we can do!" This remark was addressed to the whole crew as he looked at me and grinned. Then he told Brian to 'gun front' and the turret resumed its normal position. I took up station facing rear to watch 31A's antics behind and keep 'Stan' informed of the proceedings. CT had placed his tank squarely in the middle of the road to prevent any chance for the chasing Leopards to overtake. This tactical manoeuvre did wreak chaos with oncoming cars, many of whom suddenly found themselves playing 'chicken' with a 56 ton monster, thereby forcing them into drastic avoidance measures.

We had by now lost sight of the third Leopard which, still going 'cross country' had disappeared behind a wood. 'Stan' leant across and grabbing my shoulder, brought to my attention the fact that we were rapidly approaching a 'T' junction. Stood at the junction was a German MP to control traffic, he was obviously expecting a fairly leisurely column of Chieftains to eventually arrive. Instead he was confronted with two howling monsters with the crews waving madly for him to get out of the way. He directed us to turn left and then joined a bunch of civilian spectators on the verge, as we entered the corner slewing wildly across the damp road surface, not slowing down for fear of being caught. As we turned left the third Leopard now appeared bouncing out of trees on our left nearly killing the MP and spectators also narrowly avoiding crushing the MP's jeep. But the driver had got his gears wrong and the Leopard quickly lost momentum and their chance to cut us off was lost. By now the OC had been back on the radio, "31B, what's your situation, where are you?" 'Stan' was by now totally in his element, grabbing his mic' with no time to encode our map grid reference he simply replied "we're approx 8 miles through enemy lines and advancing, 31A also still running!" Forgetting all radio discipline the OC's reply came sailing through our headsets; "Janner you are my pathfinder, find a way through this mess, you can do it man!" I saw 'Stan's' chin jut out a further inch at this encouragement and he simply replied; "Wilco out", and then gave me a huge almost demonic grin.

That was obviously it in his mind, we would now, stop for nothing. Looking behind, I could see that the leading Leopard commander was now a raging maniac as 31A foiled his every move to overtake. Undeterred our two vehicles motored on. As we started to climb a hill with two traffic lanes up and one lane oncoming we started to slow. 'Stan' simply told Nick to start 'weaving' up the hill, slewing back and forth across both lanes. This he did and 31A followed suit behind. This manoeuvre really got the following Germans mad. Near the top of the hill 'Stan', who was studying his map, decided we should turn right towards a small village. This we did only to find a column of German 'Marder' infantry vehicles parked alongside the road on the verge. The crews were sat on their vehicles breakfasting. As we drove past we traversed left and proceeded once more to throw pyrotechnics at the Germans, all this unexpected activity threw the Germans into total confusion. A flurry of discarded breakfast and cups flew into the air as they attempted to man their vehicles. By the time they had achieved a single engine start up we were 'long fucking gone' disappearing in a cloud of exhaust smoke down the road.

The third Leopard, having extracted itself from the roadside throng, had by now caught the other two up and all three were now up 31A's exhausts. CT was resolutely standing up in his cupola 'flicking the V's' at the chasing commanders. By now I was asking 'Stan', "surely we must be 'dead' by now?" 'Stan' just turned to me and replied; "dead Malc? Never say die, and besides there's not an umpire for fucking miles to kill us!" With that we resumed our headlong assault on Germany. Once in the village ahead of us, we took an apparently wrong turn into what was, apparently, a dead end. As we stopped we saw a huge amount of enemy vehicles assembled in a nearby field. The crews assembled there didn't pay much attention to our unexpected arrival, until that is, we launched the usual explosive announcement of our presence.

As we threw everything we still had at the enemy 'Stan' ordered Nick to conduct a 'neutral' pivot turn to leave us facing our pursuers. Having completed the turn, 31A pulled in to copy our manoeuvre, but as they pulled into position a Leopard drove across their rear, thereby making the proposed turn impossible, umpires now appeared from nowhere and swarmed all over CT's wagon with 'switches' vainly trying beat them off from his cab with a shovel. 'Stan' looked at CT in his turret, waved and then told Nick to reverse, this we did and erupted through a small tree topped hedge into a courtyard belonging to a sawmill. We spun round and under 'Stan's' direction, headed down a small service road knocking down garden walls on each side as we were slightly wider than the road. Two of the Leopards followed us on our escape, as we hastily departed from the confines of the village. As we tracked up a small road we received a message from the OC telling us to stop where we were as the umpires were now losing their sense of humour. This we did, pulling up next to a farm yard. Once halted 'Stan' calmly reached out and plucked apples for each of us from an overhanging tree. As our two relentless German hunters drove past us each commander smartly saluted us, our response being hand gestures of a totally un-military fashion. So ended the 'Great chase'. To our chaps, heroes we were and heroes we remained for some time. We had ended up some twenty miles behind enemy lines and technically remained unscathed. I think to this day, that had 'Billy' our OC had the authority, he would have given Stan a field commission and decorated us with some medal of honour. However that was of course, not possible so we had to content ourselves with a few beers and a ripping good story to tell.

16. Boldly getting drunk

Bold Guards Endex having been announced, what seemed to be the entire British army assembled on the edge of BAORs' Soltau training area at Rheinsehlen transit camp area. We had erected a series of tented encampment areas to house the various units. We found our camp placed next to the camp of a Cavalry unit, namely the 9th/12th Royal Lancers, they had, in true Cavalry fashion brought many of their traditions with them. The most memorable thing they had brought were a brass bell supported on a tripod of antique lances, the entire ensemble having been won as spoils of war in some battle or other. This edifice had been erected outside the guard tent at the camps entrance, more of this later.

Safely ensconced in our C Squadron encampment we started to... surprise, surprise, drink. I headed for the RQMS' tent and purchased a bottle of scotch. 9 Troop had been allocated two tents in which we were housed, but the entire Troop had congregated in our tent for drinking duties. 'Switches' and I started to drink the contents of the scotch bottle interspersed with cans of beer. We all became drunk, pranks started and 'Stan' for some reason ended up, his feet tied to the top of a tent support, upside down trying to continue drinking. None of us were soon in a fit state to reach the toilet block, so piles of crap and vomit were soon littering our camp like a minefield. Then someone from a neighbouring Troop, ('Shelly's' name springs to mind) had the idea of 'kidnapping' someone from the neighbouring 9th/12th camp. In due course a reconnaissance (recce) party of 3 chums was despatched to seek a suitable victim. As they disappeared into the dark suitably clothed in black overalls, we continued drinking eagerly anticipating their return with information.

The recce party's return however, came in an unexpected manner. Quite suddenly our neighbours' camp erupted with loud activity. Firstly we could hear someone shouting loudly and repeatedly, "unhand me you bastards, I'm the Colonel of the 9th/12th Lancers!" Someone shouting in an equally loud, deep, Westcountry brogue; "yeah? fuck off, I'm the fucking Pope" followed this! This exchange continued for about two minutes ending with the first voice repeatedly shouting, "call out the guard!" At this request, the air was suddenly alive with the shrill sounds of whistles being blown as the guard obviously got called out. We next heard the sound of muffled running feet as a group of bodies ran past our tent. The commotion lasted some considerable time during which, we continued to drink.

'Switches' and author, night of the 'kidnap'.

My night ended up with me being unceremoniously thrown naked from our tent because I wanted to go to sleep. I then proceeded around our camp attempting to find a place to sleep, dragging my sleeping bag behind me in readiness. Apparently I entered the cooks tent to find a refuge, promptly vomited over the master chef and was ejected. I do remember walking into a lit marquee, spying a group of people assembled at the far end, drunkenly announcing to the assembled throng that; "this fucking dark corner will do for me!" and as I then pissed in the corner and, fully relieved, climbed into my 'slug', I recall a voice saying "RSM, who the bloody hell is that man?" As I came to the next morning in the guard tent, finding myself secured, tightly by belts into my sleeping bag, I was informed by the Guard Commander that the Colonel hadn't been 'too impressed' when I wandered into the Officers Mess tent the previous night. He had been even less impressed when, during the 'entertaining' of the Sergeants Mess, I had urinated in the corner of the tent and settled down to sleep.

Once I had been released from 'custody' I made my way back to my tent. It would be fair to say I never lived the embarrassment of this incident down.

On Squadron Parade that morning we learnt the reason for the previous nights commotion in the neighbouring camp. Our 'recce' party had come across a lone tent with a solitary kidnap victim within. They had at that point decided that, rather than report back and form a 'raiding' party, they would attempt the kidnap there and then. Of course, they really had picked on the $9^{th}/12^{th}$'s Colonel, who was seriously not happy at the following physical drunken assault. Our guys, having punched the Colonel repeatedly in an effort to silence him, suddenly realised their error. As they retreated, they ran past the Lancers' guard tent knocking over their prized and apparently valuable tripod of antique lances and, during its fall, denting the bloody brass bell suspended from the tripod! An official complaint had been raised against us and we were duly chastised, albeit that our OC had a bit of a smirk on his face as he did the chastising. In due course, our stay at Rheinsehlen finished, we were 'railroaded' to Cuxhaven for embarkation to the UK.

Our tanks were loaded onto a Danish container ship called 'Dana Futura' along with their respective commanders and drivers. The rest of the crews were placed on a civilian ferry for the voyage home. Once on board the ferry we heard an announcement that civilians, officers and senior NCOs would occupy the rear of the vessel, the rest of us being confined to the front. Having offloaded our meagre baggage in our bunks, we headed for... the bar. We had to go to the bar, Corporal 'killer' was celebrating his birthday. 'Killer' hadn't gained his nickname through being non-confrontational previously and this would prove no exception. As we claimed our tables we realised that the bar also contained a large group of $9^{th}/12^{th}$ Lancers obviously still smarting from our attempt at kidnapping their colonel. This, as we started our customary 'Wurzel sing along', did not bode well! Even before our anchor had been 'upped' empty beer kegs were being rapidly exchanged for full ones.

As we set off homeward, our singing was getting louder and anti-cavalry chants were winging their way through the air. The Lancers were of course retaliating with their own chants aimed at 'Wanky Tankies'. At this point my bladder was in need of relief and, in due course I exited the bar in search of the toilets carefully carrying my pint lest it get drunk in my absence. Having relieved myself I headed back to the bar still with my pint. As I walked through a foyer area I saw my mate Shane 'punchy' Greenhalgh from 11 Troop living up to his name and punching anyone whose face he simply, didn't like. A hard bunch, we Tankies! I continued on my way and, nearing the bar doors, realised that the singing competition had ceased. It had been replaced by the unmistakable sounds of a riot. I pushed open the swing doors and was confronted by the sight of one of our guys sat on the chest of a Lancer beating him senseless. I immediately cheered him on but, suddenly a fist landed in my face and I shot back out through the swing doors, landing on my back near Shane whose attention had been grabbed by the prospect of the bar fight. Shane helped me up and, as I discarded the glass handle to my pint glass, which was all that was left after my impromptu departure from the bar, we duly waded into the fray. As the melee reached new heights of ferocity bodies were falling out of the closed French windows onto the deck beyond. I clearly remember that, in the middle of the fracas a small group of drunken Engineers were sat, unmolested in a corner of the bar, singing their own songs, in the same manner as the band on the 'Titanic' played as the great ship went down.

I can't remember how the fight ended, but I know that although grossly outnumbered, we gave the Lancers a damned good dusting, just to add to their embarrassment over the kidnapping. It was an overnight passage and as I awoke the next morning I realised that I was in fact on deck and not, in my bunk. I was also not alone, quite a few of us were lying prone on deck. The only sounds, which could be heard above the sea, were snoring, and the tinkling created by empty beer bottles rolling on the deck in time to the boats' swaying. "Bloody hell" thought I as I held my aching head which felt like the 'beer gorilla' had been playing in it. The 'beer gorilla' was commonly known as a right bastard. He would pick on some poor unsuspecting soul, drag him to a bar, spend all his money on beer (and make him drink it), then beat him round the head until senseless and finally shit in the poor chaps mouth while he slept. All this just so you could wake up the next morning feeling much as I now did! My next thought was to get a 'hair of the dog!' So off I went to the bar, upon entering I could see that all that was left was a massive debris field as if a jumbo jet had crashed. I picked my way through the jumble of broken glass and bodies and, arriving at the bar, was confronted by a gorgeous blond barmaid. She was occupied with trying to clean up the devastation behind the counter. I put on the most charming grin I could and quietly asked if I may buy a drink. The girl looked up at me, her eyes flashed and she simply told me in a Scandinavian accent to; "Fuck off!" This I did, and the journey continued without further events.

When we eventually docked an announcement was broadcast through the ship; "Would all members of C.Squadron 3RTR leave the ship first". So, we weren't that popular then! But having disembarked to the jeering of Lancers up on the ships deck, we boarded our buses and headed back to 'Tiddy'.

17. 'Ranges'

I have tried in this section to cover our firing periods while stationed at Tidworth. Some experiences happened before and after Cyprus and also Exercise Bold Guard. Each year the Regiment would embark on a trip maybe twice, but normally once to practice Gunnery at the ranges. The first time I went to the ranges was when we went to Lulworth Camp in Dorset. This was also the RAC Gunnery school where both recruits and trained gunners are either, trained from scratch or taught new skills to gain qualifications up to instructor level. Apart from school staff and trainees, regular UK based units also use the ranges for honing their gunnery skills.

So it was then, that one cold winter morning we arrived at Lulworth where I had, as a Junior Leader, been trained in the art of tank gunnery. We unloaded the tanks from the 'Antar' tank transporters and lined them up on our allotted firing point. On the firing point each Troop's tanks were split across the line so that during firing no two tanks are next to each other. This is simply so that the Gunnery Instructor stood on your back decks 'spotting and advising' is not 'disrupted' by the neighbouring tank's gunfire, and of course the two guns traversing wouldn't crash into each other. Each day started with 'Ammo bashing' when the entire Squadron would go through the knuckle smashing exercise of breaking open and unpacking the ammo required for the days shooting. Having 'bombed up' the Tanks, each Troop would be called forward for its turn at firing.

This first morning, as loader, it was my duty to ensure that all the ammo was stored correctly in the turret ready for action. This involved making sure the MG ammo was open in its 'ready rack' with the end of the belt exposed ready to be placed in the breech of the co-ax GPMG. This also applied to the.50 ranging gun. We were in the habit of linking boxes of MG ammo together so that it saved time in not having to change belts a box at a time. The loader simply kept his eye on the belt and at the appropriate moment removed an empty box and 'sausage machined' the boxes up towards the MG linking a new box in to the end of the chain. All the 120mm projectiles would be stored into their respective ready racks, Sabot nearest the breech and Hesh behind. This was because Sabot shooting was the fastest engagement time. Hesh required more time as it simply flew slower thereby giving the loader more time to throw another one up the breech.

If the commander's MG was to be used that day, it too received its quota of ammo belted together on and next to the commander's cupola. With experience a loader knew that prior to firing, a good trick was to liberally squirt gun oil all over the Mg's mechanism to ensure the 'working parts' wouldn't stiffen causing the dreaded stoppages. The main tool to be kept at hand was a screwdriver, this was to prevent stoppages on the co-ax MG due to spent case build up. When this Mg fired the ejected cases were channelled down a shute to a box on the turret floor. This kept the brass cases from flying round the turret, but the box was never big enough and the shute too narrow to sometimes allow free passage of the cases and belt links down to the box. So after a few boxes of 7.62mm had been fired off, there would be simply too much volume for the shute to control. The cases and the associated metal belt links would build up and eventually stop the MG by blocking the ejection process. Then the loader would simply ram the screwdriver down the mouth of the shute to free it off.

Discipline was everything on the firing point, discipline meant safety, this was vitally important with the amount of explosives present. Once firing proceeded the tanks engaging their targets were known to be at 'Action' and each flew a red flag on top of the cupola. Any tanks that were not firing flew green flags. So firing under way we would sit behind the firing point to await our turn. The day progressed with the 'targeting' bursts of co-ax fire followed by much longer 'killing' bursts once the Gunner had found the target distance. Then the regulated bop, bop, bop of the.50 would be heard punctuated by the ear splitting crash of the main armament. Once the gunners were in full swing the noise of the Troop's 3 main armaments would reach a crescendo as they showered the targets with a rain of steel.

"Yahoo!" Yelled our Troop's crews as we were called to our Tanks, our adrenaline levels were now going sky high and we hadn't even reached the Tanks. The static firing didn't involve drivers being in their cabs so 'Stan', Brian and I scrambled up the rear of 31B and into the turret. The 'Jenny' was already running so as we settled into the turret we simply waited for the OCs radio message to go to action. Within the turret, only the commander and Gunner would wear radio headsets. As a loader it was virtually impossible to wear headsets, as the cables would seriously hamper the speed with which he could load the various weapons. So in true gunnery drill fashion we would scream the various orders and responses at each other. This really got us 'psyched' up for the action and increased adrenaline levels to bursting point.

Loaders were also not allowed to wear gloves as, when loading the main armament, if a bagged charge had been stored in a 'leaky' container the loader would not be able to feel the damp before he rammed the charge into the breech. This dampness could cause a 'misfire' the corrective drill for which involved flying a yellow flag and waiting for thirty minutes. During the wait the gun could go off as the charge would be ignited but, due to a damp slow burn, the explosion would be delayed. If the gun 'delay' fired it was called a 'fismire'. If the gun however, did not fire within the waiting time the loader would have to gingerly open the breech and remove the (sometimes smouldering) charge and dispose of it very quickly. I only had to do this once (albeit the charge hadn't even been wet) and I can assure you that it brings a whole new meaning to the term 'shitting yourself'. You are never quite sure what is going to happen as you open the breech, when shut the breech is airtight as its sealed at both ends by the breechblock and the projectile. So if you open the breech, the sudden rush of air could potentially turn a smouldering charge into a raging inferno.

Anyway, here we were, ready for the off. 'Stan' sat listening to the radio, suddenly he whooped and screamed 'ACTION'. This was the command for Brian to start the 'Gun kit' and run through his pre firing checks reporting 'ready' when complete. 'Stan' reached up and changed the flag to red and, ducking back in, rubbed his hands with glee and watched me in action. I, released the retaining clips on the projectiles, fed both the Mg's ammo belts into the respective breech, took a loaded vent tube magazine from its storage box and placed it into position in the base of the 120mm's breech block and pulled its associated Vent tube loader (VTL) 'rammer' into position. I then checked that the turret stowage was in order and, looking through the 120mm's breech to ensure there was only daylight at the guns muzzle I screamed "bore clear!"at the same time checking that my turret safety switch was 'off' thereby allowing 'Stan' and Brian to use the gun kit.

'Stan' was now peering through his sight as over the radio he received orders from 'Scouse' in his tank as to which targets we were to engage. Having digested the information 'Stan' was not long in coming out with his first 'fire order'.

"Load Sabot, Sabot dot 2 on!" He had screamed this as, using his controls, he 'laid' the gun onto the prospective target so Brian could see and engage it. An experienced commander such as ours would often estimate the range to the target, by-passing the ranging gun technique, especially at closer ranges with Sabot. Stan ordering 'Load sabot' had told me to keep ramming Sabot up the gun until he told me otherwise. Sabot engagement procedures normally involved the loading of rounds one at a time per fire order. So Stans order informed me that he intended only to engage 'emergency' short range targets initially. I now swung into action, grasping a Sabot proj I literally threw then punched it into the waiting breech, I then reached over behind the gun and hit the VTL rammer so that it sprung forward driving a vent tube into the rear of the breech block. Then I released the top of a charge bin and pulled out a Sabot charge which was then thrown and punched home behind the proj. I then grabbed and pulled hard on the breech closing lever, the breech block now sprang up closing and sealing the breech with a clang. I then grabbed another proj from the rack at the same time pulling the loaders guard to the rear (to prevent me from walking behind the gun). With the next proj cradled in my arm I then hit the safety switch to double check it was off, and howled "Loaded!" Brian in the meantime had finished 'laying' the gun on the target, replying to Stans command.. " Sabot dot 2... on!" He selected the appropriate gun to fire on his firing handle and waited for the order to fire. This procedure had taken no longer than fifteen seconds which was basically the time it took me to complete my drill. Stan now simply screamed "FIRE!" Brian screamed in reply, "Firing now!", pressed the trigger and the breech shot past me to the full extent of its recoil. As it rushed forward again, my next proj was already entering the breech as I slid through my drill again.

Brian was now screaming "Target!" Stan immediately bellowed "Target fire!" and we put another round into our target. After two or three more shots Stan started his fire order with "Stop Loading" this meant that the proj I was now loading would be the last until a fresh fire order was given. I felt utterly magnificent, the sweat was pouring off me and the blood on my knuckles felt as though it was burning. Our turret crew was now in a totally overloaded state of excitement. I was busily re-stowing ammo from rear racks into the closer ready racks in preparation for the next frenzied round of firing. This was not long in coming. The day progressed with us loosing off all our ammo types in frantic bursts of action. Having finished our post firing cleaning and gun maintenance we adjourned, reeking of the acrid smell of burnt cordite mixed with oil and diesel, to our rooms. Having showered we headed for the NAAFI where we drank heavily and discussed the days events. Stan bought me quite a few beers that night as we celebrated the fact that our crew had that day had two HESH rounds in the air at the same time on three occasions. I had gained a reputation as a fast and 'crack' loader. Over the coming years loading and radio operating were to be my trademark until I became a commander on my own Tank. Take it from me, it would be hard to beat the 'buzz' that loading gives, in just about any walk of life. I remember how our instructor at JLR had said that a good loader 'is worth his weight in gold' and that was true. For the rest of my years in 9 Troop 'Scouse' was trying to pinch me as his loader, but luckily Stan always won the contest and we stayed intact as a team.

Further range periods proved equally as satisfying, not only did we go to Lulworth but also to Castlemartin in Wales which was a training camp for the German tank units using American designed M48A1s. It was a novelty for us, seeing grey tanks carrying the German black and white Maltese cross insignia as they bombed along the Welsh coast. But that is probably a story for another time. There will be more on ranges later however.

18. The Mayflower

No, the title of this chapter may suggest that it's about 17th century puritans escaping the persecution of English law, but nothing could be further from the truth. Firstly, we could never be described as puritans and secondly nobody had persecuted us, not even the law. Instead this is about an exercise called Mayflower.

When on Squadron parade one morning, we were told about this upcoming venture we weren't quite sure what to think. The exercise would involve us driving from barracks in Tidworth and then following a laid down route. This route was along public roads for a considerable distance Northwards, passing through Marlborough towards Swindon and then back Southwards onto the Salisbury Plain training area for a Regimental exercise.

"Tank now bulled to perfection, We were at last, ready to meet our public!!!!!"

Before we could take to the public roads and also enter the public eye, we had an intensive preparation phase. This included servicing the tanks to ensure breakdowns were minimal, and cleaning and painting the tanks for 'best visual impact!' These tasks were in themselves fairly difficult given the country's financial state but somehow we managed it. Therefore after this period of 'bulling' up the Tanks, we were ready to embark on what would go on record as the largest movement of armour on British roads since the D Day preparations in 1944.

So it was that one afternoon, with our new orange flashing lights atop our turrets, we set off on our trek. It was not a trek through 'space the final frontier', nor was it a trek 'to infinity, and beyond (albeit that several of us thought it may as well be!). No, it was to quote the CO, 'a simple road march along a nice, pleasant route'. All I can say is that 'the nice, pleasant route' was soon, smothered by a huge cloud of diesel fumes from our exhausts and awash with oil from our various oil leaks. But undeterred by the dwindling numbers as various Callsigns broke down, we pressed ever onward. The REME through that day and the following night did a magnificent job. As soon as a vehicle failed, they swarmed onboard and got it rolling again as best they could. This was just as well as, the entire route was lined with spectators eager to glimpse evidence of Britains armoured might. The most stalwart of these spectators were still up and about in the various towns at three in the morning, passing up cups of hot chocolate whenever we halted due to some unseen traffic delay. It is of course highly likely that these poor souls were up at that time of the morning, due to the amount of noise we made as we howled our way past their houses. It is fair to say though that our general reception was very warm from the fascinated onlookers. Some of course, weren't exactly thrilled when, stood on a roundabout, they were confronted by a few hundredweight of steel road wheel heading towards them at an alarming rate of speed. The errant wheel had become detached from a tank when its wheel nuts failed (through over use as I mentioned earlier) and the wheel flew off and under its own momentum accelerated. Had it met an oncoming car, it would have been a major disaster. Luckily the spectators managed to get out of the way and nobody was harmed. Another group of fans were also not amused when one of our tanks 'snagged' an oncoming tanker lorry. The lorry driver hadn't quite judged the amount of room needed to safely pass. Consequently as he passed the Tank, a stowage bin caught the side of the tanker and rent a gaping hole down its side allowing its contents to spray everywhere, its contents being raw sewerage. This act mightily upset the bystanders as 'everyone copped for a bit', as the effluent quickly emptied onto the road. On through the night we hammered, 31B was a magnificent machine, not letting us down once in our mission to keep the whole of Hampshire and Wiltshire awake that night. One thing we did make sure of before departure was that the side of the orange flashing light nearest Stan and myself was, covered in thick masking tape. This was to shield our eyes from the incessant flashing that otherwise may have sent our brains into a 'disco inferno'!

Early the next morning we found ourselves leaving the roads and battering our way onto more familiar territory. This was the northern edge of Salisbury Plain. I always found Salisbury Plain a strange place. A sort of wilderness but somehow, after all the schemes we had completed within its confines, it was strangely welcoming. We had all become so familiar with its features that commanders having established where they were going on the map, discarded the map and relied on memory and landmarks. Landmarks, well, there were certainly loads of them. From natural woodland, to deeply rutted tracks. These tracks had probably started to harrow their way into the ground when our forefathers had first exercised here in the 20's and 30's. The tracks were so deep now that they had indelibly scarred the landscape. Woods were commonly referred to, by their shape on the map. 'The rings' for example were a couple of circular copses with their centres missing. Many a crew found itself towed here by an ARV. The wood was situated fairly close to a road so, it gave good access to repair crews as they brought spare parts from the workshops at Tidworth.

Another landmark was the abandoned village of Imber; this village (like so many on MOD lands) had at one time been evacuated as the then War Department took over the land for training. Many of its original buildings still stood such as the church. The church was strictly out of bounds to troops and, if memory serves me right, an annual service was held there. The village was a Close Quarter Battle Range (CQBR) and was used intensively by Infantry units training to fight in 'built up areas'. tanks were not normally allowed within its perimeter, but on one occasion we did exercise through it in support of a 'Grunt' unit which was fun. Stan and I did our usual trick of lobbing thunderflashes at anything that moved in the houses. It was obvious to me though that a tank is much better suited to warfare in open countryside. There are simply too many places for a 'Grunt' to hide in a town. One well placed shot with an anti-tank weapon and our goose would be well and truly cooked.

The infantry were always a source of amusement to us. They had an unnerving knack at doing something that made us laugh. For example, a constant source of amusement was their use of the 'infantry tank telephone' (ITT). This was a telephone handset in an armoured box on the back of the Tank, which connected into the vehicles crew intercom. In principle it was a clever device for increasing infantry/armour co-operation. In reality it was just another excuse for us to 'take the piss' out of the 'Grunts'. On one occasion we were sat 'closed down' in a fire position 'supporting' an infantry attack in front of us, then, in our headsets Stan and I could hear a bleating buzz. The buzz was from the ITT 'call button'; Stan turned his head to look out of his cupola episcopes to see if he could identify who was calling. Now, the ITT handset was connected to about thirty feet of spring loaded cable so that the Infanteer could pull out the handset enabling the tank crew to see him. Invariably the 'grunts' didn't know this and would hunch down below the rear of the Tank. This was highly dangerous of course, and not wishing to disappoint we often enjoyed engaging reverse gear thereby caused the tank to 'jump' without moving. It was normally enough to send the average 'grunt' running for his life while we sat howling with laughter. The down side being that he would drag the handset out when he ran then let go sending it whizzing back into its box, the spring tension smashing the handset to pieces on the armoured cover, yet another repair job!

So as Stan peered outside to see who was calling us he could see nobody. We selected to speak on the ITT and were immediately confronted with a little voice saying,

"Hullo, hullo, (puffing sounds as he blew in the mouthpiece), fuck me Jim, I know the buggers are in there 'cos the engines are going!" this was shouted to his unseen mate while he still had the handset pressed to speak. Once again, he attempted to make contact.

"Hullo you in the Tank, this is me out here?" He went on, "(puffing sounds again) Hullo, hullo, hullo, hullo can anybody hear me?"

Inside the tank I had switched the radio control box so we could all hear this guy going on, the result was that we were all splitting our sides at the grunt's efforts. Stan even had tears rolling down his face. At last Stan regained control and picking up his mic', spoke to the poor chap,

"Hello, and who the fuck are you?" asked Stan promptly falling about with laughter.

"Er, er, er Mike three three alpha, over". Came the little voice from below.

"What the fuck is that? Your name or your Callsign?" Stan nearly lost control of his laughing again before he could stop talking. But the grunt was persistent;

"My Callsign, over!" he informed us. Stan was now on a roll,

"Well Mike what the fuck do you want?" Asked Stan. The grunt's reply came,

"Reference that tree over there, there's an enemy MG post two fingers to its right, dug in, please destroy, over!" Well, that was it, we had now all collapsed in absolute agony at this conversation. Stan was saying between guffaws;

"Who the fuck is this? Who's put him up to using the ITT? I know they have to practice but, this is fucking ridiculous!" He promptly collapsed in convulsions again. The point was, here was a grunt crouched behind 56tons of steel, through which we couldn't see him. And yet he was pointing at a tree, somewhere, assuming we could see him and the tree. The problem being that we were surrounded by trees, whole woods of them. Stan now gave up, opening his hatch and disconnecting his headsets from his breastplate he climbed out. He then jumped onto the engine decks and cupping his hands to his mouth, shouted at the grunt.

"Oi, Mike or whatever your fucking name is, what the hell do you want?" He yelled. This went on for some time because the grunt and his sidekick who Stan found crouched beside him had, their heads next to the exhausts. This meant of course that their hearing ability was severely impaired. Stan bent down and retrieved a spare track pin from where it lay on the engine decks. Quite a weight a track pin, the grunt found this out as Stan dropped it onto his shoulder to attract his attention. For the first time I saw the fellows face, covered in camouflage cream, appear over the top of the exhaust box. Stan and his opposite number then had a conversation with much pointing and flailing arms. Finally satisfied Stan returned, chuckling to himself, dropping into his commanders seat. It transpired that Stan now knew what the Infanteer had wanted and we motored off and 'suppressed the enemy position'.

In the seventies 'Infantry/Armour co-operation' was a real 'buzzword', it was the only time I ever experienced giving grunts a 'lift' on a Tank. One cold rainy day we were told to take a company of paratroopers on board and take them to battle. This was due to the fact that 'Para's' were not mechanised. So as to keep pace with our advance it was far simpler to give them a piggyback. This we duly did, and motored off with about fifteen chaps hanging on for their lives, on the turret and perched on the engine decks as we bucked our way across the terrain.

When we arrived at our destination we were faced with a problem. The problem was that these grunts didn't want to get off the hot engine decks, and struggle through the rain and mud. In the end Stan became so frustrated that he ordered 'cooperman' to traverse the turret round and, using the main armament, swipe the para's from our vehicle. This we did, but gently as the injuries that the para's could have sustained would have been dreadful.

Of course, the Grunts loved riding on our Tanks!!

The looks on their faces were mixed with fear, surprise and downright hatred as we dislodged them from their perches. We could understand this as, one of our pastimes in such weather was that at every opportunity when we had an impromptu halt, we would jump over the turret rear and sit on the engine decks. This way we could get warm while also drying our soaked arses. Unsurprising then, that haemorrhoids within tank crews is fairly common.

As I mentioned before, that was the only occasion that I experienced Infantry riding on tanks 'a la Russian style'. Normally Infantry were carried in FV 432 APC's during the advance and then 'de-bus' during an attack on the enemy. Tactical doctrine in the seventies meant that when a battle group was 'advancing to contact' (moving forward to find the enemy) the Infantry would lead. Upon contacting the enemy the armour support would take over unless in a built up area. This was a source of frustration to the armour commanders, as an armoured formation could move across territory far quicker and more effectively than the Infantry. I'm glad to say that in the early eighties the doctrine changed and became more armour friendly. Now long sweeping advances could be made in a relatively short timespan. The Infantry would only dismount to fight or take the lead in either built up areas including woodland. The only drawback to this was that if an advance was too long and sweeping, there was a potential problem with leaving the Infantry behind in their APC's, as they couldn't cover terrain at the same speed as the armoured spearhead, this could obviously lead to delays when Infantry support was needed in clearing an objective. tanks are primarily an offensive weapon so whereas they can 'take' ground on an objective they find it difficult to 'hold' ground without the Infantry 'digging in'.

One of our more onerous tasks at the end of each scheme was at endex to return to barracks via the vehicle wash. This was of course necessary so that maintenance on the tracks and running gear was made easier, and so we didn't get the hangars and ourselves continually covered in mud. The vehicle wash was a series of concrete islands with huge standpipes and water hoses built on them. The hoses were heavy and once the water was forced through at high pressure they could be quite hard to control. Many crew members found this out when a hose sprayed them with water while out of control. Even the Squadron 2i/c Captain J.E.B. 'War Dog' Smedley's dog 'Mowgli' found this out. My old chum 'Lucy' had been tasked to look after the pooch for a day and travel around in the Squadron Landrover while the 2i/c was on his Tank. This Lucy did, but whenever the Landrover stopped 'Mowgli' would jump out and play in all that lovely mud.

By the end of the day, what had been a lovely black retriever was in fact a scruffy mud caked mongrel. When the 2i/c saw this Lucy was ordered to return the dog to its home with the 2i/c's wife. Lucy complied but made sure that prior to his return 'Mowgli' attended the vehicle wash, it being very difficult to train the heavy hose on the poor howling creature as it was thrown every where by the water pressure. We ourselves were never convinced by the washdown, it started okay with clean water but, by the time two vehicles had been washed the water had drained and been recycled through the hoses. So the wash eventually became more of a sand blasting exercise. Inevitably after washing, when the tanks dried they were still covered in a sand coloured outer layer which disguised the under lying green and black camouflage pattern.

The pattern itself was always designed so that two thirds of the vehicle was green and one third black. This differed from 'the manual' because it stated that brown should be incorporated into the scheme. We never worried though as our tanks were continually brown with mud. Well, and black with oil leaks and spills staining the dried mud coating. Oh the joys of camouflage, but, ever onwards and upwards.

19. Cadre course

During our stay at Tidworth I was informed one day that I had been selected to attend a Cadre course. This is a course to promote and enhance a soldiers leadership skills, in order that he or she may take the first step up the promotion ladder as a Junior NCO. To be promoted to Lance Corporal you first had to pass this course. The course was designed by the CO and ran under the control of the RSM. The snag here was that 'Grot' had retired and we now had RSM Dave Cowley whom was renowned for being something of an ogre. His bark was definitely not worse than his bite as many unfortunate souls discovered. This was to be his first attempt at running the Cadre course and he was determined it would be a success. I had by now completed around three years service in 3 RTR and this was the normal amount of time before a Trooper was considered for promotion. This was as it was considered an appropriate amount of time for a guy to have served in the various roles involved on the tank Park. When I joined the Regiment the average age of a Trooper was 22 to 23 years old. When I left in 1990 the average age of Lance Corporals was only 19. How recruitment trends had changed!

Our course was to take place in barracks initially, which to me had the appearance of being back at JLR. There was much drill to be practised and bulling of boots. Then the main phase of the course was to be carried out near Bath, where Charlie Mead who had recently left our number, had set up home. Along with a another chap Ron Pope, Charlie was setting up a sort of outward-bound centre. When we arrived on site, we found that our first task was to design and construct a sort of assault course. Naturally we couldn't just design and build; we had to test the damned thing to destruction. We had set up a perfectly horrific set of obstacles culminating in a death slide. To enable the slide to be a little safer we had dug out the bed of a large brook below to increase its depth. This in itself had been laborious even though we had laughed when someone, enthusiastically threw a shovel full of gravel over his shoulder, the shovel then knocking one of us unconscious.

The testing phase of the course was suitably painful. We were split into teams to increase the competition element of the affair and off we went. Our team's first run was deemed as too fast, according to the RSM's watch, so to prove our prowess we had to repeat our performance. This we did but the effort proved too much for one of our number when we arrived at a 'speed' obstacle which consisted of a five-panel door with the panels knocked out. The door was laid down over a shallow pit, through which we had to run, placing our feet through the gaps in the door. Admittedly we had completed half the course already which included sliding down the inside of a large pipe into a swamp at the bottom. Escaping from the mud at speed was bloody hard work and then we had to run up a very steep slope. At the top of the slope was this damned 'speed' obstacle. Our poor chum took one look at the door and promptly collapsed suffering from both exhaustion and an asthma attack. We ran on leaving him to the tender mercies of the RSM (who thought screaming at the lad would improve his condition!) and a Medic. We completed the course and fell exhausted to the ground. The RSM felt that we still hadn't performed correctly, so off we went again!

One morning we were taken to the town of Bath Easton. Here we found ourselves deposited on the banks of a river. Once again we were split into teams, and then presented with a task. The task being how to be the first team to cross the river using the equipment now provided. We were given; 6 metal 'jerrycans', a length of rope, some lengths of timber and a huge plastic sheet. So we began building a raft, by roping the jerry cans together, stabilising their shape with the timber and covering the whole thing with the plastic sheet to 'increase' buoyancy. In fact the plastic sheet quickly proved itself to be the opposite. As we attempted our first launch the sheet promptly filled with water and under went the raft. We then decided the sheet was only provided to mislead us as, nobody had actually said we 'had' to use 'everything' provided. So sticking with the cans and timber structure off we went. As we entered the water we suddenly realised that the crossing point had been cunningly placed next to a sewerage outlet. So as we propelled ourselves along with our feet, we found various lengths of toilet paper wrapped around our ankles. The less said about what else was seen floating by, like brown torpedoes, the better.

As we neared the centre of the rapidly flowing current, disaster struck, our raft started to drift apart. I suddenly found myself holding onto a jerrycan as I was quickly propelled downstream. As I glanced around I could see many of my mates also becoming driftwood. It was suddenly more a case of the first team to make it to the far bank alive, would win. Somehow we all made it across, but nobody could decide who'd won so a dead heat was declared. Later when we tried to enter a nearby tavern for refreshment our entry was barred by a landlord who claimed we 'stank like a sewerage farm!" I really can't imagine the fuck why!

The culmination of our stay in Somerset was to be an 'escape and evasion' exercise. These exercises, as their name suggests, were normally designed to simulate soldiers separated from their units returning, uncaptured through enemy lines to their respective unit. Once again we found ourselves split into teams. This time into groups of three, our team consisting of 2 men from A Squadron, 'Ginge' Austin, Pete 'Berny' Burne and myself. On our first night 'on the run' we were 'dropped' from a lorry on the outskirts of Bath Easton with our only means of navigation being a map. We were told to return to base camp as quickly as possible without being caught by the 'enemy'. The 'enemy' was in fact the RSM and various other senior NCO's prowling the countryside in Landrovers. So off we tramped on what, looking at the map, would be a considerable distance. As we walked uphill past a housing estate, we thought we heard the unmistakable whining of a Landrover engine accompanied by the ever present whoosh of cross country tyres on tarmac. As quick as a flash be jumped up an embankment and vaulted over a small garden hedge onto someone's front lawn. As we lay behind the hedge, the Landrover zoomed past below us. As the sound of our pursuers disappeared up the road another sound became apparent. The sound was discovered to be the voice of a small boy shouting at us from the pavement below.

"Hey, you bastards behind the hedge!" the little voice bawled.

We stuck our heads above the hedge to see who was shouting. The boy was unshocked by the appearance of our camouflage creamed faces followed by our heavy pack laden bodies as we emerged from the garden. We quizzed the youngster on who he was and where he had appeared from at this time of night. It turned out he was only eleven and had run away from a care home in, of all places, Plymouth and he was making his way back Northwards to family ties. We hurriedly discussed the situation amongst ourselves, the lad having asked to come along with us. We decided to take him with us but at the earliest opportunity we would leave him with the appropriate authorities. At least this way he would be safe with us and, having found a spare pullover in one of our packs, off we trogged. The lad had only been wearing a t shirt, shorts and sandals. It was difficult for us to comprehend how this lad had made his way so far, scrounging lifts off people who, hadn't even tried to hand him to the police or any other authority. Without doubt he was extremely 'streetwise', being able to identify cars by engine noise alone. Later when we decided to find somewhere to sleep he even broke into an empty stable so we could sleep on straw bales! We shared what rations we had with him, and ensured he had warm food and a cup of chocolate.

Next morning we got up and vacated the stable before we could be discovered by the owners. Some time later we stopped at the roadside and, having lit a solid fuel cooker on the tarmac, took off our boots and socks to soak our feet in a drainage ditch. As we sat pondering the world a school bus zoomed past us destroying our cooker and the water filled mess tin we'd put on for a 'brew'. As we jumped up we saw, waving from the back window of the bus, one of our rival teams. We unceremoniously stuck our fingers up at the three faces disappearing down the road. Later that morning we managed to hitch our first lift. The lift was on a small lorry full with sacks of coal which promptly covered us in black coal dust. Never mind, it saved our feet. Once we had been deposited at the roadside again we managed to stop an RAF minibus. The driver was a very friendly chap who, having looked at our map, offered to drop us only three miles from base camp.

Later as good as his word, the driver dropped us outside the entrance to a large, imposing house which looked like a stately home. As we unloaded our equipment from the minibus a Landrover appeared behind us. Staring wide eyed from the passenger seat was, the RSM. A very angry looking RSM at that, as he climbed out with steam pouring from his ears. Our immediate reaction was to run like mad twats in any direction other than towards him. This we promptly did, running into the gardens of the mansion before us. Here we were confronted with another angry face. The face belonged to an elderly woman stood on a raised terrace, waving her walking stick at us and using some really quite unladylike expletives. She wanted us to leave the grounds quite rapidly before we trampled any more of her prize rose bushes. More? Yes well, we had caused a fair amount of damage to her borders in our escape from the RSM. We were now torn in deciding which way to run, but inevitably the RSM's ranting won the day. He was upset at our having got a lift. As he said;

"It doesn't ruddy matter that 'everyone's done it', you're the fuckers what got caught"!

With that we were made to run the three miles back to camp and then stand for two hours at attention in the sunshine. Doesn't sound too bad? Well you try it wearing a respirator! We had of course noticed that during the skirmish in the rose garden, our little friend had disappeared into thin air. We spent that evening telling our story to our comrades, having reported the incident to the CO who contacted the police.

Having completed the field phase in Somerset, we returned to Tidworth. There we prepared for the CO's parade on completion of the course. During the parade the best member of the course would be presented with an 'instant' promotion to Lance Corporal. The rest of us having to wait for our various Squadron Leaders to recommend us for promotion when deemed 'ready'. The parade over we were released from course duties to rejoin our Squadrons for tank Park duties. I'm glad to say that even after the 'hitching' incident I passed the Cadre Course and returned to C Squadron to wait for promotion.

It was a policy that once a soldier had passed the Cadre, that soldier would be required to carry out an 'admin' period. This would be a job such as Officers or Sergeants Mess steward for four to six months to 'broaden your experience'. Luckily for me I had spent time in Cyprus as barman so my admin requirement was already complete. It merely remained for me to continue working hard and hopefully in due course I would be promoted. I could then carry the flag of NCO to uphold our traditions and be a leader of men.

20. Bye-Bye Tiddy

We were informed in 1978 that we would be moving back to BAOR in 1979. We would be stationed in Paderborn situated in Nordrhein Westphalen. Suddenly things started to whirr in our routine, preparations for handover started in earnest in early 1979. Once more we found ourselves bulling tanks and equipment like crazy. The difference was of course that, like our predecessors, the 4th/7th we found that our exercise commitments would take us nearly up to the handover. I also had to attend a Control Signallers course at Bovington. This course was my next step up the career ladder. When the Squadron leader told me of this decision I was actually dismayed. Signals? Me? Oh no! I had wished to pursue my training in the Driving and Maintenance (D&M) field. But, as I was informed, my experience thus far had mainly been as an Operator/Loader so my future lay in signals. Within our Regiment D&M and Gunnery were given a higher importance than signals. This was driven mainly by the main functions of the Tank. Most things were measured on how effectively a tank was maintained and how accurately it could shoot. Therefore signals, being fairly unmeasurable, tended to be somewhat neglected. Consequently Control Signallers and indeed, Signals Instructors were continually in short supply. I wouldn't have minded so much except, Signals was by far the hardest subject to learn! All the various codes, voice procedures, radio frequency theory and different types of equipment had to be learnt. The course was lengthy and all I could see before me was boredom.

Once on the course however, I discovered that the course was far from boring. Okay, so all the various subjects had to be learnt but, the Instructors tried to make it as interesting as possible. I was actually on the first 'Con Sig.'s' course to teach the new 'Clansman' range of radio equipment. We had already started to receive and use this new equipment as I had departed on course. The days of 'Larkspur' interference ridden communication were gone forever. These new 'wonder sets' were a huge improvement, now, instead of an essential item of tuning kit being a hammer, we simply dialled in a VHF frequency. Once we had tuned to the desired 'output power', we simply talked into a headset and boom microphone combination and messages were sent and received 'interference free'. The messages could also be sent over vastly increased ranges compared to the old C42 sets. Our new set was the VRC 353, its only potential drawback, was its antenna tuning. As I mentioned, the antenna was tuned to a power output, the problem that could arise was, that if somebody tuned to the highest output (50 Watts) while somebody was grasping that antenna, they could light up like a Christmas tree! The 50-watt setting was 'out of bounds'; the setting was only for use in emergency having tried unsuccessfully to contact anyone by using other, lower settings or by moving the tank to 'higher ground'. But it was possible to inadvertently tune to the setting, so all crews were specifically told not to climb on tanks using the antenna base as a 'hand hold'.

Another problem was the use of voice procedure. Suddenly here we were with a means of communication over which, individual voice characteristics could easily be identified. Previously on the C42 the static and 'mush' interference had helped to disguise voice patterns. The 'Clansman' range of sets were, however, an enemy 'intercept operators' dream. The operator could sit, listen and identify our voices and gradually build a picture of what and who we were and what we were doing. The Soviet bloc forces were masters at recording this information and then using it against their foes. So voice procedure suddenly became a 'hot' subject, we were to ensure our voices were kept at a constant pitch and tone and that when speaking we were either to use code or disguise any uncoded messages. This had always been the case but now it would be enforced with a vengeance. A member of A. Squadron found this out while on exercise. When we were on scheme we had long wondered who 'Natasha' was. Many were the nights when, as a Squadron we were bashing across the countryside on 'radio silence' (when we were strictly forbidden to talk on the radio), when from nowhere the Squadron radio net would come to life. Firstly there would be a crackle and pop then the customary hissing of the 'mush' interference. Suddenly a quiet voice would speak...

"Naattaasha, Naaattaaasha, ooh Naaaaattttaaaaasha". Then silence again. This would happen on every exercise, the interference from the radio assisting in disguising the culprit's voice. However, with the advent of 'Clansman', the culprit was quickly identified as a member of A. Squadron who, had tuned into our frequency in order to try and drop us in the shit for 'breaking' radio silence procedure.

Anyway, I passed my course with flying colours and was recommended for an Instructors course in the fullness of time. When I returned to Tidworth I was regarded as a bit of a guru as, I had also been trained in the art of test and repair of headsets etc. I could also test radios for problems but not repair them, for that we had the REME. A previously unknown piece of radio equipment was now issued. This was the infamous crewman's helmet which we called the 'bonedome'. This was a fibreglass helmet fitted with headsets and a 'boom mic'. The idea being bump protection inside the vehicle, the protection it didn't provide however, was against the helmet itself which had an awful tendency to feel like a vice on your bloody skull. This was due to the headsets being spring loaded to maintain pressure on the ears for hearing efficiency. Of course the pressure wasn't meant to be so great that it made us feel as though our brains were being pushed out of our eye sockets.

Before 'Clansman's' arrival we had also seen the introduction of our first Chieftain Mk 3G, this was of course not a brand new Tank, rather a reworked and upgraded Mk 2xy. It went straight to SHQ and was given to my old pal Lucy as his to drive. It raised a few eyebrows in the Squadron as it was the first tank we had seen with the new No.6 NBC system fitted to the turret. We had long since got used to the appearance of laser rangefinding equipment to replace the familiar Bop, Bop, Bop of the.50 Browning. The.50 stayed in the turret as the balance of the main armament relied on the.50's weight so that the gun control equipment wouldn't be thrown out of synchronisation. Eventually this much loved gun would be taken away and replaced simply by a weight to replace it. We could not understand the decision to scrap the.50, as its heavy calibre was ideal for light armour penetration instead of wasting main armament ammunition. But as I said the new NBC pack created interest as it was so much improved on the old system. The turret no longer looked as if it had a small tin attached to its back. Instead the new pack became an extension of the turret rear, creating on its top, flat surface, a new sleeping place.

But this sleeping place was used only if we were unable to erect a shelter over the warm engine decks at night as we were in a 'battle hide'. tanks at night move into 'hides', a reserve hide is normally a wood to the rear of the Troop or Squadron battle positions. Safely tucked away in our wood, we would put the main armament squarely over the engine decks and, then strap a tarpaulin along the top length of the barrel and tie its sides down to both sides of the Tank. The crew would then curl up in their sleeping bags on the decks, their armour staying warm all night. A 'battle hide' was a wooded overnight position where we were concealed in our actual firing position. Our main armament would remain 'gun front', ready for immediate action. Normally we would sleep in our crew positions but, we may have permission to sleep outside on the turret or available engine deck space. If this was the case, crewmen could be found sleeping in all manner of strange positions. Sleeping in crew positions was a particularly unpleasant chore. Imagine the gunner being squashed in his seat taking on the form of a Chinese puzzle. The driver would of course, have the best nights sleep, fully reclined in his sealed cab. The commander would order the gun to be elevated, allowing him to sit upright but stretch his legs on top of the main armaments breech. The operator? I can clearly remember many a night, curled around the turret ring on top of the ammo charge bins, with a jacket rolled up as a pillow. The main problem with vehicle sleeping was the overnight drop in temperature, I mean it was fucking cold. Our warm breath would circulate creating condensation on the turret roof, this in turn would drip on our slumbering bodies creating more misery.

Upon waking, when in a reserve hide, our routine would normally be to get up, stow all our equipment and the camouflage nets. The previous night before retiring, the operator would have gathered the compo tins for breakfast, and placed them in the BV ready to go. Having ensured our stowage was secure and that nothing would be left behind, we would depart from the hide ensuring that the BV was switched on. This way, by the time we reached our new location and had erected the awful 'cam nets' the BV would have finished heating our food. There was nothing quite like a Bacon burger buttie and cup of tea for our groaning stomachs. This ritual of up, stow, move and get to a new location was really a survival exercise. Its aim was to remove us from the danger of an enemy who had been watching us overnight, preparing to attack us at dawn. So before 'first light' it was up and get out. I suppose you could liken it to the Infantry ritual of 'stand to' at dawn, where they all man their foxholes ready to fight off any aggressors who'd 'fancy their chances' as daylight approached.

As the year rolled on so the tempo of our handover preparations increased until, they were at fever pitch. Along the way many of our pals departed the army, choosing to pursue civilian jobs and stay in the UK. This was always a trade mark of postings in Britain, manpower tended to turnover at an increased speed. I think it was because the temptation of seeing jobs in the vicinity of home and family that did it. Also, soldiers formed relationships with partners and decided to forgo the trauma of separation through long periods in Germany. We, for example were destined to stay in Paderborn for nine years. Armoured units always received long postings I believe, due to the fact that the bulk of our armour was in Germany facing the Cold war threat of communism.

Some of the faces who departed were 'Snake' Butler, Phil 'Ollie' Olbrechts, 'Sam' Boundy, 'Rabbit' and, to my surprise, 'Stan Janner'. When, over a beer I discussed his logic in leaving, his answer was simply "Malc, its getting so that the fun of Tanking is going down the tube, people are taking this army lark far too fucking seriously!" This shocked me but, never the less Stan departed to become a policeman in Bristol. And so it was that a good proportion of experienced crewmembers left the Regiment. At least some of my friends were staying, such as Gary 'Monklet' Monk, Pete Lip and the ever-faithful 'Lucy' Taylor.

Also, during our stay at Tidworth the RTR said farewell to the 'Hackle' a plume of feathers in the RTR colours which fitted behind the cap badge of our parade 'No 1' beret which, unlike the hackle itself, nobody missed when it too, disappeared!

We that remained had our farewell parties including a night in a marquee. This night was C. Squadrons farewell to Tidworth and a cracking good night it was too.

'Switches' was actually found availing a young lady of his sexual charms behind a stack of straw bales in the marquee we'd set up for a farewell party. Found… during the bloody festivities as we all drank and made merry.

In due course having said our farewells and handed our tanks over, we departed for Germany in late 1979. Next stop, Germany.

21. Deutschland Über Alles

Here we were then 3 RTR, October 1979 and firmly ensconced in Barker Barracks, Paderborn. The Germans simply referred to our barracks as Panzer Kaserne. This name dates back to WW2 when our barracks housed SS tank units. Paderborn itself is a spacious, typically modern German city. This, I have no doubt is mainly due to a major rebuild after the ravages of the Americans 'taking' the city in the war. The city and its surrounding area at Sennelager bore numerous barracks that once housed units of The Fatherlands finest. Now they all housed we British, while the German Bundeswehr were housed in fine new abodes.

Panzer Kaserne certainly showed enough evidence of its previous occupants. On the approach to the main gates, on the perimeter wall, could be seen where the German eagle and clutched swastika had been chiselled off. On the end wall of each barrack block we could still, but only just, make out the old block names and the shape of what looked like a running man. Inside the blocks could be seen the original wall racks for rifles. Our barracks were shared, one half for us and the other half for 25 Field Regiment Royal Artillery who, also hosted 5 Ordnance Battalion and an American detachment within their area.

The blocks in our section of the barracks were large three floored affairs with a windowed attic space and cavernous cellar. The cellars had been segmented into rooms. These rooms were used as individual Troop offices and stores, or as we called them 'cages'. One cage was the Troop office and the other contained spare tools and equipment for the Tanks. The blocks ran parallel to each other with HQ Squadron and D Squadron sharing the block at the top of the slope and then C. Squadron, B.Squadron and A.Squadron respectively across down the hill. The top floor of our block contained our band, and Christ, the racket could be monumental. The top floor of B.Squadron block was the Corporals Mess and atop A. Squadron was the Training wing. Running at right angles to these down the hill were the Sergeants Mess and the NAAFI below. RHQ was below the NAAFI, and was a semi detached building with the Artillery HQ in the other half.

On the other side of the Sergeants mess from our block were the tank parks. These were long brick built hangars with individual bays for the vehicles but as D.Squadron had been formed and shared part of both our and 'Bumbles' tank parks we found vehicles doubling up. Luckily the hangars appeared to have been designed for Tiger Tanks, so our Chieftains did fit. Our park was at the top of the hill with 'Bumbles' below and A.Squadron who shared with Command Troop (RHQ) at the bottom. Below that, right at the bottom was the REME with their HQ LAD sharing with our Quartermaster Technical (QMT).

Not to forget the Squadron LAD's each LAD being situated on the end of each Squadron Park. The Officers Mess lest you think I'd forgotten was at the top of the camp next to a railway track with the sports fields between them and the tank Parks. The Officers Mess was the only modern building on camp. On the far side of the tank parks was the SSVC cinema, and beyond that on the perimeter was an old disused ammunition compound still with all its grass covered bunkers intact.

When we'd arrived at Paderborn we had left our trusted REME fitters at Tidworth as they were posted to different units independently normally on a two-year cycle. It was a shame as we always accepted our REME guys as if they were one of us. So on arrival we inherited a new bunch of fitters. Now being back in Germany, the CO had allowed us to have Squadron bars again. This vital piece of our life had been missing in the UK due to NAAFI trading rules. So, top priority was to build and operate the bar. Soon the Friday 16:00pm 'happy hours' began again. However they were known as 'Dutch O' groups to disguise the fact it was a drinking session. Our lives were governed by 'Orders'; these were displayed in our blocks on a notice board. They were split into two parts, 'Part ones' being Regimental orders containing, information on guard requirements from the Squadrons and fatigue duties and other Regimental notices. 'Part twos' were generated by the Squadron office and contained the detail requested in 'part ones'. In other words if C. Squadron were providing men for barracks guard duties the names of the poor individuals were displayed here along with any Squadron notices. A good example would be;

> NOTICE: The Squadron will parade on Friday 17th November at 16:00 hrs, in the Squadron bar where the OC will be conducting a 'Dutch' O Group. All members of the Squadron will attend for briefing.

Attend for briefing? Yeah who were we kidding, briefing spelt D R I N K I N G. It was on one of these drinking sessions that I met Tony Seery, a fitter in our LAD, and a man for telling yarns. You see every ex NAZI barracks inhabited now by our nation, contained some cracking ghost stories. Tony was a guy who was only too willing to tell us of our camps history. Our block for example had a good ghost story about an

SS soldier who 'came a haunting'. Apparently the last unit had gone on 'block leave'. This meant that apart from soldiers who were on essential duties the entire Regiment went on leave. Even the chaps on duties were moved into one block. The empty blocks then had chains and padlocks fitted to the corridor doors leading to the stairwells for security. Well, the story went that one guy was on leave in England and having no transport, he decided to hitch back to Paderborn. It would appear that he was more successful than he had anticipated and arrived back a day early. When he reported to the guardroom, he was given access to his block but had no key for his room. He then decided he would sleep in the corridor in a borrowed sleeping bag from the guardroom. Then next day the rest of the guys would return and everything would be fine. However, very early next morning he was awoken by the sound of hobnailed boots crunching along the corridor. He emerged from his 'slug' and peered down the corridor to see a guy walking away from him wearing only khaki coloured breeches, jack boots and carried a washing bag and towel. The chap's head was shaven and as the waking chap challenged this intruder the head turned to see whom this was shouting at him. The guy then ignored the challenge and disappeared into the washroom. Having put his shoes on, the returnee ventured to the washroom to further investigate the intruder but, on arrival found the room empty with the windows secured. When later that day his colleagues returned from leave, he was found quivering and burbling about ghosts and SS soldiers. I can only say to this, Bollocks, we never had any incident with the mysterious soldier. We did however, that night, find one of our young Troopers running naked, up and down the corridor screaming. He had awoken in his single man room, to find a tall figure clad in black with SS insignia on his uniform standing over him. The figure was apparently holding our guy by the throat while laughing demonically. We put this down to drink-related hallucinations. But who knows?

Another myth in our camp was; 'the underground tank park'. The story is that when, during WW2 the American forces came to 'liberate?' Paderborn they were confronted with fierce resistance. The American commander's information was that a complete SS tank unit was offering this resistance. With the war in its closing stages the commander decided to surround the city and 'blow the sucker to pieces' with the SS tanks being prime candidates for destruction. Having well and truly blown the city into the next year, the Americans advanced but, were surprised to find only a couple of 'knocked out' Tanks. Now, they'd had the city surrounded so, knew that nothing had escaped their hail of death. So, where were the SS? Somebody decided that within our camp there was a huge underground bunker where all the tanks had, in Arthurian style, driven into the concealed lair to come out and fight at a later date. Unfortunately the vehicles and crews didn't get out again and, to this day the tanks and their dead crews are parked underground. Yes well, you can imagine how we laughed at that one, until, one day a group of German scientists were allowed access to the camp. They brought with them masses of X-ray equipment and started scanning the landscape. When later, we discovered they were looking for the underground park, we had to give some credence to the story. Certainly there was an extensive network of pedestrian sized tunnels under the camp as some chaps had found them. They were so extensive that they seemed to extend beyond our camp perimeter. We assumed that our camp was therefore only a shadow of its former size. The local inhabitants were quite unforthcoming about the military history surrounding our camp. The local mayor however was particularly forthcoming when he wrote a letter of complaint to our CO. His complaint concerned our wearing of black coveralls. We had always gone on town visits to the bank and so on, during lunch breaks still dressed for the tank Park. But in Paderborn the locals took umbrage at our black clothing as, it brought back memories of the SS heritage of this once staunchly National Socialist stronghold. So that was it, overalls ban in town. When later, a member of C. Squadron returned from UK leave selling us 'Adolph Hitler - European Tour, 1939 – 1945' t shirts which we wore around town, it certainly prompted another letter to the CO.

The residents of Paderborn were not the most friendly of people towards our presence, and remained fairly aloof. Annoyingly, I speak German and so, could understand much of what was said. 'Bloody Englanders', 'Shit Tommy's' and 'Island apes' were fairly commonly heard in bars containing members of the older generations. But in the main we led a fairly peaceful existence and only felt 'tolerated' occasionally by our German hosts. I don't think the attitudes of the Paderborn residents were in fact that different to anywhere in the world where a large military garrison was stationed. After all I have already given examples of the work hard, play hard syndrome and it must be hard for people who witness events but have no understanding of them.

It didn't take us long to adjust to our new surroundings, the drinking haunt down in the town was the 'London Pub', if we wanted to go to a club there was the 'City club' a place of easy drinking and easy women. As you can see there is a knack that the Europeans have of taking fairly monotonous English terminology and using it to make their mundane establishments sound a little more exotic. Another example was a club in nearby Schloss Neuhaus called imaginatively 'Love Story', here you could dance the night away with German girls who actually liked the English. Of course it has to be said that the naming of bars and clubs in the area also cunningly attracted British soldiers like a magnet. Such bars seemed to prosper very well I assume, due to the vast quantities of alcohol we consumed. On every street corner in town stood the wonderful 'Schnell Imbiss', this literally means quick bite. The 'Schnellie' as we called it, provided fast food in the form of sausages such as Bratwurst grilled fresh over charcoal and served with a slice of bread and mustard or ketchup. If a soldier was buying one it would be ordered with chips. There was only takeaway service so it was stand and eat even when wobbling after a drink.

This then was Paderborn, our home for the next eight years.

22. 'Activate your Edge'

Having assumed our duties in BAOR we became liable for what was called Exercise 'Active Edge' – designed to test the Regiment's ability, at very short notice, to mobilise and 'crash out' of barracks ready for war. A Regiment was made Active Edge liable for a period of time simulating a fairly quick political build up, leading to a Soviet military invasion across the Inner German Border (IGB) separating East from West. During this period our tanks would be geared and equipped for war and ready to go at a moment's notice.

'Crash out' always happened at night, announced by an immense siren on the roof of RHQ. The noise alone was enough to wake the dead, let alone the Squadron Duty NCOs running from room to room, kicking and cajoling us from our beds. Not only did it wake us, but probably most of Paderborn as well. And I wondered why we weren't so popular? As soon as we were up and dressed, we would grab our belts with the ever-present respirator pouch attached, and run for the armoury downstairs. The armourer would be there throwing both personal and tank weapons at us (after we'd signed for them of course) and it would be hell for leather to the tank Park. Having stowed our gear, SMG's and mounted the machine guns in their various positions the by now throbbing engines would roar and we would pull out onto the park. Frequencies would now be tuned onto the radio's and we would place them on standby so that we didn't inadvertently break radio silence. In time of war this would be the most critical period for us, waiting to deploy to our 'survival areas' which were pre designated parts of the countryside in which we would hide having escaped our landmark barracks. Once in the survival area we could safely wait for further orders as to what our next missions would be.

Sat waiting I used to wonder what it would be like to really 'crash out', and pursue a land war. Maybe, drawing on my peace time experience I may write another story in the line of 'what if?' The wait would not be long and soon the OC would appear and by word of mouth we would be drawn forward with the rest of the waiting Regiment. Then as if someone dropped a flag 'We were 'orf!' Storming out of the barracks gates our engines roaring and our heavy exhaust smoke choking the occupants of the Artillery Guardroom. As we exited we would swing hard left onto the main road and hammer off into the night our orange flashing lights illuminating the nearby fields. Of course in war any lights would be extinguished except the small convoy light on the tanks rear, this was so that in darkness there was a small light, to prevent over enthusiastic drivers ramming up the tank in fronts' backend. An orange flashing light would therefore be firmly thrown in the nearest skip. I can't imagine anything more attractive to a Russian Hind D helicopter gunship. It would be as good as a crew standing on top of a turret 'mooning' in broad daylight while shouting;

"Oi, come over here big boy and shove one up my arse!"

Having seen film evidence of a Hind D's firepower it wouldn't be something I'd encounter without it totally ruining my day.

Our journey from barracks culminated, after a short journey, on our small training ground called the Goldgrund. This was our survival area for the purpose of our exercise. In the event of real war our survival area would be much more distant the location of which was kept secret behind lock and key. Having arrived we would go into our hide routine putting up cam nets, digging trenches and posting sentries and radio watch in our turrets. 'Runners' would be dashing round relaying orders to Squadrons from the CO. The CO would come round himself to check on our progress. Progress? Oh yes, you see the whole exercise was NATO administered so some very senior people would appear at our side at any time to inspect what we were doing. They could demand anything from "show me how to make a cup of tea!" to stripping the complete toolkits out to be checked against the equipment schedule. These teams did appear but I was always fortunate not to have been involved in any of their checks. The following day having officially ended 'actively edging', we would pack up and move back to camp. But first of course we had covered our tanks in mud so? Yes, washdown. Now the Goldgrund facilities were sparse to say the least. They were simply not designed for a Regiment of 62 MBTs at a time. So washdown took an absolutely outrageous amount of time. We would form a queue and simply wait, but in due course we would have eventually washed the vehicles and head back down the road to camp. At this point in time our biggest prayer was that we wouldn't break down.

When we reached the tank Park we would 'de- kit' the tanks ready for maintenance and return all our guns, cleaned and oiled to the Squadron armoury. Dependant on time we may have then either returned to work on our steel steeds or attend a debrief in the Troop cage. But one thing was for sure, the Squadron bar would soon be open!

From this point on I will be, once again leaving the chronological order of events in Paderborn and simply relating occurrences in specific areas of operations. I will attempt however to keep the flow of each section in the right chronological order.

23. BATUS

The British Army Training Unit Suffield, Suffield being a small settlement in the middle of the Canadian prairie, some 4 hours coach ride south east of Calgary in Alberta. The nearest, significant, town to this area is Medicine Hat about 2 hours car drive away. Or at least if you stuck to the low Trans Canada Highway speed limits it could be two hours away. The training area actually belongs to an Indian tribe who rent it to both the Canadian and the British governments. Its size is massive it takes a tank two good days travelling, to motor from one side to the other in battle conditions. I believe its size is about the same as Wales, but could easily be bigger.

BATUS sunsets – bootifull!

To describe the prairie as per a tourist brochure would be difficult. If however you can picture a barren, desolate and rolling hilled Arabian Desert but covered in dry scrubby grass, you won't be disappointed should you one-day visit? If you look at a map of the area it just looks monotone in colour, with contour lines denoting the heights of the 'look alike' hills. In one or two sections of the map you may, if you look really hard', see some small green dots. Now European maps have whole woodlands, but these green dots actually represent individual trees. If memory serves me right, about twelve in all. In the centre of the map is a point named Jadex Junction and from it radiating outwards are circles that are physically tracks in the ground. Cutting through these circles are tracks with names such as Rattlesnake road, Badger road, Antelope road and Dragoon trail to name but a few. Also on the map are manmade landmarks such as 'Coke tower' this really is a huge coke can on top of a wooden tower. These were erected to aid vehicle commanders in what is otherwise, a very difficult terrain to circumnavigate. This is due to safety constraints more than the ineptitude of commanders at map reading.

Why do we train in BATUS? Put simply, it is the only place where we could put down a complete battle group and its support elements with enough space to really practise the arts of war in their entirety, the only thing missing was an enemy firing back at us. In firing practices for military forces, all firing ranges have what is called a Template. This is the area for safety if a shell or projectile misses the target and flies off into the beyond. The template is set to allow for ammunition being at the limit of its natural flight when it would 'run out of steam'. In Europe the templates have, understandably been shortened to accommodate the size of range being fired on. There are on the map also out of Bounds areas marked. These are normally places belonging to the Canadian Department of Research and Experimentation who in the past have supposedly carried out some 'nasty' experiment or other, now rendering the ground unusable. Indeed Jadex junction itself was designed to be 'ground zero' for an atomic bomb test in the 1950's, which never happened. The radiating circles therefore were the 'rings' on the ground to allow measurement of the resulting shockwave.

The base for all this? BATUS itself contained staff from the Canadian army and for the British, soldiers drawn from all parts of the army on posting. These ranged from administration to vehicle repair. Also there were the range safety staff who, zoomed all over the prairie in Ferrets with red paint all over them. These guys followed us everywhere controlling how we 'fought' ensuring we kept within safety limits. The camp for the exercising battle groups was a 'portacabin' style series of huts for our accommodation before and after scheme. We also had a cookhouse with a seemingly endless supply of tasty food, and of course, a bar. The bar could get quite rowdy from time to time with so many different units installed. The accommodation was pretty rudimentary consisting of a huge room filled with bunk beds, enough of which there were to basically accommodate half a squadron's men. This array of buildings was called Camp Crowfoot after the native Indian tribe indigenous to the area.

Just outside camp Crowfoot was the vehicle park, known simply as the dustbowl. It was of course exactly that. An area bordered by a simple wooden fence to denote its boundary from the onset of the prairie. The exercise season each year was split into seven sections of approximately 6 weeks duration. Each section was known as 'exercise medicine man (med man)', suffixed by the numbers one to seven in that order. The season ran from spring into the start of winter but more on 'med man 7' in due course. So the vehicles based there saw some very intensive service to say the least, in fact they got 'fucking hammered' would be more apt!

So the routine would be, in a nutshell, fly to Calgary on an RAF VC10 of 1960's vintage, stopping at Iceland to refuel, the journey time taking around nine or ten hours. Once at Calgary it would be a quick transfer to a 'Greyhound' style bus, and then about four hours to BATUS on the Trans Canada Highway. A mind numbingly boring journey to say the least. Having arrived at camp and been allocated our accommodation, it was off for a briefing. The highlight of the talk was the Royal Military Police detachments instructions on Canadian laws on driving, drinking and, of all things, sex. Strange as it may seem we were told which girls in Medicine Hat to steer clear of in respect of, their being under age or, having some strange sexual disease. Quite frankly they might as well have not bothered as, squaddies 'with drink' wouldn't give a 'rats arse' who they slept with. Well, some of them anyway! After the briefing, regardless of 'jet lag' it would be 'beer then bed', but mainly beer. Then the next week would be preparing the vehicles followed by four weeks in the 'uluh' as we called any exercise area. At the end we would prepare the vehicles for handover to the next 'Med man' and depart for rest and recuperation (R&R) which, dependant on flight times could last up to around ten days. Lastly of course the flight homeward.

Having now given you the quick itinery, lets dwell on individual events. The flights could be quite eventful, flying out to Canada; I mentioned the refuelling at Iceland. When approaching the island, we always seemed to approach from the wrong direction this then involved a fairly low level fly past out to sea followed by a gut wrenching 180 degree turn to come back in to land. On one occasion we arrived at Iceland in a gale force storm. Undeterred the pilot swept out to sea and performed his usual 'stand the 'kite' on its wingtips' manoeuvre, leaving our stomachs miles behind us in the slipstream. We all swore later that the breakers from the stormy waves below were touching the wing tip. As he quickly descended on our approach, the chaps on one side realised that the crosswind was so severe that they could clearly see the fast ascending runway in front of their eyes. An instant before touchdown the pilot straightened the aircraft and with a bang followed by bouncing thuds, we arrived at our destination. Without exception, we all rushed from the plane to the bar and rapidly had a drink. As we watched the standing area through muggy, damp lounge windows we saw the aircrew come towards us. I assumed the one with the handlebar moustache and glint in his eye was the pilot. 'Fuck me, he looks like he's come straight from the 'Dambusters' raid!" I exclaimed. This only resulted in more frantic drinking from all present. As we waited to be called back on board our 'flight to hell' we all thought that we might be grounded. The weather had deteriorated to a truly alarming level. But no, we were called out to the plane only minutes later. We all sat down and pulled our seatbelts as tight as was humanly possible, "after all", thought I, "the RAF have never lost a VC10 yet!" As if reading my thoughts, Lucy, sitting next to me said, "Ha fucking Ha there's always a first time for everything!" Oh how very fucking comforting. Anyway we got under way and before long, were soaring above the weather front that had so very nearly brought me to tears.

On another occasion we were on a flight home, we had all fallen asleep as we'd left at night, and after about two hours of the flight had passed, we were awoken by a bell ringing. We all assumed that, for some obscure reason, someone had packed an alarm clock in his hand baggage. Much shouting ensued with people verbally assaulting the culprit with;

"Shut that fucking alarm clock off!"

A steward went forward and the bell was silenced. We relaxed again and fell back into our slumber. Around an hour later we were roused once more, this time by the captain announcing that;

" We'll be landing at Calgary international airport in approximately one hour".

"Fucking 'ey? We left there three hours ago!" exclaimed I to my neighbour.

Our questions of; "what the fuck is going on?" Were dealt with quickly by the stewards, who answered simply that we had ' a slight technical problem'. Later after landing we found that the 'slight technical problem' had in fact been an engine with sixteen feet of flame shooting out the back. Due to safety regulations, we were not allowed to fly over the sea with less than full engine power! Oh, how comforting. We had now assumed we would simply arrive, be put in a terminal and await the next flight out. But no, we were put on buses and driven back to BATUS, once there we were told to rest until the next flight. This we did... for about twenty-five minutes, then with an announcement that the next flight was awaiting us, we got back on the buses and away we went to the airport. Upon arrival at the airport, we waited on the bus until called to the plane. We sat and watched the ministering of the engineers as they prepared the 'Vicky 10' for its return journey.

"What the hell are they doing?" Someone said. The attention of everyone was now drawn to a team of blue overall clad workers on top of a wing. They were stamping on something with their feet.

"Oh my fucking god, they're sticking something down!" Someone said. And so they were, they were in fact using thick adhesive tape and sticking it over the air brake flaps on top of the wing surface. An RAF 'Bod' came to the bus and informed us;

"We've had a fault with the airbrakes on the port wing and we're unable to fix it here. So we've disconnected both wings and are sticking the flaps down to secure them, no need to panic guys, we'll be perfectly safe". With that he quickly departed to rejoin his colleagues 'Morris dancing' on the wing. I wasn't sure that I liked his suggestion that 'we' would all be safe as, he quite clearly was ground crew so wouldn't in fact be on the plane. As we climbed the steps to the planes door, we looked at the wing with a Tankies eye, as if we could assure ourselves that the 'bodge' had been carried out to the best of 'our' ability not the RAF's. The wing simply looked as if it had been 'band aided' all across the wings surface. In due course we took off and by the time we reached our cruising altitude of thirty two thousand feet, the tape was quite happily flapping in the wind with the brake flaps threatening to break free. To say the flight wasn't comfortable would be an understatement. But, after another quick first aid repair at Iceland we duly arrived safely in Europe.

The bus ride! Well I could think of more interesting subjects but I would like to pass comment on some of the things that left an impression on me. This was the first time I'd been to Canada; in fact it was for all of us. BATUS had, I believe only opened fairly recently in 1975. As we left the airport and headed through Calgary's suburbs I was struck by how different everything was. This was the Seventies and having left the UK I was surprised at how big everything seemed. Cars, trucks, buses and the buildings seemed huge. But the impression I got was the fabled American decadence, in that, due to the ramshackle appearance of everything it was as though a policy of build it, don't repair it, let it crumble, knock it down and rebuild it was in action. As we left the city and headed into the Prairie the highway before us stretched to infinity. The only things I saw which impressed me were the trucks. Their drivers seemed to have such pride, as the vehicles were immaculate. Having seen the film 'Convoy' I could now see the real White, Kenworth, Mack and Ford leviathans toiling along the road. Mighty impressive they were too, way bigger than anything I'd previously seen. Their big, chrome stack pipes belching diesel fumes seemingly saying; " Get outta my way, I own this fucking road and my drivers soul". Okay, I admit that sounds romanticised, but I've always liked big machinery. As our journey progressed we found ourselves halting at every railroad crossing. The driver explained this as the law. For the safety of his passengers he was required to halt, open the doors, check up and down the line for oncoming trains and then cross with caution. Once across the line he would shut the doors and resume normal speed. This made us think that the trains must be supersonic; I mean you could see up and down the track for absolutely fucking miles, from miles away. But as we once found, nothing could be further from the truth. We sat on the bus watching as a train rolled by, at the front, three huge locomotives thundered by at about 10 MPH, then, what seemed like hundreds of wagons followed by another two engines thumping away at the back. We timed that the train took nearly an hour to clear the crossing, that was indeed, some train.

Further along our route we started to see 'nodding donkeys', these are pumping stations with huge swinging arms swaying as they tap into Canada's huge natural wealth of gas and oil. The stations themselves were simply wooden outhouses next to the 'nodding donkey', unmanned and with vast distances between the stations. Occasionally we would pass through a town, these being more like desolate settlements of old. But the signs for hotels and gas stations showed that people definitely lived here. I now believe, after numerous visits to Canada that many buildings and vehicles simply look 'tired' due to the extremes of weather that they experience. Especially Alberta with its magnificent expanse of prairie. To try and explain the vast distances on the prairie to the uninitiated is very difficult, but imagine this, we once witnessed corn harvesting, and counted some fifty combine harvesters wing to wing and they didn't cover a half of the fenced field area. To water the crops huge wheeled water sprinklers are seen like spiders legs stretching out to fill a circular radius of some five hundred meters at a time. The country certainly is huge, I can say no more other than if I found myself needing to emigrate, of all the foreign lands I've visited, Canada was and still is my all time favourite.

BATUS could be seen from miles away on the highway, even though it was miles from the highway. All towns and settlements have a huge, bulbous metal water tower rising up above them. The tower at Suffield was painted in a red and white chequer pattern and could be seen across the seemingly endless waste.

Once there we were ready for the RMP briefing. Once it started we were soon laughing at some of the information we were given as 'light entertainment'.

"Contrary to one squaddies opinion which he voiced to the Medicine Hat police when being arrested while pissing up a parked cars wheel arch, it is NOT legal in Canada, when caught short, to urinate up the pavement side wheel arch!"

"Take a bottle of scotch from the closed brown paper bag it will be sold to you in, break the seal but don't take a drink, and the police can arrest you for being drunk and disorderly!"

"Beware of a girl called Helen in "the Hat"(Medicine Hat), She's only fourteen and has the 'crabs'". On that occasion we'd seen the evidence of this on arrival. Two of our guys had arrived ten days earlier on 'advance party' to prepare for our arrival. They had both been 'familiar' with Helen, and the 'crabs' had grown so big, when we arrived they were racing them on a window sill and taking bets on the winner. They thought it strange when later, on scheme, they found themselves exiled to a small two man tent away from their crews! Their only comment was; "I'll be fucked if she looked only fourteen!" How very apt!

The drinking laws in Canada are quite convoluted and to explain them all would take too long, lets just say that, unless the laws have changed, the evidence I saw in Calgary was that it was simpler to buy drugs on a street corner than alcohol from a 'liquor store'. More of drinking and drunken cavorting later. Let's now continue with the real reason for our being at BATUS, exercising.

24. 'Prairie dogs'

10 Tp C Sqn in the assault.

Right, having 'prepped' our vehicles on the 'dust bowl' we were now ready to depart and 'let slip the dogs of war'. As we departed clouds of thick, lung-penetrating dust immediately engulfed us. It didn't matter how much protective gear we put over our eyes and mouths, it still choked us. How were we to survive this? It was simply a matter of adjusting to the atmosphere over a relatively short amount of time. We had already become accustomed to the prairie dogs or 'gophers' as they are known. They were simply everywhere, sat watching on top of burrow mounds only to scurry under as we roared by. We had also been warned of the rattlesnake presence and many of us would see them. Especially if, when parked the cry "Rattler" would be heard. We would immediately rush to inspect the beast, prodding it from a relatively safe distance with an antenna section. On one occasion 'Trigger' Duckworth's beret was Frisbee'd on top of a snake, which, promptly took it as protection and curled up, hissing and rattling beneath its new shelter. It was consequently some time before trigger could reclaim his hat. On another occasion a Troop Leader SSGT 'Nosher' Cadman, a chap of great joviality, went on a 'shovel recce' carrying his spade and toilet roll. He promptly returned with his overalls still around his ankles shouting "Fucking Rattlers!" it would appear that he had attempted to dig a hole in which to 'drop a log' only, having prepared to relieve himself he discovered that he had in fact disturbed a rattlesnake nest. In the face of the writhing mass he departed 'pronto' back to our leaguer.

A cunning ruse to hide a Chieftain Dozer?

To explain, a 'leaguer' to the uninitiated, is a protective parking formation when in open ground due to a lack of woodland cover. In those days SHQ's 3 MBTs would firstly park line abreast facing any expected enemy frontage. Then the sabre troops would come in behind at each side 2 troops left and 2 right in line ahead formation. The troop's guns would then traverse outwards for 'all round protection'. In line abreast across the rear would park the REME vehicles with the Squadron ambulance parked in the middle of what was now a 'ring of steel' box formation. Once parked, bivvies would be erected against the tanks on the inside of the box, having first checked for 'wildlife'. The crews could now adopt the normal routines for 'stand down' activities including guards etc. This formation would always be adopted in Canada because as I explained earlier, there were only a few trees to be found. Even then, many vehicle drivers tried where possible, to be the man to 'remove' a green dot from the map! Still, trees or no trees, we could still erect a camnet – we were duly issued camnets WW2 desert vintage camnets but, with no woods, hence no branches we couldn't lift them off the vehicle to disguise it's shape – hhmmmmmm… not too clever.

During the exercise we would be given maintenance days where we would remain leaguered to carry out essential tasks to keep the vehicles in order. Also on these days we would be offered the chance of a shower. Sometimes we would be ferried to the 'mobile shower unit', this was a tent with a heated water supply fed to showerheads inside. If for whatever reason that wasn't available such as on our first visit to BATUS, it would be 'all aboard the Crowfoot express'. This was our MT troop with old American 'Deuce and a halve' trucks ready to shuttle back to camp. Dirty we were on departure, dirty we were upon our return. All due to the dust thrown up on the journey. I remember on one occasion our OC's operator; 'Mad' George Palframan went on a shower run. He and a couple others managed to stay in Crowfoot all day, eventually returning late that evening, drunk of course. The OC had retired early to the bivvie that evening. Somehow George, who was now strangely naked apart from his boots, appeared on top of his turret with a sandwich in one hand and a bottle of Labbatts 'blue' beer in the other. His naked expanse gleamed in the reflected glow from our lights, which, as we were 'non-tactical', shone everywhere. Then he proclaimed from his lofty perch; " I CAN FUCKING FLY! I CAN FUCKING FLY!" And launched himself from the turret in a magnificent belly flop on to the bivvie below. The resulting eruption was hilarious, the OC awoke and immediately exclaimed; "I say, what the fuck was that?" He was now waking the gunner Ian Jones who had also just retired after drinking. "Jones, Jones, wake up, what the hell's happening? Someone just fell on the bivvie, where's my bottle of scotch? Come on! Get up I want to know what's happening!" By now George's inane cackling had come to the OC's ears.

"Corporal P' what the fuck are you doing?" The OC received only a loud "Fuck off!" For an answer. The OC was now fighting to get out of the bivvie to grab his assailant, still shouting for his bottle of scotch. George, on the other hand, had different ideas. Quick as a flash he was up and running, departing the leaguer, his white arse disappearing from view as he reached the end of our lights' glow. Apparently there was a stony silence in that turret for a couple of days.

The actual exercises were excellent we saw many things in action that we had previously only heard about. One example was 'Giant Viper' this was an explosive packed hose that the Engineers could propel with rockets across a minefield. The explosive would then be detonated, creating a 'minefield gap' through which we could safely pass. We could watch the Artillery create barrages on enemy positions or in fact, on our positions. I say this as our REME packet of vehicles were parked watching our Squadron on an attack when suddenly; CRUMP, CRUMP, CRUMP a shower of shells fell on their position. The resulting radio messages were chaotic, the upshot I imagine, was some poor artilleryman or 'dropshort' as they became known getting a really bad time off someone. 'Dropshort' being the name for rounds of ammo

~ 148 ~

which fall short of their target area, the rounds in question falling some four thousand metres short of the objective. We weren't too fond of the Artillery to say the least. They also for some reason, thought their self-propelled guns were Tanks! I should think not! It was Artillery in BATUS who after a man extinguished a cigarette one night in the dark on a bagged charge, (when he shouldn't have been smoking in the vehicle) illuminated the prairie for bloody miles when the M109 SP Gun he was in, exploded. The resulting firework display was fantastic, miraculously nobody was hurt in the incident but the M109 was effectively 'melted'.

Another memorable incident on my first visit to BATUS was the ranging gun of a tank firing on another Tank. During an assault, somehow a Commander got slightly out of line, and with a jolt suddenly heard a ping, followed by ping, ping, ping on the outside of his turret. In a complete panic he screamed across the radio net, "STILL!" This was the accepted emergency call for everything to literally stop instantly within a tank as a crewmember may have spotted something life threatening. It could also be employed as an emergency stop signal across a radio net in this case the Squadron net. The commander had realised that he had been hit by ranging shots from a.50 browning. All I can say is that it was lucky that this happened before we received laser rangefinders. For the rest of that 'Med Man', during slow periods of battle, operators could be seen being despatched from their turrets, running to a neighbouring tank with a two-pound hammer in their sweaty hand. The operator would then climb up the side of the tank and bang the hammer hard three times. For a while this provoked a reaction as commanders stuck their heads out to investigate, only to find the offender on the ground below 'mooning' his arse at the now irate commander. This was quickly stamped out as you can imagine. It was never discovered who had ranged in the first instance, luckily for the commander of that Tank. But, by Christ we knew who had been hit, I shan't name him to save his embarrassment should he read this. Members of the Regiment who were there will know exactly who it was.

The days of the exercise seemed at times never to end. We once spent 72 hours closed down in fierce heat, in simulated NBC conditions, ammo was plentiful and we joyfully banged away at the targets. But in those conditions the exertion was pretty extreme. Even the main armament once warmed by firing added to the internal temperature of the turret. This meant that the operators had better have remembered to fill the turret water tank or face the consequences of not being able to drink for the duration. The wrath of the crew being the deterrent against this. But within the cramped confines it was maddening.

The only daylight available came through the various sighting equipment for each crewmember. The commander was obviously in the best position, followed by the driver with both gunner and operator only being able to look through holes some three or four inches wide. So it could, at times become very fraught within these conditions. The driver being closed down in his fully reclined seat was quite comfortable. But everyone else was basically glued to their seats in a sitting position. As operator, at least I could wedge myself against the turret ring, using the clip on loaders seat and an ammo rack for my head I could get an element of comfort. I could assume this position when the tank was also in motion. I admit it was not the most serene of positions but when you are dog-tired you can sleep anywhere. One night we were on a night march and I fell asleep, when I awoke I found that we must have had a rough ride as various pieces of stowage were lying everywhere. But somehow I was none the worse for my ordeal. tank crews are masters of adapting to their surroundings, it is amazing how, given a bit of time we could somehow make all that steel quite comfy.

Exercise Med Man 7. These words are indelibly printed in my brain. This was not to be my last exercise at BATUS but it may have been. Prior to this escapade I had been promoted to Lance Corporal and had been internally posted to Command Troop due to my signals expertise. There instead of working in the back of a Command converted APC, I'd been put in charge of the ferret scout car section. These ferrets were rebroadcast stations, in a nutshell 'rebro' stations are, in this case ferrets which, when the CO can't speak to the Squadrons due to the distance and terrain that block radio signals. A 'rebro' is set up by the ferret getting up onto high ground between the two stations.

The 'rebro' itself is the linking of two radios together, one receiving, and the other sending but on the same frequency. In other words it 'boosts' the signal onwards. Anyway this Med Man 7 I was meant to be driving the Regimental Signals Officer (RSO), Lieutenant Phoebe in a ferret. The temperature in Crowfoot prior to leaving on scheme was minus 36°c by the time we were in the prairies depth with a wind chill factor, the temperature was minus 45°c. as you may imagine this is fucking cold!

We knew we had problems before we left Germany, every previous winter scheme at BATUS had been cancelled due to the extreme Canadian winter. But no, off we went on the plane. Now here we were, freezing our nuts off in Crowfoot, being issued with arctic sleeping bags with extra lining. Oh shit, this was really going to happen! Then as I was contemplating four weeks in a ferret with no real shelter due to its construction, good news. It would appear that the last battlegroup had wrecked my ferret. It was in workshops for refit! I could have danced for joy, had my feet not been fucking frozen into the permafrost layer beneath them. I was to be the operator on the Regimental 2i/c's Tank, as he wouldn't be on it, make what you will of that!

This Tank's crew were Sgt 'Sid' Collins commanding, Robbie Thornton gunning and Jan 'old man' fuller driving. If the 2i/c had been on the tank Sid would have been operator. Not that I cared, the thought of warm engine decks at night outweighed everything. So having bought balaclavas for our faces and extra gloves from the 'Canex' (equivalent to our NAAFI) we lumbered off on exercise. On the first night out we had an accident. With the ground being so hard we could drive everywhere freely as if on roads. Earlier we had suffered a breakdown, which separated us from the rest of the troop. Once fixed and with night having suddenly fallen like a theatres safety curtain, we motored off to find the troop. Jan was making best speed, which I found worrying, as we could see absolutely nothing.

Pitch black doesn't explain this darkness it was frightening. Every internal light was switched off in an attempt to improve our vision; Jan had refused to use his night sight. The driver's night sight was an image intensifier or 'II' device, it functioned by absorbing star and moonlight, magnifying it and giving the driver an eerie green image in his sight window. With experience and dependant on the night's brightness the picture could be interpreted in shadows and light representing hollows and bumps in the worst instance. But in good conditions it could be likened to a green TV picture. On this night there was no light whatsoever, therefore Jan decided to 'drive out the corner of his eye'. This is an old trick you can try, if in darkness, turn your head away from the direction you are going in but keep your eyes looking forward. The corners of your eyes will give you better vision in the dark. But even this was failing for Jan; we were bombing along when suddenly we could no longer hear the rattle of tracks. These couple of seconds seemed to take minutes. All we could hear was the wailing of engine above the whistle of the winds. The IC sprang to life as, I believe it was Sid started to exclaim; "FUUUU... He never finished as suddenly we came down with an immense crash shaking not only the entire Tank, but also me, like a cork from a bottle I launched from the loaders hatch. Had I not somehow grabbed a lifting bracket on the front of the turret I would have fallen in front of our own vehicle. Death, I'm sure would have been certain. As it was, I hung on until the tank came to a rolling halt.

The jolt had caused Jan to bump against his cabs internal light which came on. I could see from its glow Jan's face unconscious from a blow to the head. His bonedome hadn't been much use it appeared. Sid had also been flung half way out of his hatch but had managed to hang on and was now gathering his senses. Robbie had also managed to stay in one piece but was suffering from very bad shock. How the bouncing main armament didn't kill him I'll never know! I managed to bring Jan round, Sid, by now ranting at Jan for being a "blind old cunt!" Put his spotlight on to see what on earth had happened? As he shone it behind us we could see we had left the track we'd been travelling on some time ago. Instead we'd been cross-country and had managed to ski jump our way off of a ten feet high vertical embankment. We were all lucky to be alive at the speed Jan had been driving. Chieftain suspension was hard at the best of times but this had simply been too much for it to cushion. But having picked ourselves up we motored on, Sid made a wise decision and we put our headlights on. When we got closer to where the troop was leaguered we still couldn't see further than the headlights beam. Sid radioed for help requesting the troop "shine a light" This they did and the beams from the skyward pointing spotlights were the most welcoming sight I could imagine. The end of my stay with Sid came a day later with the news that my ferret was ready for collection. I was to meet Lt. Phoebe at BATUS and bring him on scheme.

Upon arriving at workshops there was Lt. Phoebe waiting for me. We loaded our gear on the ferret and departed. Now the ferret was not designed for this weather, in Europe they were equipped with detachable windscreens to fit over the main drivers hatch keeping out the elements. Not so here, no windscreens. Okay, I could close the two smaller Battle hatches to my front left and right, I could even close the main hatch in front of my face, leaving the smaller integral battle hatch ajar for vision. But no matter what I did I couldn't shut out that fucking wind. It whooshed past my ears and buried itself into my commander's crotch, which was behind my shoulders. We quickly realised that driving at 50mph in this weather would severely hamper our future chances of rearing children. So on his orders, Lt. Phoebe and I dismounted every five minutes and beat the crap out of each other to keep our circulation active. That was the best order I'd been given by any officer.

When we eventually arrived at the troops location, I was ridiculed like crazy for driving a ferret! The next problem was, where to sleep, there being no way that I would be able to sleep on the frozen ground beneath us. Lt. Phoebe had no such worries, he headed straight for the erected 'penthouse' tent attached to the back of a command vehicle. "Bastard", I muttered as I pondered my predicament. Then I thought, if I wedged the small engine decks open with cans they would be level, even at six feet tall I could curl up, encased in my slug, on them. So I set about my mission, firstly using the vehicles tarpaulin and two borrowed main armament cleaning staves from Sid, I erected a strange wigwam affair over the engine. I ensured the canvas draped over the back covered the engines exhaust louvers and kept the engine running ensuring hot air blew into the tent I'd constructed. I then prised my slug from its stowage bin and put it in my shelter to thaw so I could unfold it and get into its duck down interior. Once satisfied that all was ready, in I climbed having shut off the engine. 'Snug as a bug' was I, and very proud of my improvisation too. Next morning we all went through the ritual of trying to get water from our frozen plastic 5-gallon jerrycans. This normally involved big blokes and very big sledgehammers. We had to try and smash enough ice within the top of the can allowing the shattered ice crystals to fall out and be thawed and subsequently boiled for morning tea. We were all by now convinced that we were guinea pigs being used in some experiment on survival techniques.

We were under orders not to wash or shave due to the temperature against our quite brittle skin. Our petrol stoves would only work after hours of preparation. The tanks needed constant injections of 'easy start' to kick them into life. And me and my ferret? No such problems I simply fucking froze!

While in the latter stages of this 'retreat from Moscow' I became a casualty. Lt. Phoebe had an annoying habit when dismounting of, staying seated so I couldn't exit through his turret hatch. This meant I had to struggle out of my main front hatch while wearing all my gear plus two parkas! For a man of my bulk this was extremely difficult. One night during my acrobatics I committed the ferret drivers cardinal sin. As I pulled myself out I became entangled, so I put out my hand and clasped and leant on a battle hatch. I should have known better after my experiences in Cyprus. These hatches were prone to snapping shut for no apparent reason. In this weather the springs were frozen and suddenly... Smang! The hatch slammed shut on my hand, and I flew out of my hatch, my hand still trapped in the battle hatch. Suddenly the pain penetrated the cold and fuck did I scream? Oh yes I certainly did scream, very loudly, in fact.

The Regimental 2i/c and his Landrover driver came rushing over to investigate. Having freed my hand and removing the two pairs of gloves covering it, they took one look at the blood pumping out but congealing almost instantly in the cold, applied a first field dressing and sent me to the Regimental Aid Post (RAP) for further help. I was dispatched in the 2i/c's Landrover with his driver Clive (Snoz) Newman at the wheel.

After a somewhat hectic journey we arrived at the RAP. My old pal 'Charlie' Chaplin greeted me and shouted for the Medical Officer (MO) to come and see. The MO had other ideas however; I could see him through my pain-racked eyes, hunched over a vehicle wing, busily pumping like mad at a 'tilly' paraffin lamp, and then attempting to get it to light. He glanced across at our small gaggle of bodies and; "hang on Charlie, I think I've nearly got it, fuck, fuck, fucking thing..... AAAAAARRGH! Came sailing through the air closely followed by the offending lamp. With that the MO strode across to us as we stood in the glare from the Landrover headlights.

"Right, what's this poor fucker done?" he enquired, starting to unwind my blood soaked dressing. "Soon have this off!" he said, and with that, quite literally ripped the dressing pad complete with the last of the bandage from my hand. In the process the congealed blood was torn away and once more I found myself shouting in absolute agony. "Ah, sorry sport, didn't realise you're a real casualty, thought it was for exercise purposes!"

WHAT? thought I, not real? What the fuck is this pumping out my hand? Mock blood? What on earth did this muffin head think he was doing? My thoughts were interrupted by intense pain as he tested my hand. "Mmmmm, X-Ray job this" he murmured to himself. And with that he asked Charlie if SSGT Chadwick was about. Dick Chadwick was B. Squadron's SQMS who had stopped on his way back to BATUS where he would collect supplies. He had seen the RAP and although not a part of 'Bumble' he had stopped to see if the RAP needed anything. In his packet were the usual trucks including a diesel bowser driven by two guys from the, 'Rickshaw Cab &Taxi or RCT, but to give its proper name Royal Corps of Transport. I found myself squeezed into the cab with these two chaps and we departed for BATUS. Along the way Dick stopped to help any 'strays' we came across. He was so enthusiastic about his duties, at one point the diesel bowser found itself refuelling a 'hard target' (wrecked, obsolete tank used as target), Dick assuming the crew to be asleep! Having realised the mistake we hurriedly departed. Eventually that night we arrived at base. I was dropped off at the Medical centre where two medics put me in a bed, stinking though I was to await the Doctors arrival. The doctor arrived and after inspecting the damage, packed me into a Landrover ambulance and I was taken to hospital in Medicine Hat. There the nurses were most attentive, ignoring my sweaty, diesel laden stench and unshaven grubby appearance I was given coffee and got ready for an X-Ray. Having discovered that the only damage was severely smashed muscles and a couple of hairline fractures in a bone we were told we could leave. As the medic and I were descending some stairs, two civvie ambulance drivers approached us and told us we had a flat tyre.

We went to our Landrover and sure enough the rear tyre was flat. The medic was mechanically inept, so it was I, the patient who with a bandaged arm was trying to jack up the rear end to change the wheel. Two ambulance drivers came over laughing about 'Brit' medics and how to treat your patients and, using an inflatable jack attached to our exhaust, saved the day. Repaired we made the long journey back to camp, where I realised that in the rush to evacuate me, all my gear, including washing and shaving kit were still in the ferret. I managed to scrounge soap and a razor from the medical centre and returned to my accommodation block. Luckily I had some spare coveralls and underwear in my suitcase left under my bunk. So finally showered and shaven, all I had to do was find someone to turn the heating on and then sit back and wait for the return of my mates. Upon their return, the amount of 'piss taking' over my early departure was horrendous, everyone seemed sure I'd self mutilated myself to get off the prairie. As I sat cradling both my hand and ego, I thought about the pain I had endured and knew I would have swapped that agony for anything. Another fortnight on the prairie would have been preferable. WHAT? Who was I kidding?? The weather had certainly been different to conditions on a previous Med Man 5 where, we had sat in the tanks shade to get out of the heat, watching 'dust devils'(mini tornados) skirmish through our leaguer lifting berets and playfully whipping them away from their owners. Mind you those temperatures had their drawbacks, particularly mosquitoes. We were once broken down between two small lakes during 'mozzy' breeding. Lake to lake they flew via our bloody Tank. Even with the fine mesh cam net we had erected to protect us they still got through. The insect repellent we'd been issued only seemed to attract them more. On that particular occasion I had been gunner on an SHQ tank, Callsign three Charlie, 3C.

Our commander had been corporal 'Lofty' Halford a towering chap with massive feet who lolloped more than walked. Our driver was Rupert 'look at the size of that bump' Harrison and operating was Steve 'Crosslet' Cross. What a team!

I had quickly gained a reputation with Lofty as 'a gunner who could hit the left testicle of a gnat at a distance of two kilometres' no matter how hard I tried missing, to release me from the gunners position. Lofty was a gunnery instructor, and I could do no wrong at shooting! But after a night drive where, over the IC all we could here was our 'nig' Rupert exclaiming; "look at the size of that rock!" promptly followed by a large crashing and jolting as he drove over the obstacle which he could have so easily avoided. Once? Okay that would have been acceptable, but continuously? No chance, I found myself driving next day. As dozer Tank, we were detailed one day to go to an infantry position and help them 'dig in' their APCs by creating 'scrapes' in the ground. Off we went and as darkness fell we found our destination. A grunt sentry approached us and, having satisfied himself as to our identity, he told me to follow his green torchlight. As he walked off in front, I dutifully followed him keeping his green torch squarely in front of me. I then inquired on the IC; "what are all these black circles on the ground?" much discussion on top of the turret was suddenly cut short by crosslet

~ 156 ~

exclaiming; "fucking hell, this berk is leading us over the twatting grunt foxholes!" This had been realised when a grunt was seen departing his foxhole in fright after we had driven over it. When we arrived at the positions to be dug, we enquired of our guide; "why?" his reply was simply, "didn't realise I'd done it!" And they wondered why we called them grunts?

Tuning in the '353'.

Endex brought each Med Man to an end, and our prayers went skyward that on the way back to camp we wouldn't break down and delay our exit from the prairie. Recovery over these distances could be an horrific experience. On one Med Man 7 an MBT broke down and after the crew were evacuated the vehicle was left for dead on the prairie through the winter. A magnificent photo in an office shows a Chieftain 'floating' a foot above a massive orange flame when, the offending MBT was blown out of the permafrost which had frozen the vehicle to the ground. It had simply been quicker to blow it with plastic explosive from its resting place in spring and then tow it back for repair.

More of BATUS exercising later. Now its time to move on to post-endex drinking and more specifically R&R.

25. Resting but not recuperating

After a very long night march.

R&R, a term which always filled our hearts with joy at the end of our arduous training period at BATUS. Before we went on scheme we had already booked with a travel agent, who'd set up a temporary shop on camp. There were all sorts of package deals to be had from 'working ranch' holidays to flying to the USA. On my first visit to Canada I wasn't earning enough money to pay for anything extravagant, so I opted instead to stay on camp and take day trips to sample the delights of the 'Hat'. Our R&R on that occasion wasn't longer than two or three days anyway as I was destined to leave on one of the first flights. So it was that three or four of us 'chipped in' for a taxi to the 'Hat' one evening. The driver's instructions were simply "take us to a drinking hole" This he did and we ended up at the Assiniboa Inn, other wise known as the 'sin bin'. What a place, a bit rough would describe its interior fairly accurately. As we entered we were confronted by drunken crowds at the tables watching a floorshow, with large armed waitresses dodging between them carrying jugs of beer. These jugs or 'pitchers' seemed massive and the girls were carrying four to six at a time.

As we found a table to sit at, a waitress came to us and asked; "whatta ya have ta drink fellas?" We asked for the appropriate number of beers and sat back to wait. In due course the beers arrived, a slight problem was that there were two beers per man. We asked the waitress if there had been confusion over our order, and she said "No, you ordered four beers and here are your eight, now pay up!" Our heads span and we hadn't even started drinking, "eight?" I questioned, "yes, fucking eight" she retorted holding out her hand, waiting for cash. After much discussion we discovered that an old custom from the cowboy era was, the first round ordered by a cowboy was always one beer but two were supplied. The first one to wash the dust down his throat, the second being for enjoyment. I call it a damned good ruse for squaddies to buy more beer! Having drunk our beers and had a conversation with some locals, the cheaper option was now to buy a pitcher of beer between us, first lesson in Canadian drinking learnt! This we did and later that night returned to BATUS very drunk.

On another occasion, my mate 'Lucy' and I booked a return Greyhound bus ticket to Calgary. Before we knew it four other chaps had asked to join us. As we said, we weren't their bosses so they could tag along if they wanted. Having finished the exercise we reported for R&R, jumped on our escape vehicle and headed off. We arrived at the Greyhound depot in Calgary and walked off into the city. Our plan was to simply find a hotel and book in. This quickly proved easier said than done. Every hotel was fully booked but, eventually a receptionist took pity on us, made a couple of phone calls and told us of a hotel in the suburbs with rooms available. We said our thanks and hailed a Shamrock cab, and then another to get all six of us to the hotel. The cabs deposited us at the entrance to (if I remember correctly) The Westgate Motel, a sprawling motel type structure. We launched ourselves into reception and after all the niceties of "Oh, you're English?" and "What lovely accents!" Lucy and I found ourselves in a twin room with the other four in two other rooms. That night we ventured to the cocktail bar and ordered 'Turkey sunrises' more commonly known as Tequila sunrise. This was sheer luxury, relaxing in a bar with a piano player crooning out songs and civilised people all around. The pianist then started to bash out 'Beatles' numbers in honour of the "English guests."

A couple of days then passed visiting Calgary's many attractions including, the Tower, Glenbow museum, Devonian gardens (somehow, nothing to do with Devon), and many bars and restaurants on a huge 'pub crawl'. On the third night Dave 'Luigi' Lomax, a Plymouthian born and bred, and myself decided to try somewhere new. A Shamrock cab ride later we were at the 'Trade winds' Hotel where we entered a club. During the evening we chatted to various people who seemed to find us 'fascinating'. At the end of the night two girls asked us if we needed a lift to our hotel. They weren't exactly the most beautiful girls we'd seen but that is cruel, they were genuinely nice people. As soon as it was announced that one had just taken delivery of a new Pontiac Firebird we couldn't refuse. We left for the hotel but detoured to an all night diner where, the girls sat staring adoringly as we played up our English accents. On leaving the diner we managed to get into a race on a rainy freeway with a pickup of which the engine was so vast its chromed top was blocking the windscreen. The speed at which we were zooming along the road had Luigi and I, desperately clinging to our seatbelt clasps. But in due course we arrived back at the hotel safe and sound.

Having met our new friends, Luigi and I couldn't shake them off, they kept calling for us and then taking us everywhere. One day they turned up in their fathers 'station wagon' and took all six of us to the magnificent 'Heritage park', a collection of historic buildings that had been dismantled and rebuilt in the park. It was possible to travel round the park on a 'Casey Jones' steam engine stopping at various townships. We had a great time, every building was attended by people wearing period costume who informed us of 'frontier life, of that era. The 'Mounties' log cabin even had Mounties playing guitars and singing old folk songs. My mates thought it hilarious when one of our friends and I were pushed into a cell, and locked in, my pals then hurriedly departing. I had a bit of a fight on my hands as the young lady thought it an instant excuse for 'romance'. The visit to Calgary was ended by the girls inviting us to their family home for a barbecue. It turned out that their house that we visited was the 'town house'. 'Daddy' actually owned a cattle ranch on the prairie. Outside were parked six cars of various sizes from 'compact' to 'fucking big truck'. The father had slaughtered one of his herd and the torso was on a spit in the back garden. To say we had a great time would be an understatement, and everyone was fantastically friendly. The girls' mother was originally from London's East end and her pseudo cockney/ Canadian accent was as hilarious as her sense of humour. It was genuinely with regret that we said our goodbyes to this friendly, warm and welcoming family.

I spent many more periods of R&R in Calgary, at the same hotel with various chums. A good time was had by all, we were once invited to a Royal Canadian Legion by a Canadian soldier we'd met. When we'd been signed into the guest book and introduced to the manager we were taken into the club. Hells teeth, our eyes nearly popped out of our heads. All the waitresses were wearing french maid uniforms complete with fishnet hosiery. We enquired if we'd come on a theme night and the reply was that this was the normal uniform. What a night! We simply didn't know where to look after so long on the prairie, legs everywhere! The 'Legion' there, bore no resemblance to the British equivalent. It was also huge, the manager showed us round taking care to show us the chilled rooms for beer storage, each one seemed to be for an individual beer. We had just completed a 'dry' scheme(no beer) due to the Labatts brewery being on strike. When we asked how they had beer? Had they bulk stored prior to the strike? The answer was that the 'Legion' was guaranteed a delivery every day without fail. So even if the brewery's management donned overalls, the 'Legions' beer would be brewed. I never understood whether this was simply a business promise or because of the respect for the organisation. Either way we had lots of beer and legs on display so, couldn't care less.

I never ceased to be amazed at the warmth of welcome in Calgary the people seemed so open and friendly. Although the city police responsible for law inside the city limits weren't particularly communicative. The 'Mounties' however, when we saw them outside city limits, were communicative pleasant and helpful. Mind you, we never broke the law, otherwise they may have not been such a pleasant bunch. The French - Canadians however were not such a bundle of joy when faced with 'Brits'. I never visited Quebec but met a couple of Canadian reservists in BATUS who came from those parts. We were left in no doubt that they regarded themselves as more French than the French themselves! And it appears that even today there is a certain hostility between 'English' and French Canadians politically. General Wolfe may have had something to do with that! But all Canadians seem to be united in one thing, a genuine dislike of their American neighbours. Canada is however great, its America without the Americans!

More reference to Canada later, for now we'll return to Europe.

26. Picking our Winkles

When serving in BAOR, for us the mere mention of 'Winklepicker' could fill our hearts with dread. Earlier I mentioned escape and evasion exercises during my Cadre course. Well, 'Exercise Winklepicker' was normally an annual event, if other regimental commitments didn't prohibit its execution. Our Regiment deemed survival as a high priority for its crews and the great idea of 'Winklepicker' was born.

With the early 80's swing in tactical doctrine towards armour-spearheaded thrusts, this increased the chances of tank units becoming 'marooned' behind enemy lines. I believe it was always calculated that the 'Eastern bloc' could rapidly roll through Western Europe, albeit they may not be able to effectively 'hold' ground. This would mean encirclement of any pockets of NATO forces while the main thrust continued. It would be fair to surmise that they wouldn't have it all their own way as, all bridges in their way would be demolished in what would amount to a 'scorched earth' policy by us. Therefore the Russians developed a massive amphibious and engineering capability to counteract this threat. Many of their vehicles from utility to armour were fitted with schnorkelling devices. Our own Chieftains were also supposedly 'amphibious capable' but I wouldn't have liked to risk it, at least not by the way that rain poured in through every orifice.

So as the Russians advanced, the likelihood of our becoming detached from friendly forces would increase. Therefore the art of escaping from, and evading the enemy would be very important. Part of a tank crewman's life was always 'Baleout' drill. This was normally always trained and tested on Troop training. It would involve evacuating the crew in the quickest time possible, including any casualties. The casualty was invariably the gunner, buried in the depths of the turret. As the crew baled out of the Tank, the gunner's job would be to dismount the commander's machine gun and the box of ammo to take with us. The operator would in the meantime be, passing out the turret crews SMG's, magazines of 9mm ammo, the ground conversion MG butt for the commanders MG and maybe spare ammo for that, then wrestling the webbing equipment from the exterior turret basket for the crew, only then jumping from the tank to escape. The driver meanwhile would grab his gear and gun and exit the cab. The Commander would grab any maps and coding documents, the signal flare pistol and then stand on the turret top. In the time all this had just taken he would now only have time to grab his SMG, beat off the advancing Mongolian tribesmen from the turret top, and protect the operator who, would still be wrestling with the overcrowded turret basket. Or at least this was my vision of baling out; it was a lengthy process if done 'by the book'. Our experience taught us short cuts; such as the webbing harnesses were stored on the exterior of the turret, hooked onto projecting bin work. Therefore as the crew departed they simply snatched their equipment and jumped. SMG magazines were in fact stored in their pouches clipped to the webbing. Webbing consisted of a belt and body harness, attached to which were your Field dressing, respirator, ammo and back pouches and your waterbottle. This was known as CEFO (Central European fighting Order) and was designed for speed and mobility. In our uniform pockets we would carry our 'home made' survival packs contained normally in tobacco tins. In here would be wet and dry matches, fishing hook with line, plasters, pins, a garrotting wire (for snaring animal and human life forms) and anything else that was of use and could fit.

Of course Exercise Winklepicker was 'by the book' so, we had all the equipment to carry and to top it off, our backpacks and 'slugs'. Were we to try removing our sleeping bags from the tank 'for real', it would have been very difficult. We used to stow our 'slugs' in the rear bins next to the engine decks. This used to dry them out with the engines heat and keep them warm for the following night. But, fitting them into the bins was hard work; so getting them out was no fast job. The reality of baling out would have probably been our guns, our webbing, little more and us.

But 'for the purposes of this exercise' it was everything but the kitchen sink. So there we were with more equipment to carry than the comic character 'Union Jack Jackson' with the prospect of normally sixty or so miles to walk. We would normally be dropped off from vehicles without knowing where we were, simulating the sudden 'knocking out' of our Tanks. We would then make our way through a series of checkpoints (simulating a resistance or special forces network) on our way back to friendly lines. We were only given the map grid reference of the first checkpoint. When we reached the checkpoint we would then be given the 'grid' for the next checkpoint and so on. The allotted time limit to complete the exercise varied but was normally three days. The 'enemy' was provided by either; non-involved members of our regiment or by other units of Infantry. The Army Air Corps also provided helicopters for spotting our poor escapees. The exercise was usually run by tank crew but in a couple of cases we acted as entire Troops. In the following sections this will become apparent. The 'teams' were also marked on a point's basis. 'Enemy' capture being rewarded by point's deductions; a memorable occasion was 'Nosher' Cadman's team who were found asleep in a wooden 'hut' bus shelter. The 'enemy' simply found a note pinned on the front saying;

> *TO OUR ENEMIES.*
> *Fair cop mates!*
> *Please deduct points from below!*
> *Luv Nosher.*

Or at least words to that effect. I think he had had enough on that occasion! I remember that exercise well because the weather was dreadful. At that time I was in Command Troop and we were participating as enemy. A mate of mine Kim and I 'volunteered' early that morning to ascend in a Gazelle helicopter of the AAC to act as spotters. As we climbed into the rear seats of this Perspex bubbled contraption, the pilot was already firing up the engine. Once it had reached the required engine speed and, Kim and I were shaking in a suitably aviator fashion, the pilot engaged the rotors. As they increased speed the whole aircraft started to vibrate in a quite alarming manner. Outside the woodland surrounding us was difficult to see because of the weather conditions. However we could see the trees bending in the high wind. The rain that was beating down on our Perspex shell was being blown into tiny droplets as it was forced down by the rotors' down draught. Our headsets which we had been given, were buzzing with life as the two figures in front cackled through the pre flight checks. The pilot then said;

"Fucking weather's murder, oh well let's see if we can get her up!"

With that we lurched off the ground suddenly swinging violently to one side. My stomach didn't know which way to go, one second down, the next, off in the opposite direction to our swing.

"Ho ho, there she goes!" came the response from our pilot.

"Fucking hell!" chorused Kim and I.

Then with an increase in noise we rose upwards, and then the nose dipped and away we went out of the hover, gaining forward momentum. I looked at Kim and he was already looking green, I'm sure he saw a reflection in my face.

So we grimaced in a sickly manner and experienced the most uncomfortable helicopter ride of our lives. At one point we were skimming along when Kim suddenly announced;

"I could have sworn I saw a team down there"

"Where?" queried the pilot.

"Back there on the right" explained Kim.

I suddenly felt as though my torso had been removed from my limbs as, we executed a gut wrenching turn towards where Kim was pointing. My response to this was grabbing Kim's arm and shouting above the noise with the mic' turned off.

"DO NOT EVER FUCKING DO THAT AGAIN!" I could instantly see by the look of horror and sickness on his face that Kim wouldn't!

Later we found ourselves hovering high above a village, trying in vain to spot our prey through the rain. With an air of resignation the pilot said, "not a fucking chance of seeing anything in this" and the helicopter dipped forward to get moving again. Dipped? I looked over the shoulder of the navigator in front of me, and still remember the vision I saw. Chimney pots! And we were diving straight down them. Suddenly, just as it seemed we'd reached the point of no return, the pilot yanked on his stick and we frisbee'd across the roof tops of the houses below. Just as I was about to say, "screw this for a laugh, can we go back?" The pilot announced that this was now his plan of action. It was with joy and relief that we greeted our return to the ground, thankful that we weren't being removed in carrier bags from some one's bloody chimney.

On another 'Winklepicker' I was part of a 12-troop crew with my friend Sergeant 'Gorgeous' George Brighty as commander, me as operator and 'Zippy' Wellington (unfortunate, that long scar down the back of his neck!). We were also joined by 'Babbsy' Babbs from the SQMS' stores. This was because we were short one man to make up the crew. 'Babbsy' turned up with a massive display of knives strapped to his legs and the little 'Action' war comics you could buy. One of the titles was quite apt, 'Fighting to live' it read. Well, bugger me, we thought this was a little extreme. We were escaping and evading our 'enemy' the Royal Green Jackets, not, fighting the fucking Afrika Korps for Tobruk! Anyway having been lumbered with the GPMG because of, 'Zippy's' scar and 'Babbsy' being hardly able to walk due to his iron mongery, George had nominated me. By the end of the third day my neck had a ridge across the back, from the guns weight on the sling.

The first night found us somewhat lost due to thick dense fog. Never the less we found some concrete by the light of a dim street lamp, and settled down for some sleep. Next morning we were woken by a short fellow wearing a trilby and farm workers clothes. I had a conversation with him in German and yes, he was a farmer. In fact the farmer who's barn door we were bloody well blocking!

He had however, parked a tractor in front of us making us nigh on invisible to passers-by. His wife appeared and brought us a platter full of cold meats, bread rolls and butter. She also carried a large flask of steaming, sweet coffee. We proceeded to gorge ourselves, thankfully, on this feast. Meanwhile George was trying to find out, on his map, where we were. The farmer suddenly grabbed the map in his enthusiasm to be of assistance.

He started stabbing his grubby fore digit at the map and then at the ground. I translated that to mean that this point was where we were. Later he even loaded us into his tractor, trailer 'combo' and took us to the top of a hill. Having said our farewells, we trudged off, only shortly afterwards to be spotted by an 'enemy' detachment.

"Bollocks, lets get out of here, fucking move it!" Shouted George as he heard the grunts running towards us. We ran like the wind, all except 'Babbsy' when one of his knives worked loose and promptly impaled his fore leg. We were now vaulting low, wire fences like Springboks in our desperation to get away. The grunts were gaining as they carried only guns. We on the other hand, must have looked like lumbering great lumps of camouflaged rags and equipment as we evaded capture. Luckily we made it to a nearby tree line and slipped away into its depths. The grunts for some reason didn't follow.

Later that day the rain absolutely thrashed down on us, the only wet gear we had was the issued poncho. I must have resembled the sail on a clipper, with my poncho stuck out each side due to the length of the GPMG. But undeterred I bashed on until, having tried to negotiate an extremely high anti-deer fence, I managed to catch my foot in the top wire and found myself hanging upside down. The GPMG and sling took on the attributes of a noose around my neck while I screamed "get me the fuck down from here!" into the night. The other lads managed to free me and, after some deep breathing exercises, I found myself underway again. Georges only comment was "fucking hell Malc, all the noise you were making, wonder we weren't caught!" yeah, thanks a lot George.

That night we were walking down a woodland track when suddenly, from the darkness a voice said, "Wer da?" We all stopped short. George switched on his torch, and swung it into my face, effectively blinding me with its light. "Are you taking the piss with your German?" he enquired. "Am I fuck as like!" I replied. George swung back round shining his torch to see if he could identify where the noise may have emanated from. As he did so he nearly smashed it into the face of a German paratrooper sentry who loudly exclaimed "Verdammt!" Having calmed him I quickly explained who we were and what we were doing, and we were allowed to pass. We had walked straight into the middle of a German exercise. We spent the rest of our journey that night leaping off the road for cover. This was because the Germans were using little Quad bikes, which sounded like Landrover engines. One over enthusiastic leap took me some fifteen feet, headfirst down a bank, as I was towed by the weight of the GPMG.

My last recollection of 'Winklepicker' was when I was nominated as 9 Troops Sergeant. On this occasion we were dropped as a troop from a Chinook helicopter, at night, from ten feet up as the crew had misjudged their height in the dark. Having picked ourselves up, we headed for a light we could see through some trees. The troop leader, an officer, led us into a woodland restaurant and, covered in mud we lay his map out in the reception area. Having identified where we were, he promptly rang a cab company to pick us up. Long story cut short, we found ourselves in a nightclub. Disaster, as the German speaker, people bought me way too many beers. Result, next morning I found myself lying under a propane tank nearby. The troop had laid me there that night. Troop? Where the fuck was the troop? Nowhere in fucking sight was where the troop was. Having waited for an hour, and deciding I had been deserted, I removed the 'just in case' map from my pocket and set off. The next two days were a nightmare. I walked some 100 kms back to the base camp which was the final destination, there being no checkpoints on this occasion. But, I decided to play it by the book and avoid capture. It must have been a strange sight, a lone soldier dashing about the German countryside, diving for cover at the faintest sound of a 'chopper' or Landrover. When I came to cross the river Weser I opted to avoid bridges. Instead I made my way to a ferry shown on the map, once aboard, I stood in the middle of an empty deck, legs splayed and hands on hips. I reminded myself of a picture of a General as he crossed the Rhine in WW2. I eventually made it to my destination, there sat the troop asking where I'd been? Where I'd been? What about where the fuck they'd been? But that's another story involving 3 German girls, a house and a carving knife. So endeth the 'Winklepicker' lesson.

27. Rickety Rackety Road

You may be forgiven if you think that the title means I'm about to start a diatribe about a classic Hollywood musical. But as usual, nothing could be further from the truth. I mentioned earlier, the Soltau training area, and that is now what this is all about. The training area now relinquished back to the German government, stands on the heath land in the vicinity of Fallingbostel. To reach it from Paderborn was a complete chore. Firstly we would have to prep the tanks for travel on the railway. This involved stripping every piece of removable bin work from the turret. That included the search light which though, not projecting over the side a great deal, it could potentially hit a railway bridge.

Having removed the clutter from the various mountings and strapped it all to the engine decks, we were ready to depart. So, a quick trip through the city outskirts, dumping oil on the roads and polluting the air of course, down to the railway yards. Once there, a Bundesbahn railway official would greet us. He was the man responsible for the accurate loading of our vehicles. When I say accurate, I mean accurate, the bastard even had a slide rule with which to measure our track 'overhang' each side of the truck. This he did with typical German precision, to the very millimetre. If not satisfied he would demand that the tanks position be adjusted. Now tanks might be pretty manoeuvrable but, to adjust by a millimetre or two was beyond the steering systems capability. Therefore there was much "back a bit, forward a bit, whooooah!" until the tank was positioned according to 'Heinrichs' satisfaction. On one occasion Steve 'Stumpy' Evans having got totally pissed off with the German train 'Fuhrer' and his slide rule screamed:

"What the fuck do you think this is? Fifty six tons of fucking ballerina wearing tracks?" that only resulted in more shunting about!

Once the tanks were secured with wooden chocks and adjustable chains, we would speed on our way. Speed? No, not exactly, as I mentioned earlier, the Bundesbahn prioritised cattle before us. The distance to Soltau could be covered in around three hours by car. So how the hell did it take us two days by train on one occasion? Our trips to Soltau were fairly frequent as there were no other significantly sized areas for tanks available in BAOR. Even Sennelager on our doorstep was only used for 'demonstration' purposes, at least as far as we were concerned. You see it was classified as a NATO Lager (no, not beer, it means camp) for the use of visiting nations, and the German army of course. Here we were then on our way north, the only other method being a trip on an Antar tank transporter which albeit slow, provided entertainment. The entertainment came in the form of the driver and his 'mate'. These would normally be 'older' Polish fellows in British fatigue uniform belonging to an MOD organisation called MSO (Military Service organisation) the workers earning the nickname of 'MoJo's' for their trouble. I don't know how they came to be there but I believe it had something to do with the war. I know of a 'camp' in the depths of Devon, which I believe may even now contain the survivors and their families. These guys were seasoned veterans of transporters. To them it was simple to load a Chieftain and 'burn rubber' onto the German roads with their burdens. Naturally an Antar stood more chance of exploding than 'burning rubber' at about 25 mph 'convoy speed'. I seem to remember that 'best speed' was a hair-raising 27mph! No wonder then that, through nervous exhaustion, the drivers of these charging monsters endlessly consumed, vast quantities of vodka as they whizzed up the autobahn. Many were the tank drivers that arrived in a drunken stupor having availed themselves of the copious amounts of vodka given with Polish hospitality.

Once we and the tanks arrived at Rheinsehlen camp, we would frantically ensure that everything was mounted back where it belonged, all our kit was correctly stowed and away we would go. Sallying forth across the landscape of Soltau. To say that Soltau was an area of land that had been 'over exercised' would be an understatement. The area was in fact a collection of small areas linked by 'commuter routes'. One of these routes was simply known as the rickety rackety road. It was of course not a road at all, but a track always awash with a high volume of water. Driving along it was always an 'interesting' experience as, under the water there seemed to be a layer of boulders. The boulders were unseen, as was the whole bed of the track. Therefore it was particularly hard for drivers to gauge how to drive. One minute everything was fine the next... bang! Down in a big dip or over a big bump. When looking at a convoy of tanks coming down the track, their strange lurching and juddering motion earned the track its name.

Soltau itself had been so overworked by British 'scheming' that it was hard if not impossible to find a blade of grass in some sections. These areas consisted of the region's sandy mud with pine trees stuck up like some sort of distraction to the mud. Even under the trees there was no grass, just firm layers of decomposing pine needles and cones. The earth had even taken on a form similar to the ocean. It seriously looked like the sea with a heavy swell. I've never worked out how these ripples in the land occurred. I can only assume that the constant heavy traffic and its motion, have exaggerated the lands natural contours into this form. To travel along in a Chieftain over this terrain was tortuous in the extreme. No matter how hard our drivers tried to compensate, by hitting the ripples at angles to allow the tracks and suspension to absorb the effect, we still felt seasick. The constant drone of the engine up and down as we rose and fell would quickly become monotonous. Practising 'fire and movement' could be, in some areas, classed as little more than a joke. But in true Tankie style we used to make the best of a bad thing.

The area was also interspersed with plantations and was marked as such on the map. These, as the name implies, were where new fir trees were planted, fenced off with red and white posts and made 'out of bounds' to everyone. The plantations also made movement difficult at times. Many was the Squadron or Troop Leader who, while planning some grand assault, had his way barred by a small clump of saplings. The other area of note was the Schwindebeck. This was a large area of marshland with designated transit routes through it. Stray from the route and you could be seriously 'for it'. Not only was it a form of nature reserve in places (which was guaranteed to make the OC mad should you stray), but also physically your tank could become 'bogged' rapidly. It was also, for some reason quite hard to navigate due to the myriad of tracks, which seemingly bore no relationship to the map. I remember as a commander at night 'swanning' through this area only to find my driver throwing us in a ditch. The real problem was that the ditch contained a freshly laid pipe. By the time we'd extricated ourselves, we'd ripped out about 700 metres of the pipe, oops!

Over exercised?

Our favourite wood must have been 'strip wood'. No, it had nothing to do with wanton debauchery and naked women. It was simply a strip of woodland across a commuter route. God knows how many attacks and defensive battles those trees had, over the years witnessed. I remember as a commander in 12 troop, an attack that started in strip wood. It was during troop training, 'Nosher' Cadman was troop leader with 'Bert, James Henry George' Hammond as troop sergeant and me as troop corporal. Nosher gave Bert and I our briefing before the attack,

"All right Bertie and Malcy, we're gonna put in a bit of an attack towards the tank bridge (another landmark), My tank'll be the 'firebase' for your fire support. You two can hammer in on the objective and I'll watch to see how good your tactics are, I'll send the orders in code to make it proper like, all right?" Bert and I had no questions so we returned to our crews. On the way Bert looked at me and smirked. The reason was that, at times Noshers tactical logic could be likened to that of a lemming. "Ere we go then Malcy" giggled Bert's Plymouthian lilt. And with that we climbed on board and awaited Noshers orders. Once received, decoded and I'd plotted it all on my map, I glanced across at Bert to see him with his arms up and shoulders hunched as if in question. The reason was also apparent to me; Noshers grid reference for the objective didn't make sense. It certainly wasn't where he'd shown us on the map at briefing. Still, maybe he'd changed his mind? In any event, Bert laughed and pointed ahead, and off we went. Over my headsets Bert came through loud and clear on our 'illegal' chatter net on the 'spare' radio.

"Four two this is one, you take left I'll go right, out!"

Following his instruction I flanked off to the left of a plantation as he disappeared off to the right. Before we reached the far side of the saplings we heard Nosher on the Squadron radio net;

"Ello four one and four two this is four zero, in firebase, bringing down fire now, out!"

Bert and I now joined forces again and, cresting a ridge, bore down the far slope onto our objective. But what an objective! There sat Nosher's tank with Nosher, stood in his hatch drinking tea and eating a butty. The look of surprise on his face a picture of bewilderment as we clattered past him. I looked across at Bert and he was howling with laughter. Nosher had only called the attack in on his own position! Nosher of course accused us of misunderstanding the orders. But eventually he calmed down when he realised he had got confused with the map!

That particular troop training had got off to a ropey start anyway. It was dark when we'd set off from Rheinsehlen, I'd assumed we'd be moving tactically. Nosher had said, "This'll test your map reading Malcy, you lead". I, on the other hand, realised it would have probably been more of a test of his map reading! But seriously his, like all tank commanders, standard of navigation was above average. It was just that nobody enjoyed it at night. So I instructed Sean 'Tommo' Thomas to switch off all his cab lights, inside and out, my gunner and operator dimmed the interior turret lights and off we went. Quite quickly I realised we may as well have not bothered without lights. As we bumped and banged across the area I cursed Tommo for the rough ride.

"Not my fucking fault, can't make out the bumps properly!" came his reply over the IC. I stood up in my hatch and looked at where the ground should have been in the moonlight. Instead all I could see were shadows jumping around, as the light seemed to flicker. I turned and, there behind us were Nosher and Bert's tanks lumbering along with their headlights on main beam!

"Fucking hell, its like Blackpool fucking illuminations up here!" I exclaimed, "Fuck it, put your lights on Tommo, you'll never be able to see with this bloody circus following!" Tommo did as I asked and we trundled onward to our wooded 'hide' for the night. Once we had reversed into the trees, my crew and I set about 'camming up' and getting ready for our night routine, as silently as possible.

Nosher and Bert's tanks reversed noisily into the tree line crashing through the undergrowth. Once halted Nosher's 'jenny' ran for ages, I presumed Nick Allen; his operator was using the BV. Noshers voice rang through the night, "Come on Nick, ain't tea ready yet?" A wartime vision of Russian Special Forces, knives clasped in teeth, running towards our location flashed through my mind. Then, echoing through the trees came; "Bertie! Malcy! O group my tank now!" an 'O' group is; collect in a group to receive 'Orders'. I really can't explain it more simply than that. I made my way in darkness to where Noshers tank obviously was, I say obviously as the flashing of torches and general noise that emanated from it was wondrous to behold. I met Bert on the way who was also astounded at the display from our troop leader. We found Nosher sat on the back decks tucking into a plate of stewed steak and mash, a steaming cup of tea next to him. His Tank's 'Jenny' ran down and switched off as we drew near. "Fuckin' smashin' this Nick" he bawled at the turret. Nicks head appeared, his face highlighted by the glow from the interior lights, "Ssssh," intoned Nick, who was also obviously confused by Nosher's relaxed attitude. "Ssssh fucking what?" replied Nosher seemingly unaware that this was meant to be war. As Bert and I appeared out of the gloom, Nosher saw us and waved us up onto his sweltering engine deck throne. Once we'd clambered up Nosher said; "Right then boys, tonight is the last time we do this, from now on we's tactical". "Okay Nosh", chorused Bert and I. Next night, Bert and I led our move into another wood as silently as, on a 56 ton monster, we could. Noshers arrival took down a tree, followed ten minutes later by, ringing through the night air; "Bertie, Malcy, O group, my tank now!" It did get better I promise you because; at the end of troop tests we'd won. 12 'Cock' Troop was the best. I put it down to, not only being the best skilled troop but, also having the best morale because Nosher was, one in a million.

Over the passage of time we as commanders became very familiar with Soltau. So as with Salisbury plain, we would consult our maps to see where we were headed and, having found it, throw our map down and away we'd speed. This all changed however when, one February we went to Soltau and, it had snowed. What we were now faced with bore no resemblance to the Soltau we knew and grudgingly loved. It was a carpet of deep virgin snow, with no recognisable features. Map reading now took on a whole new meaning. But, somehow we managed to come, unscathed through the exercise. At the end the OC decided we'd set up a Squadron hide in a wood and each troop could have a 'smoker'. He didn't want a Squadron smoker as he wanted us to be restrained because the CO would be visiting and he didn't want drunken Tankies besporting themselves in un-soldier like behaviour. Therefore we could have a troop fire so long as it was a compo can of petrol soaked sand! And to add to the misery we could only have two beers per man. I was incensed as my charge bins were full of Paderborner (our local brewery) 'silver tops'. We needed to drink these badly. Anyway, as I departed for Nosher's tank I'd left my operator Kev 'animal' House in charge of organising the 'fire' and festivities along with Tommo and my gunner Trev 'Smudge' Smith. I should have known better; Kev was a Corporal like me, he'd lost command of a tank and been put as my operator. His loss was because, his tank had broken down on exercise, the REME from a workshop came to change the engine, Kev who'd been drinking Brandy while waiting, had taken offence to the unknown faces who now appeared before him. The result was Kev assaulting a REME bod. Result? Reduced to radio operator on 12-troop corporal's Tank. Meeting with Nosher over, I was returning to the site of the forthcoming smoker when a shout in the dark anounced; "Stand back this fuckers gonna blow!" greeted me through the darkness. The following WHOOMPH! and resulting illumination of the entire wood was scary. Kev had supervised the collection of any fallen trees that could be found. He had then poured a cocktail of different oils, followed by most of the contents of our petrol supply onto the pile of wood. The resulting pyre was amazing as it pushed flames high into the surrounding treetops. My crew was stood around rubbing their hands with glee in the light from the bonfire. Also in the light from the fire I could see our entire supply of beer stacked against the tank. As I arrived Smudge pushed a bottle of Paderborner at me. The heat was already so intense that I decided a drink was more than welcome. I noticed that tree trunks had been positioned, as seats around the fire. At this point Bert and Nosher complete with their crews arrived on the scene, without hesitation Nosher exclaimed; "too late now, might as well enjoy it!" And with that our drinking session started.

During this exercise I had taken to wearing a WW2 German helmet complete with SS runes on one side. I'd worn it when off the tank as a bit of a trick to raise a smile and a laugh in the bitterly cold weather.

I was seen leaping through snowdrifts in my greatcoat. Only a couple of we 'old Fally lags' had greatcoats left. Shortened, they were warm and comfortable on a Tank. Mine had only been shortened to just above the knees. So when, combined with my Jackboots (purchased to replace our regulation 'lace ups') and my re-enactments of the siege of Stalingrad the effect apparently, was quite good. So it was then that on this fateful night, I was sat by the fire dressed as a NAZI Stormtrooper. Soon 9 and 11 troops also had raging fires and the sound of singing could be heard. Then out of the gloom, the CO, his 2i/c and our OC appeared. The CO (Colonel John 'Woody' Woodward) walked to the fire, surveying the mass of empty beer bottles strewn in the melting snow and asked; "So how are we men?" As soon as I'd seen the group arrive I'd removed my helmet for fear of reprisal. Nosher was now nudging me and whispering; "Malcy, put yer 'elmet on, go on, go on!" Plucking up the courage, I slapped the helmet on and stood up, clicked my heels together, saluted and reported in a German accent; "Herr Oberst, Stalingrad vas a complete laugh, tomorrow vill find uns at ze gates of Moscow!" Kev was now also jumping drunkenly through the raging inferno before us. The entire troop collapsed in a hail of guffaws, the CO looked shocked at my outburst then politely laughed, the 2i/c, Major 'Wardog' Smedley, ran from the fire's glow and disappeared behind a tree. He could be heard laughing loudly, meanwhile our OC, Major Wheeler glared as if to say "You'll get yours, wait and see!" The party of officers then departed to review another troop.

And see we did! Next morning I crawled from under our engine decks shelter, peering bleary eyed off the back I was met with a dreadful sight. The snow, which had so easily melted last night, was now rock hard with beer bottles frozen in limbo into the ice. I jumped down immediately wishing I hadn't, as my head had definitely hosted a party for a whole tribe of beer gorillas the previous night. Having relieved myself against a tree, my attention was drawn by loud shouting. I looked around for the source of the ranting. Up the nearby track I saw Nosher, he was stood at attention while the OC stood shouting and angrily gesticulating before him. When the OC had successfully vented his spleen, he approached Bert's Tank, took Bert to the track and once more let loose a verbal barrage. Next, my turn, boy did I get it! Comments like; "who the fuck did you think you were? Heinrich fucking Himmler?" and "what the fuck was Stalingrad? Thousands and thousands died there, it's not fucking funny!" were hurled at me. His last statement was; "Corporal C' you're one of my most senior corporals, I expect more from you..., now, where the fuck is that idiot Corporal

House!" he glanced around just in time to see Kev, his head stuck out of the bivvie, ejecting vomit all over the back of our Tank.

The offending helmet.

The OC threw his arms in the air and stormed off to the next troop due to receive his 'words of wisdom'. Later I met up with 10 troop's Sergeant, my old pal Lucy. He immediately took the piss, but then said his night was crap as, their troop leader, a Lieutenant had 'played by the book, and their smoker was fearfully boring. Lucy had ended up drinking at another troop smoker nearby. The OC hadn't been amused at their antics either.

All good things must come to an end and Soltau was invariably one of those. In the exercise periods we came to somehow accept its rules and regulations and actually enjoy the exercises. I have so many memories that it would take an eternity to write them all down. But one last sobering thought is; once during troop tests, an A. Squadron crew arrived at the 'prisoner-handling stand'. Some surrendering 'Russian prisoners' were thrown at them and were knocked to the ground by a crewman. The troop then 'summarily shot' the pretend 'commies'. When the testing officer asked "why?" The crewman simply replied; "what would we feed them on? How would we transport them? Who would we give them over to? Would we set them free to fight again? Na, fucking blow 'em away, that's what I say!" The testing officer gave no reply simply shrugging, but that troop definitely didn't win troop tests that year!

When we heard of the incident it started a debate. What would we do with prisoners? Officially we would; disarm them, tend to their wounds and care for their welfare handing them to SHQ for transport to the rear echelon and consequent interrogation and imprisonment. But in reality would we? True, we wouldn't have enough rations for ourselves let alone prisoners. Would we have the expertise and supplies to administer the level of first aid they may need? Would we care for them? Hardly likely as they were our enemies! The buggers were trying to kill us! Hand them to SHQ? Days sometimes went by without seeing SHQ, okay so we saw the SQMS more often, but only once in 24 hours! What would we do with them in the meantime? Strap them to the engine decks? Let them runaway? Or simply shoot them? The debate ran for ages but we simply couldn't decide. My solution? I don't know, but my leaning was probably a bit towards the shooting unless we were close to someone to hand them over to. Sad but true. Okay, Infantry who, would have been better prepared to deal with prisoners would have accompanied us. We on the other hand wouldn't be able to spare a man to guard them. The survival of our crew and the vehicle we tended would be more important to us.

Soltau was used by the British army to hone our crew, troop, squadron and regimental professionalism into focus. This it undoubtedly did but, there were many questions which were left unanswered. We were never to experience total war involving armour. Perhaps the men and women who served in conflicts such as the Falklands or more recently the Gulf Wars could answer. But maybe not, humanity is a strange thing, the most precious piece of it being, your own life.

28. Banging at Hohne ranges

I described in an earlier chapter, ranges in the UK. Now lets ponder a little over Bergen Hohne once more in the vicinity of Fallingbostel. Hohne as we simply referred to it, was a massive expanse of heathland bearing the scars of many years tank firing. It was once again a pre-war training ground for the forces of the Third Reich. Consequently a major feature of the landscape was at its centre. This feature was a massive and battered concrete blockhouse known as the Hitler Hof. In its day Hitler and his staff had used this bunker as they gloated over their marvellous, SS and Wehrmacht's training. The landscape was littered with all manner of targetry from the normal canvas screens to the scrapped remains of tanks known as 'hards'. Once more the firing points were a mixture of static points with their concrete standing areas, and the battle runs, their tracks disappearing through the landscape.

As I've just mentioned, the area was used prior and during WW2 by the Germans to train for their dreams of world domination. A chilling reminder of this lies a short distance from Hohne. The name is infamous and irrevocably connected to misery and death; I refer of course to Bergen-Belsen. As the Second World War drew towards its finale, 3 RTR was one of the units that discovered and liberated Belsen. We all know the history of these shocking camps so I won't dwell on the horror.

But visit the site a few of us did, and it has left a scar imprinted on my mind. When we entered the site there was a small museum consisting mainly of shocking pictures of the suffering and squalor that the poor souls within had been subjected to. Once we entered the site into the remembrance area we were amazed at how vast the camp had been. We were informed that the heather and trees had been transplanted as mature examples. This being the only way to get plants to survive on the despoiled topsoil. Dotted around the landscape were large, heather covered mounds, on one side of each was a stone tablet simply informing us; 'Here rest 2500 souls', some mounds containing even more. How could we fail to be impressed by the solemnity of the area? We were told that no birds fly over nor sing at Belsen, but I can't honestly remember if I heard a bird or not. We were glad to leave this place, its peacefulness and isolation gave us an eerie feeling, difficult to shake off.

Back on the ranges we quickly got into the ammo bashing, bleeding knuckles and screaming atmosphere that is so much a part of firing practise. Each firing point had, at its rear, the infamous 'Thunderboxes'. These were buildings erected over a large cesspit. Inside basically a long plank had been placed above the abyss with 'arse sized' holes at regular intervals along its length. To maintain a little privacy wooden partitions were put up between the holes creating doorless stalls. So there you would sit with a procession of blokes parading before you as you tried to conclude your business. Each hole had a floppy rubber cover to 'seal' the hatch. I once witnessed the perfect 'booby trap'. It consisted of the seat covers being dropped beforehand, then when the poor unsuspecting soul entered the events would follow thus. Firstly a Chieftain track pin would be wedged into the end of a thunderflash. The chap with this 'grenade' would now silently enter the building. He would get as close to the perching victim as possible without alerting him, lift a nearby seat cover, ignite the thunderflash and launch it into the sewerage below. The weight of the track pin ensured that the thunderflash was embedded as deeply as possible in the mire. The resulting deep and resonating 'Crump!' and splashing sounds accompanied by a scream of "What the fuck… aaaaaarrrgghh!" was a wonder to behold. The poor chap had risen from his seat to find his backside encrusted with a brown lunar landscape the shape of the hole over which he'd been squatting! Disgusting I know, but bloody funny at the time!

Ranges varied in duration but averaged about two weeks. During this time I lost count how many 'bomb loads' were un-boxed, loaded into our tanks and then dispatched post-haste down the range.

By the end of the firing period we knew from the pains what we had been doing. After a long days firing we used to emerge from our steel clad beasts covered in sweat and reeking of burnt explosive. But by god what a feeling it was, we were the kings of the battlefield and felt like it! Our faces and other areas of exposed skin were black from the oil and smoke that for the duration of firing became part of our being. The end of the day would be rounded off by the gunner and operator 'stripping' the breech mechanism of the main armament down, cleaning, oiling and checking the mechanism for damage. Once complete it would all be carefully reassembled and left ready for the next day's activities. All that remained now would be the stripping and cleaning of the GPMG's to ensure that all was well for next day. Then, onto the waiting buses and back to 'transit' accommodation at 'Fally'.

Ranges were not a place where we turned up and simply let loose with everything we had. On the contrary, gunnery training was a constant training process. In our Gunnery training wing was the turret simulator, this was an accurate reproduction of a Chieftain turret operated electro/hydraulically. The big difference was that there was no armour. Instead the steel shell was filled with large cut out portions covered with metal grills for safety. This way the assembled group could watch the activities of the turret crew as they trained. The ammunition was 'drill'; in other words they mimicked the real thing in every way except for firing and exploding. When the main armament was 'fired' a mechanism pulled the drill projectile and charge up and out the end of the barrel, ejecting it into a trolley below. So it was as real as it could get without being able to explode the buildings walls through a hail of real gunfire.

Various punishments were regularly meted out to offenders who, carried out drills in an incorrect or dangerous fashion. Favourite of these was to run around the buildings exterior with a drill HESH 'proj' held, at arms length, above your head... three times. Shit, but your arms were aching at the end of that! But it soon put your drills and duties into sharp focus! Even as a gunner you are taught the commanders fire orders, this is to ensure you understand what is required of you, but also to ensure a hopefully, smooth transition to the commanders seat when your time comes. tank crews all multi task to ensure that if needed the 'weapons platform' as it's sometimes known, can continue to function. In theory a Chieftain could, at a push, function as a three-man crew. Maintaining the vehicle however, requires four men. During a 'track change' for example, it wasn't uncommon for the entire troop to become involved to increase the speed of this back breaking, weight lifting exercise.

But, having trained ourselves to the level of uttering fire orders and responses in our sleep, off to ranges we went. The Hitler Hof which I've mentioned, although not a monument, was out of bounds for target practise. But often to announce our commencement at Hohne the OC may order an engagement on the distant lump. This would normally be a 'long range' shoot using 'Live' HESH, yes, the real ones! All the Squadrons tanks would line up and 'lay' their guns onto the offending target. The loaders would 'bang a live HESH up' the breech and we would wait with baited breath. The OC would begin a countdown and upon the command " FIRE!" all hell would break loose. As one, all fourteen of our 120mm's would explode, belching fire and smoke from their muzzles. Quickly sticking our heads up and out of our hatches, the operators and commanders would watch the trace elements of the projectiles as they arched up in the sky. The rounds would then lazily start to fall, converging as they approached the bunker. Then the skyline would quite literally erupt as the fourteen rounds hit the target. All that could be seen were bright orange explosions and a huge pall of dense black smoke would billow skyward. Some minute later we would hear the solid CRUMP which rumbled as all fourteen explosions happened simultaneously. It was like an unearthly, massive and stomach turning clap of thunder. It felt so good to watch this event that even today, the hair on the nape of my neck will stand up at the thought. Testament to German build quality was that the bloody Hitler Hof always remained after the smoke cleared!

As the period progressed we would move from the static firing points out onto the battle runs. These were lively affairs as we trundled at a relatively constant speed down the run. The range safety staff in their German army 'Unimog' control vehicles always closely shadowed us. Their job was to ensure that we didn't endanger anyone's life including our own. They also controlled the targetry and decided which target would be 'presented' to which tank for firing on. Battle runs could be quite a fraught affair as suddenly the commander and gunner would have there eyes darting to and fro ensuring that a presented target didn't escape unnoticed. The driver would also be scanning the landscape for signals which signified; 'shoot this bugger over here'. The loader meanwhile would be stood with the main armament loaded, his next round cradled in his arms.

When the fire order came, the drill was slick, the driver would maintain his engine rev's at a constant pitch, the gunner would identify his target and the commander would be watching to ensure that all was proceeding to plan. When the gunner pulled the trigger, the main armament would buck backwards into the recoil cycle, as it 'ran out' to the ready position, the loaders would already have the next round up the breech and preparing to finish the loading procedure. This sounds simple enough but I can assure you that its anything but simple. The motion of the vehicle combined with the recoil of the gun makes the turret interior come alive with activity. If you don't keep your wits about you, the consequences could be dire indeed!

I vividly remember one of my battle runs as a commander. I had recently acquired a new driver in the form of trooper 'ugly' Thompson. New driver was indeed the operative word as, he hadn't yet passed his tracked vehicle driving test. More ammunition which Lucy could use to 'extract the urine' from me. I was that commander who, lined up ready for battle run nine (each range had a number), with a large 'L' plate swinging from the rear of the tank. Oh, the bloody shame of it! I had, after some intensive training, given Tommo the chance to be my loader. 'Smurf' Murphy was my gunner, therefore I had a totally inexperienced crewman in each job.

I need not have worried, as we sallied forth the excellent training each of my three lads had received meant they swung into action as a well oiled team.

We went to 'action' and having changed our flag to 'red' I sank back down to watch Tommo. Nervous at first but, quickly gaining confidence as I coached him along. Once he'd reported 'bore clear' I started to brief 'Smurf' on his 'Arcs of fire'. These Arcs are the left and right extremes of an individual tanks area to shoot within. They are linked to overlap between the tanks of a troop and are designated by the troop leader. This 'mapping' of arcs will then continue to be co-ordinated between troops by the squadron leader. The CO will co-ordinate arcs between squadrons, forming a regimental 'firing screen' across a wide frontage. God help an enemy who strays into what is then termed the 'killing zone'. The arcs are identified by using easily recognisable features such as woods, buildings or, on the ranges, lettered boards stood down the range.

Firing on the move is an art, it effectively simulates the engagements as the tanks advance into an attack. Therefore the engagements tended to be short range 'emergency Sabot' shoots. After I had briefed 'Smurf' and 'Tommo' about what I expected of them, I started to brief 'ugly' on his duties over the IC. "Okay, Ugly, listen up, when we go unless I tell you different get up into third gear as quick as you can, then keep her ticking along at constant revs. I want as smooth a ride as possible. We are going to knock the shit out of these targets as quick as we can. No way are we getting back with ammo that needs reboxing! Do you understand?" I asked. "Okay Malc!" came a somewhat feeble and nervous reply through my headsets. To reassure him I said "Don't worry we all have a first time, you'll be fine". 'Famous last words' sprang to my mind later that day.

Smurf meanwhile was busy with his laser rangefinder. We 'lased' various reference points on the range. I would then use these, allowing for distance travelled, to estimate the range to a target. The targets would be 'identified' for shooting by, small smoke pots set off from the Unimog and its staff. Once this smoke was set off, we would be timed on our 'engagement speed'. This is the time between identifying and hitting the target. Sabot shooting should be 100% a first time hit.

Nosher spoke on the radio, "Hullo four one, four two this is four zero, move now out". Having told 'Ugly' to move off, all of the six main engine exhausts belonging to 12 troop belched blue smoke as we roared off. The adrenaline now surged through our bodies as we searched for targets 'popping up'. In our ears Wagner's 'Ride of the Valkeries' came to life. This was because I'd built an old car radio/cassette into the turret. The music was piped to the IC by a clever use of signals wire between the cassette player and the radio harness control box. So the result was, radio orders in one ear and music in the other. The music really 'hyped' us up as we stormed along. Suddenly I saw our first target, I used my gun controls to 'lay' the 120mm onto the target while screaming, "Sabot 1300, tank on!" 'Smurf', looking through his sight eyepiece would see the target I'd identified and lay the 1300m aiming mark on. As he did this he screamed "Sabot 1300… ON!" As he finished the laying of the gun. Tommo by now had bawled "loaded!" And all that remained for me to do having checked that all was ready was to scream.. "FIRE!" Smurf's Reply of "Firing NOW!" Was punctuated by the roar of the gun as it belched its destructive cargo forth. The target we'd engaged was a hard and, I watched as the sabot round hit and flashed its magnesium trademark. "Fucking Target fire!" I bellowed, Smurf, with Tommo having completed his task, fired again, "TARGET!" yelled Smurf, having this time, seen the flash himself. "Target stop!" I commanded, still with Wagner belting away in the background. "Well done you hard bastards!" I said, "first engagement a fucking resounding success, now lets do some damage!" The battle run continued with us hitting everything, using all our firepower, presented to us.

Having reached the bottom of the run, we would normally turn round with the gun now over the engine decks 'down range', and return the way we'd come. This we now did but, instead of simply driving, this time we were to 'fire over the decks'. The CO had decreed that the regiment must practice this as it was important never to runaway from the enemy without fighting! I briefed Ugly on how important he would now become as, with my back facing our direction of travel, I wouldn't be able to gauge any bumps. So if there was a bump imminent he must tell us not to fire! The reason for this was that the turret reacted to the hull's relative position using 'limit switches'. These were electronic sensors built in to the gun kit. For example if when traversing the turret over the Tank's side, the gun was too low to miss hitting the engine decks as it crossed over their top. A limit switch would cut in, automatically causing the stabiliser to elevate the gun above the collision danger area. Therefore, if travelling 'gun rear' the gun attempted to depress downwards towards the decks, the limit switch would throw the gun barrel skywards. So we would, on this occasion have to be very careful when we fired. Ugly and Smurf briefed, we set off back up the run engaging targets as we went. Then the ultimate disaster happened. We were in the middle of an engagement, Smurf was just shouting his intention to fire when, the tank suddenly lurched and we headed downwards into a large dip, too late! The 120mm shot upwards just as Smurf shouted "NOW!" With a huge bang the gun erupted and I watched the trace in the tail of our Sabot round disappear upwards at an alarming angle, eventually, having probably gone into orbit, it vanished from sight followed by my scream of "Fucking hey, what the fuck was that?! The OC was straight on the radio giving me a good bollocking for unsafe firing. His bollocking was however, nothing to what Ugly received later from me. Having finished our battle run we returned to the assembly point and carried out our end of day cleaning routines.

Lucy appeared on our turret, and of course he was merciless in his humour at my expense. He was pointing to me and laughingly exclaiming "Jellyhead" a term we used to express a cock up in general. This was sometimes also used to express joy at someone's misfortune if someone managed to trick someone into an action. For example if someone walked up to you and sent you on a false task, you'd be classed as a 'jellyhead' the act having been termed as a 'jelly'. I had the last laugh on my pal though. The next battle run that 10 troop went down on, Lucy suffered a first engagement misfire. He duly changed his flag to yellow, then during the thirty minute wait period, he suddenly noticed that his 'very experienced' loader had not fitted the 120mm FNA (firing needle assembly) without which, the gun couldn't possibly fire. I could just imagine the scene in his turret upon this discovery. It wouldn't have been a pretty sight as Lucy, a strict disciplinarian, would be beating people around the head. He, like me, insisted on the best so, incidents such as we had experienced that day smarted like mad. Later that day I simply went over to his tank and pronounced, "Hey, you old twat, who's the fucking jellyhead now?" his only reply was to screw up his face and stick one of his middle fingers up at me. Later that evening we sat, drinking a beer and recollecting on similar incidents in our past lives.

Once on Hohne, we had the pleasure of seeing our first Abrams M1 MBT. This was the American army's newest addition. We had got used to the M60 As being fairly commonplace. But this? Well, this was new! The American unit to whom they belonged were on the next firing point to us. In due course a few of us wandered over to inspect this new machine. The Americans were friendly enough but, wouldn't let us inside. We had a good look around the outside though. Across the back of the tank was a massive grill, this covered the exhaust from the tanks revolutionary Gas Turbine power pack. Would wonders never cease? A fucking jet powered Tank! Above this grill on each Tank, in true American style, were stencilled the words 'Whispering Death'. This was obviously aimed at the tanks distinctively quiet engine, combined with its firepower.

This 'quiet' engine was in its early stages fairly controversial. When it had first driven on German roads while on exercise, it had fallen foul of German 'convoy dodgers'. We referred to German motorists as this because, when overtaking a convoy motorists would ignore the tanks crew trying to give traffic signals. Instead they would accelerate fiercely, weaving madly between the tanks in an effort to get past the slow convoy before them. On the occasion in question, a German car driver mistimed his overtaking manoeuvre and, found himself swerving. That is, swerving straight bloody back in under the exhausts of an M1. As the driver attempted to slow down before he careered under the Tank's rear end, he saw the paint on the front of his car 'peeling and bubbling' off his bodywork. This was because the fierce heat generated by the M1's turbine was more than BMW had allowed for in their design. The resulting article in the German 'Bild Zeitung' had us howling with laughter and, the Americans modifying the M1's exhaust outlet.

Anyway, the Americans were just as impressed with Chieftain, even though it was outdated in many respects. More importantly the Yanks were interested in swapping articles of uniform and equipment. That is their uniform and equipment in exchange for? Would you believe our compo rations? Oh yes they were mad for our food. Their own rations may have had tooth picks made of candy and packs of 5 cigarettes, even soft toilet paper but, nothing could beat a tin of our steak and kidney pudding! Even a tin of apple pudding could persuade a Yank to part with his GI helmet! "Fucking lunatics!" Was all we could ever say about these allies of ours!

Anyway Hohne over for another year, we would make our way wearily back to Paderborn to make our tanks ready for the final event in every year... FTX.

29. Into the breach, Dear Heinrich

September of each year brought with it FTX (Field Training exercise). This was for us silly season, we could spend two or three weeks on Soltau and then move swiftly into the long and arduous FTX for a further four to six weeks. The FTX was when we were allowed to exercise in the wide expanse of normal German countryside. This gave us chance to train in, what in real war would be, our home ground. So names such as the Sibbesse gap would become second nature to us. Other names that became common to us were the River Weser, Hannover plain and small place names such as Coppengrave. We needed to know these places because, should we find ourselves attempting to stem the 'red tide' as it flooded across Europe, it was here that we would be fighting.

For 3 RTR with its excellent record and skills, we were part of 1 (BR) Corps reserve. This meant, as the name implies, that we would be used to 'plug' holes in our, or our neighbours' front lines. What this actually meant was that for the first week or so of FTX we were held in reserve. This involved occupying a hide, as a Squadron in some massive forest in the middle of nowhere. Time would pass slowly as we polished our training in 'ancillary' subjects. These subjects included AFV (armoured fighting vehicle) recognition, so we knew who to and not to shoot. Also mine warfare was a subject, not to be confused with coal excavation, but things that went bang when you drove over them. We had to learn how to detect, identify and disarm landmines of all types. NBC training (of course!) and map reading, to name but a few. tank commanders often went on TEWT's, (Tactical Exercise Without Tank's). This was to improve our skills on tactics and ground appreciation.

Also during this time we would unofficially hone our other skills out of boredom. For example Lucy's operator 'Trigger' Duckworth would enter into our cooking competition, this was a contest to see who could make what dish using only compo ingredients along with whatever 'fresh rations' we had available. I for my own part could make tasty fishcakes from washed and de-boned 'pilchards in tomato sauce' mixed with potato powder, covered with egg and freshly rubbed breadcrumbs, sautéed in margarine. Trigger always attempted to go one better and once managed to produce fried mock steaks with onions, from a tin of 'stewed steak'. Lucy and I often bet the occasional beer on the result. It was always popular to crews from other tanks to see if they could learn anything.

As usual, this for us, 'phoney war' would come to an end, normally abruptly. Sometime one night, our 'minutes to move' alert would come down to twenty minutes. At that time our kit would be stowed and we would take to sleeping where we could find a spot on the steel casing around us. Our tanks and routines after all this time had become so familiar that, we knew where to stow everything for maximum speed and efficiency. I remember once when travelling in a dawn convoy how, all our tanks even though in the 80's looked like they'd been snapped in a photo during D-Day 1944. We had our camouflage nets rolled in the hessian which, we used to lay on the tank first to prevent the net snagging on all the various projections to be found. The hessian layer also prevented any 'shine' from wet metal surfaces. The nets would be seen as large rolls on the top of the turret NBC pack behind the commander's hatch. There would also be a smaller roll normally wrapped across the glacis plate in front of the driver. Hanging from the turrets rear bins would be the turret crews CEFO webbing. Cooking 'Dixie's' may also be seen hanging from the turrets various bins and baskets. Yes, in the first artillery barrage the lot may have been blown away, but the simple fact was that all our bins would be blown away too. So did it really matter if our equipment was inside or out? I think not. Anyway we could access our 'common use' equipment much more speedily in this way. On the engine decks would be the odd spare can of oil that wouldn't fit in the already crowded commanders basket, and maybe the crews ubiquitous black bin bag, full of rubbish. Once upon a time we'd disposed of rubbish with our tracks as we departed a wood. But the new 'ecologically sound' army insisted we take it with us. Also, in real conflict we couldn't leave evidence of our whereabouts for Soviet Special Forces to use as they plotted our locations.

Twenty minutes to move may be cut to five or ten minutes to move. This resulted in crew positions with fingers on the engine start buttons. Then, normally through word of mouth as we'd have been on strict radio silence, the orders to move would come. With a note of relief our engines would chorus into the signature tune of howling Chieftains as we roared off into the night. We normally found ourselves thumping along roads in a convoy for up to fifty or sixty kms. Finally reaching our 'drop off' point before dawn, we would howl off the road heading for fire positions in the darkness ready to counter the enemy push already overwhelming the existing defences to our front. This tactic was known as a counter penetration and always provided excitement.

Once while on an FTX I'd been 'loaned' to 9 Troop as their Troop Corporal. My crew was 'paddy' Coombe driving, 'Moose' Claydon operating and 'clutch' Sprague gunning. The FTX started promisingly enough, we found ourselves 'dug in' for about a week, on the outskirts of a small town. Our Callsign 12 was detached on the far side of the town nearest the expected enemy push. The Troop leader, Lieutenant Dixon was parked near the centre, next to a newsagent's stand and a 'schnellie' (no cooking for them). The Troop Sergeant Martin Woods was up a hill on the far side from me. When the push came we would simply move forward about 500 metres into our fire positions and engage the enemy. On this occasion our enemy was a Bundewehr unit of 'Recce' vehicles, these vehicles were the 'Luchs' or Lynx armoured cars. Quite unique as they were quite large and had a driver at each end of the vehicle, effectively giving it no reverse just 'push me pull you'. The days passed with me wading a small river under a rat infested bridge in order to visit Mr Dixon's tank for briefing, collecting a newspaper on the way. During FTX we could sometimes pick up 'intelligence info' from the German press who in turn got their info from press releases about the exercise. For example they would give residents information about when huge armour movement would be expected in their area. All useful stuff to us!

Then one morning the radio silence was broken and we found ourselves driving forward to our fire position. We could see the German 'push' assembling at the bottom of the valley before us. Then, without warning our 'Jenny' coughed, spluttered, lowered its rev's sounding very sick indeed and cut out! "Fucking hell Paddy! What's up?" I inquired over the IC. "Fuck knows! It seemed alright, but it's just died!" He replied. "It smells bloody hot back there!" said Moose sniffing the air. Paddy now interjected, "could have overheated, I wouldn't know as the fucking temperature gauge is buggered!" We were now sat, effectively as dead ducks in front of an enemy force. "Start the Main engine and rev at over 1000rpm, bring the generator on line!" I instructed Paddy. "Aw shit." Came the reply, as this was a horrific experience for drivers, as they had to sit with their foot stationary on the accelerator. As soon as the main engine generator came on line the gun kit whirred back into life. It wouldn't take long however for cramp to set into Paddy's right foot. I meanwhile encoded a message explaining our predicament. SHQ eventually replied telling us to wait for the REME to contact us. In due course the REME told us to drive to a grid reference where we would meet a field workshop. Here they would remove our stricken Jenny and give us a new unit. I now got us to put the gun rear and put it in its travelling clamp (the gun crutch). Now I would have to stand in my hatch looking over the front of the vehicle as we moved off. Moose would face the rear to control the traffic as they tried to overtake our Tank. As we pulled out through the town Mr Dixon waved at us, while eating a Bratwurst and chips and laughing like a bloody drain. Typical, here we were about to go into battle and then, breakdown. Sod's law! Flashed through my disenchanted mind.

The journey proved quite eventful. We forced a car off the road into a ditch when it lost a game of 'chicken' against us. The car had been full of 'green party protesters' who were spending the duration of our exercise protesting against war and NATO, earlier in the exercise a party had even attacked us by throwing pots of red paint at us from their overtaking car. Fine if that's what they wanted to do! But now, they were not forcing ME off the fucking road. Later we entered a town through which we had to travel, as we trundled through the outskirts, a strange phenomena occurred. Suddenly with a roar, all I could hear in my headsets was the roar of the engine. Moose meanwhile had started shaking my shoulder and was pointing frantically at the engine decks. I turned and, there behind us was a ten foot long flame belching from each of our exhausts like the Knight Rider car of the 80's. This I had seen before, it was the prelude to our main engine 'running away'. If this happened it would be the end of our main engine. I had once seen an engine 'run away' it simply kept running no matter how the driver attempted to switch it off. Gradually the engine revs would increase until they reached their maximum limit. At this point the engine would keep going until, BANG! It would internally explode, sometimes putting parts of the engine out through the armoured decking that covered it. In light of this, my action was immediate, "Paddy pull over the fuck NOW, and switch the fucking engine off, come on, get on with it!" The tank suddenly veered right into the kerb and ground to a halt. Paddy threw his switch and the engine spluttered but then died. I breathed a sigh of relief; we had just caught it in time! Then I realised that the exhausts still had flames rising from them. Also there were flames crackling out through the engine deck's louvers, this was obviously due to the wasted oil and debris in the engine compartment igniting under the extreme heat!

"Right we're on fire, so everyone out, Paddy pull the extinguishers!"

We evacuated the tank and I walked to the back to survey the damage, suddenly there was a huge cracking sound as the bottom of the engine split apart under the heat. Oil spewed from under the Tank. Paddy had left a 'belly plate' off for ease of maintenance. We now had gallons of engine oil spilling onto the road! I then noticed where we were; we had stopped at the kerbside between the entrance and exit of, a petrol station. The forecourt was a mass of drivers rushing to get their cars out of danger as our flames were getting higher! I walked to the front to find a red faced Paddy fighting to pull the fire extinguishers into action.

"Moose!" I shouted, "Get in this fucking cab and pull the knobs, NOW!" I continued. Moose was a strapping lad of great strength, the problem was, the fire extinguisher knobs couldn't be tested to find out if they were serviceable without setting them off, flooding the engine decks with foam and putting the culprit in real danger of disciplinary action! Therefore in instances like this it could be hit or miss whether they worked! Moose climbed into the cab, shortly after came a twanging sound. Moose grinned and held up a red handle attached to an inch of cable! The metal cable had deteriorated and snapped under pressure. 'TWANG!' The other handle broke free without any cable at all! Okay we tried the two external handles! Same effect, and no extinguishers going off. By now the fire had increased in intensity (second only to the voracity with which I now swore) catching light to our rubbish bag, which we dragged from the decks and stamped out. We now got the rubberised engine sheet, which we normally used as the back deck bivvy, and threw it across the decks in an attempt to smother the flames, result? It melted in the heat! There went our bloody easy to put up night shelter! Things were now serious; I was stood on the turret removing pyrotechnic charges from the gunfire simulator before the heat set them off. I then radioed SHQ to report our predicament.

Our last resort was the five small hand held extinguishers, we came, we saw, we tried, we pissed in the wind! Some 45 minutes later the flames had now started to subside of their own accord. There was now quite a crowd gathering to inspect our stunning example of British engineering. A rather attractive girl came up and, having discovered I could speak German, volunteered that her brother drove a Leopard 2 and 'this never happened!' I at that point could have knocked her down on the pavement and stood on her throat! How bloody dare she? At that moment our Squadron ARV turned up. It overtook us and pulled into position ready to tow us to the workshops. Then with a 'glug' the ARV emptied part of its bloody hydraulic oil system on the road. This had turned into a right mess. I was now attracted by shouting on the other side of the road, there was clutch, frenziedly beating off some 'greens' who were trying to haul 'clutch' in through the open roof of their Citroen 2CV in an attempted kidnap while he was directing traffic. 'Clutch' was beating them off using his metal 'lollipop' designed for traffic control not, beating the shit out of hippy's. Having extricated himself and the 2CV having disappeared in a cloud of exhaust. Clutch then narrowly avoided causing two buses to collide when he got 'confused' controlling the traffic. And now here we sat with the ARV, both broken down and all of us looking shame faced! Either way, eventually we were sorted and the exercise continued.

When we went on FTX all commanders were issued with a 'damage control card'. This acted as a warning to vehicle commanders what the potential monetary cost of damage to the MOD could be. Everything was listed, kerbstones, lengths of tarmacadamed roads, roadsigns, traffic lights and crops in fields by the square metre! Most farmer's crops would be gathered by the time FTX started, but it was common to see crops left in the fields. This was a clever ruse, if for tactical reasons we had to leave the road, the farmers would recover the cost of their crops from the MOD and still be able to salvage most of the crop for sale at a profit. So it wasn't only the huge EEC farming subsidies, which paid for the Mercedes on the farmers drive. Many was the occasion when, in return for a crate of beer, a tank crew did a little 'ploughing of its own'', or indeed drove over a farmers plough. Next season the farmer had a new plough, I hate to think that he could have 'conned' a new tractor into the bargain but, who knows?

Roadsigns? Now there's a sport. Sport? Oh yes, an experienced Chieftain commander could use the 120mm to effectively 'joust' his way down a road. "Oh look, a fucking warning sign!" He would exclaim, as he grabbed the gun kit controller and swung the turret to the right! 'SMANG' down would go the sign. Another one to his tally which he kept on the damage control card he'd been given. "Oh, what larks", he would chirrup as he drove relentlessly onward damaging everything he could! This is obviously a blasé look at the way we were, I'm not saying it didn't happen but not with the regularity I've implied.

Another episode of damage in which I was involved was when I was driving 'Gorgeous George' Brighty. I'd agreed to drive instead of operate for the duration of an FTX, this was due to a shortage of experienced drivers. One day we were hurtling down a country road when George missed our turning onto a field track by misreading his map.

"Oh bollocks! Malc turn left through this field, we'll get on the track further up" came his instruction. I immediately obliged, descending an embankment into the field. As we pushed across the turf of the field, I started to get a feeling we were slowing. I changed down the gears until we were in first gear but, hardly making any headway. Suddenly our tank leant quite violently to it's right and sank up to the height of the commander's bin on the turret! I scrambled my way out of the cab to stand on terra firma. Firm earth? Yes it certainly was, but what the fuck? The ground had wobbled under my weight. I immediately bent down, grabbed a handful of freshly 'Tanked' soil and...? "It's fucking peat George!" I shouted.

George, who had been on the radio explaining our situation, lifted his headset and said, "Bloody what?"

I repeated what I'd said. George stepped quite literally from his cupola to the ground (normally a backbreaking 12 feet). He grabbed a sample of soil and, like me, rubbed it between his hands.

"Well fuck me!" he uttered bemusedly.

I'd never before, seen a field look so perfectly normal but be so treacherous. It was immaterial now, we were quite literally stuck in it up to our arses. The gunner, Jerry 'psycho' Taylor (the only bloke I knew to buy a box of Mars bars and not share them!) and the operator 'Zippy' Wellington, now also emerged. They were 'nigs' and didn't understand what George and I were on about. Zippy suggested we dig ourselves out, George told him to "Fuck off stupid!" Then George told him to make a brew as we could see the BV's steam rising from the open hatches. Zippy had forgotten to turn it off.

What now happened was a disaster of the first order! Firstly our own Sqn ARV and its crew were so busy that they would take too long to come to our rescue! So an ARV from the neighbouring unit, the 4th/7th Royal Dragoon Guards (would you believe it? Bloody donkey wallopers) was sent to our rescue. Upon their arrival they nearly met our fate as they tried to enter the field behind us. Luckily our frantic arm waving and shouting averted that catastrophe.

The REME commander, a Recovery mechanic or 'reccy mech', as we knew them, strolled, laughing, towards our stricken tank. As he drew near he pushed his beret to the back of his head, which he was now scratching.

"Jesus Christ! This is some fucking mess you're in!" he said, stating the obvious. "We'll soon winch you out, though," he added.

He returned to his ARV waiting on the road. Once there he guided the ARV into the field on the opposite side of the road to us. They then dropped the large blade on the ARV's front into the ground, to give the ARV purchase as it exerted its might into the task of pulling us out. In due course its stout metal winch cables were stretched across the road and our field and then attached to our tank.

The ARV driver now engaged the winch clutch and released the brake. The cables tightened and our tank moved... a whole inch, then stopped. The reccy mech adjusted the pulling power of the winch and off we went again. In the end the ARV was pulling us but the peat was acting like a sucking machine, trying desperately to hold us in its clasp. The rescue was going laboriously slowly when, over the hill came three 'enemy' bridge layers. These were Chieftain hulls with huge, single-span bridges clamped to the top. They approached down the road in the opposite direction to that in which we'd been travelling.

The commander in the leading bridge layer saw our activities ahead and decided to cut into the field behind the ARV, cross a drainage ditch there and, rejoin the road. His two other vehicles decided to follow suit, and a clever move it would have been except, all three vehicles got bloody well stuck in the drainage ditch!

At the sight of these ungainly vehicles struggling to extricate themselves, the ARV crew and ourselves were howling with laughter! We laughed so hard that we had tears streaming down our grubby faces. Meanwhile, a small car was approaching down the hill. The reccy mech told his driver to brake the winch and allow the cables to slacken and lay on the road. This was done before the car got too close and the reccy mech waved the car across. We don't, to this day, know how it happened but, as the car was straddling the cables, the ARV driver's foot slipped, the cables tightened and flew up, with the result that they caught the cars rear axle and ripped it from its mountings. The car stopped with a jolt and was physically thrown backwards, like being shot from a catapult!

At this sight, we four were rolling on the ground, bellowing with uncontrolled laughter. What a bloody mess, it was so unbelievable that, it was comical in the extreme. Even an author with the imagination of Tom Sharpe couldn't have imagined it into one of his wonderful creations! Eventually the car was recovered by the ADAC (German AA equivalent), the bridge-layers got out of trouble, but not before they wrecked a drainage culvert and a section of road in the process!

That left us and the ARV back where we'd started, alone! Well not quite ... a group of local farmers had gathered to witness this spectacle. Darkness was falling and this merry band were stood betting crates of beer with each other on whether we'd get out or not! Eventually that night we did get out but, the ARV had buried its blade so deep that its hydraulics couldn't lift it back out of the ground! So there we soon were, with spades, trying to dig it out. Having accomplished this task we found that we were unable to move our tank of its own volition! The REME discovered that the 'Twiflex coupling' between engine and gearbox had melted due to our attempts to try and help our escape by reversing. The resulting overheating in the coupling had put it into self-destruct mode!

The result was us being towed to a nearby village where we could be repaired. We skirted the village trying to find somewhere out of the way to park. The reccy mech spotted a pull in area next to a barn on the other side of which was, a farmyard. It was now one o'clock in the morning, and the strain was showing on our faces. The ARV reversed us into the allotted space and then having uncoupled, started to reverse in next to us. It was then that the ARV commander misjudged the space and collapsed a section of the barn's supporting wall! We were truly cocking this one up, our tank was leaking oil next to a haystack and the ARV was demolishing a barn! Early next morning I was, as the German speaker, sent to apologise to the farmer. Imagine his and my surprise when, as he bleary eyed, opened his door to see me, he was the poor sod who's car had been destroyed by the ARV's antics the day before. Having apologised, rapidly, and listened to him ranting, I returned post-haste to the Tank. We were all really grateful when, later that morning we were pronounced 'fit' and off we sped leaving the scene of destruction behind! Our bad luck wasn't finished yet! Driving along I felt that all was not well, the tank seemed to judder as we drove along. Some five miles later whilst steering through a long left hand bend, our tank suddenly, and I mean fucking suddenly, steered of its own accord, sharp right and buried its nose in a drainage ditch! The impact was so fierce that the retaining catch holding my hatch cover open, snapped! The heavy armoured cover shot across and luckily hit my bonedome, this cracked open like an eggshell under the stress! I don't like to think what would have happened had I not been wearing this helmet!

Later, when the REME arrived it was soon discovered that our final drive and sprocket had seized. No doubt a delayed reaction from the previous days exertions. Not all FTX's were this eventful, normally everything went, boringly for you readers, with typical military precision. Remember, these are true, but selected anecdotes from many, many experiences of training for war. War is a serious business but, there are events over which we laugh, that occur even in our 'darkest hours'. It was during this exercise that we encountered our first Challenger MBT's. The Royal Hussars had been issued first with these new warhorses and this was their first foray on an FTX with them. Our squadron was withdrawing through the Hussars front line, I was full steam ahead, driving up a farm track towards a wood. Each side of us were the Challengers covering our withdrawal. Inevitably, as we climbed the tracks gradient we started to slow as we lost power and momentum. Then as if from nowhere a Challenger overtook us. It wouldn't have been so embarrassing had it not been in a ploughed field and, travelling in reverse! "Fucking posers!" Was George's only grudging comment into the IC.

This then, hammering past us, was the future! All things must change, and warfare and its machinery is by no means different. In fact quite the contrary, most of the worlds technological advances are owed to the military. How sad, why can't we invest more into peaceful development of measures to help humanity instead of killing it? I am not by any means a pacifist. Soldiers, as I once explained to some Germans, are in their profession so that other, unwilling souls don't have to soldier!

30. God Save the Queen

The year is now 1985 and a special year it was for the RTR. I'm afraid I now need to explain some regimental history to you again. Every unit of the British army has what is called 'The colours'. The most spectacular event involving these is The Trooping the Colour parade marking the Queens official birthday each year. The reigning monarch is also however, the Colonel in Chief of the Royal Tank Regiment. This honour was bestowed on the Regiment between the world wars. After WW1 it was believed that tanks were no longer required, this belief being fuelled at the War office by, bloody Cavalry traditionalists. tanks were seen as a threat to the Cavalry's history and its future. At this time the tanks were simply known as the tank Corps. The King however, was a man of perception who saw the tanks future cast in the very steel they were built from.

Subsequently, having told the old warhorses at the War Department to 'piss off' the King gave the tank Corps the prefix title of Royal. This then would eventually become the Royal Tank Regiment. The King presented the Regiment with its 'Colours', which in the RTR are called Standards. Each Regiment, which made up the RTR getting its own standard. These Standards are kept in each Regiment's RHQ behind armoured glass. When any rank of soldier passes the Standard he must salute it. This is to show respect for the Reigning Monarch who presented the Standard and also the men who gave their lives in any of the battle honours embroidered on its hallowed cloth. Should the Standard be required to leave RHQ to be displayed elsewhere, it was always accompanied by armed guards. Such is the esteem with which the Standard revered. The Standard has been blessed by the hand of the monarch who is god's representative on earth. Romantic notion? Ask most soldiers how important their Colour or Standard is! I hope the modern army is as proud of their heritage as we were. New Standards are presented to the Regiment by the monarch, every twenty five years. 1985 was the year where we would receive the new Colours from Her Majesty the Queen.

The 'Standards Parade' was to be held at Sennelager on a massive area overlooked by a windmill. This site was the only place big enough to hold a parade on this scale. Big enough? Oh bloody yes, this was also the first time in many years that all Four Regiments which made up The Royal Tank Regiment, were all stationed in BAOR at the same time. The venue being Sennelager meant that we in 3RTR would be the 'host' regiment. The bullshit that was about to encroach on our peaceful Panzer Kaserne was unbelievable. We were seen weeding the cobbled roads through camp, washing them down with fire hoses to ensure their cleanliness. The outside areas of the blocks were cleaned and, in some cases redecorated. And of course there were the tanks themselves. We painted them all green, we then painted them green and black. We then painted them green and black so that every tank in every squadron looked identical (frowned on in normal circumstances). We serviced, preened and bulled them almost to destruction. Four HUGE German beer marquees were erected, one for each Regiment, for a post parade party of gargantuan proportions. Soldiers and their families were chosen and rehearsed for meeting the Queen. The preparations were endless, even our uniforms were issued especially for the occasion. The entire regiment was to wear 'Dress' black overalls. This was the accepted dress code for 'mounted parades'. Yes, this parade was to be done on our Tanks. Just imagine the sight, over two hundred MBTs on parade! AWESOME! With our overalls each Regiment was to wear a silk cravat in their Regimental colour, ours being Brunswick green. Also apart from our badges of rank we were to proudly wear the 'Tank Arm badge' on our sleeves. This, as I've mentioned before, was normally only worn on parade No. 2 dress or the RTR ceremonial 'blues' No. 1 dress. God, but we looked bloody good, proper 'fanny magnets'!

Our tanks transported to Sennelager and ourselves being pronounced ready the great day dawned. We found ourselves inside our tanks at the start. The spectators view being a huge, long and deep block of tanks in front of them in the distance, backed by a wood. Starting at the left were the Chieftains of 1 RTR, then 2RTR's newly issued Challengers, then us in our Chieftains and finally on the right the Chieftains of 4RTR. At a pre arranged signal we all emerged from our hatches and the commander and operators stood to attention in their hatches. Another signal and the massive throng moved off as one, advancing to the front of our area bordering the huge concrete standing in front of the spectator stands. As we advanced, huge smoke pots behind us were set off, behind each Regiment the colours of that Regiment appeared in the form of billowing clouds of smoke. Once halted we were to dismount and form two ranks before the front line of the Tanks. This done The Queen arrived accompanied by a 21 gun salute fired by the scorpion reconnaissance vehicles assembled from each Regiment. The Queen was then driven past us in her open backed Range Rover reviewing her Regiments. One of, without doubt, my proudest moments. That over, the

Queen returned to the saluting dais. The next time she left the platform was to touch each Regimental Standard as she presented it to the Colonel of each Regiment. The CO's then gave the Standards to their RQMS's stood atop Spartan APC's, the Standards also flanked by two SQMS's as an armed 'Honour Guard'. Once the Queen was back on the dais, we remounted the vehicles and prepared for our drive past. According to the spectators, the ground and stands shook with the tremors created by the massive weight of the armour as it trundled past the Queen each tank traversing and dipping the 120mm over the front right wing in salute to the Queen. The pride I felt as our tank went past was and still is, beyond description. At the end of the main drive past, an old WW1 Mark V 'Male' tank slowly led a march past of 'old comrades' amid much cheering from the assembled spectators. That done there was one more trick to be displayed. From one end of the parade area concrete, out of sight behind a tree line a lone Challenger of 2RTR appeared. It came into view at full speed, its turbo charged engines deep growl supplemented why the whistling of the turbo, and charged straight across the front of the stands. As it reached the far end of its run, the driver jammed on the brakes, bringing all 64 tons to a rapid halt, engaged reverse and quickly accelerated to full speed as it sped backwards across the area, once more disappearing out of sight! This display brought a roar of approval from the crowds, and a grudging mumble from us Chieftain boys. "Fucking posers" I muttered.

The rest of the day was spent back at our barracks with the Queen visiting various displays we'd put on and meeting her soldiers and their families. Once the Queen had departed, the festivities increased in tempo. Irregardless of which individual Regiment we were in, we were all Tankie brothers, the feeling of belonging was immense. There were no rivalries or dislikes on display, this was what has always made the RTR so special, belonging! It was also a good opportunity to catch up with old pals from training. 1 RTR had music from the North and North West thumping from their tent. 2 RTR had managed to get Chas and Dave to come and bash out some cockney songs, 4 RTR had their Pipes and Drums wailing like banshees across the fields, also putting on sword dancing displays and having a great time. 3RTR? Well, I thought we'd engaged 'Shag Connors and the carrot crunchers' along with their chicken manure covered piano, to stomp out some Westcountry folk in the style of Adge Cutler and the Wurzels. The truth is I don't remember as I was very, very drunk! That evening after darkness we were treated to a 'son et lumiere' display, depicting the advent of the Tank. It was fantastic, the finale was a gigantic firework display firstly filling the sky above with showers of red, white and blue. Then lastly the night sky was absolutely filled with exploding rockets which illuminated most of Paderborn with a brown, red and green glow. As these Regimental colours were exploding above us, the roar of approval that soared into the night must have been heard in Berlin!

After this display, we returned to our tents for drinks. The party went on virtually all night. I do remember a piper from 4RTR entering our tent and playing magnificently to our cheering. He was so good we wouldn't let him go, instead we just plied him with more Scotch! In return he was requested to continually play that rousing march, 'The Black Bear'. This he did with relish, but I bet his lungs hurt the next morning!

The festivities over we retrieved our tanks and returned to normal routine. But that parade was such a talking point in the Squadron bars for weeks.

31. Design what?

While in Paderborn I used to vent my interest in our Regimental history by helping out occasionally in the small Regimental Museum, contained in a room in RHQ. It wasn't a grand affair but held a lot of information on the men and machines of the Regiment through the years. I had, even as a child, a great interest in tanks. Over the years I've spent many hours at the wonderful tank Museum in Bovington, pondering and investigating tank development. I said earlier in the book, I'd like to write about this subject, so here we go! These observations are seen from my soldier's perspective, based on fact but seen through my eyes.

Okay so everyone knows that with WW1 came the advent of trench warfare and the machine gun, that efficient killer of men. This had the boffins at the War Office scratching their heads in dismay. The trick of soldiers standing up and walking slowly towards the enemy didn't work. Why? Well... because that was exactly what the Hun expected them to do!

"Bugger!" said one boffin to another, "We'd better try something else!" But that failed dismally too. After all, just because the men now stood up and ran quickly at the Hun, didn't make an iota of difference. The German machine guns were a hell of a lot quicker than the Infantry.

"Bollocks!" exclaimed the boffin as he scratched his oversized bald head. "We're in trouble if we don't think of something new, and quick!"

His colleague, who had been thinking to himself, resignedly muttered, " I wish I was as clever as that Leonardo Da Vinci!"

The first boffin looked up. "Bloody bugger! Of course! Didn't he draw some sort of land machine that could protect its crew?"

They scoured their reference library, eventually finding the design they sought.

"Shit, we can't build that! We'll be laughed off the battlefield!" said one to the other.

"I never said we'd build it," his colleague laughed. "All I want to do is steal the idea, modify the design, modernise it and when it's finished tell the sceptics it was us, and ask who the fuck was Leonardo da whatsisname anyway?"

Having thought carefully about their problem they threw down their pencils in disgust.

"Jesus!" said one. "How the hell are we going to do this? These flippers we've drawn will be as much use as tits on a fish for a land vehicle! We may as well take one of those newfangled American agricultural tractors designed by that fellow Holt, with its thingies, oh you know... tracks, that's them, and use that!"

"Hey, that's not such a bad bloody idea," said his partner, scribbling furiously with his pencil. "We'll cover it in iron or steel plate, which we'll call armour, but what do we call the vehicle?"

The pair now stood at the urinals. His pal, glancing down at his neighbour's appendage laughed; "What a little willy you've got!"

"Bloody good name, that!" retorted the other boffin, thoughtfully. "The Boche will never guess what the fuck it is from that name!"

And so the first prototype tank – 'Little Willy' – was born...

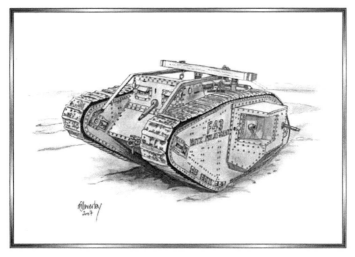

Mk IV Male, F43, 'Fritz Phlattener'.

When the trials were finished and the Admiralty had accepted the concept of a 'Little Willy', they decided that a machine named after a scientist's penis was a little distasteful. So after due consideration and their knowledge being mainly to do with water, they hit on the name 'tank' – after all, that's what it looked like, a huge water tank! So it was, that in due course, the first Mark 1 'Mother' tanks rolled from the production line onto the French and Belgian battlefields, scaring the shit out of the Germans on the way.

From the beginning, Britain's 'men in white coats' have struggled with the design of tanks. Okay, we invented it. The 'others' have always 'copied' it. So why have we continually 'bodged' it? We know what the three main characteristics of a tank are; we thought of them! Firepower, protection and mobility. When correctly balanced this leads to the battlefield characteristic of flexibility. But to look at some of the designs we've come up with, you could be forgiven for thinking that we didn't have a clue!

After the 'Mother' had taken to the field, it was quickly modified to increase its trench crossing and steering capabilities by, putting a huge pair of wheels on the back! This only met with limited success, after all, the ferocity of German artillery barrages that met the appearance of tanks in an attack, soon ripped the wheels off! The boffins drew, modified and thought up all manner of things. tanks suddenly became 'Male' or 'Female', the difference being that 'Males' had larger pieces of field artillery fitted, 'Females' on the other hand were armed with machine guns. Later in the war newer designs were built, the rhomboidal shape of the tanks was lengthened by adding a 'Tadpole tail' which did, successfully increase the tanks trench crossing ability. tanks appeared one day, lumbering slowly forward, their ungainly shapes carrying, perched on top, huge bundles of wood. These were known as 'Fascines' and when a tank approached a deep trench, the fascine would be rolled into the trench, and the tank could drive safely across it. This was, the fore runner of the modern Royal Engineers AVRE with its demolition gun or 'dustbin chucker'.

The newspaper articles of the time hailed the tank as 'The War Winning' machine! I, as a Tankie, do believe this even though the sceptics say that it was not. Let's face it, imagine you are a German foot soldier in your trench. The continual barrage one morning lifts and, there before you trundles a huge metal box, heading straight for you spitting fire and lead in every direction, smoke belching from its exhaust. Crap yourself? I should think so! The tanks may not have been much faster than walking pace but, unlike the Infantry, they couldn't be stopped by machine gun fire. Then they are on your position, travelling up and down your trench line raking your previously safe haven with, thousands of unstoppable machine gun bullets. Behind them come the enemy Infantry, and there are thousands of them, they've come safely through your defences, and having now emerged from behind the cover of the advancing Tanks, they can't wait to stick their bayonets right up your arse!

Now, while this mayhem was happening all along the front line, where were the Cavalry? Well, with the advent of WW1 they had, in the face of artillery and MG fire, found themselves literally blown from the battlefield. Certainly in many tank actions, the reason for eventual failure of the attack was, that the cavalry were so sceptical about 'breakthrough and exploitation' that, they simply chose to remain undercover. The cavalry officers deemed tanks as a 'flash in the pan', sat as they were, behind a wood out of sight, their officers were heard to say; "Let the tanks cock this one up, we'll rest a while, Rupert pass me another glass of port, there's a good chap!" The tanks speed did not match its 'shock action'. The mechanical technology that existed at the time could not exploit the effect that tanks could have on the enemy. Not to matter, the boffins were working on the 'cavalry solution'.

"Right then, which one of you blithering idiots wants to own up for this little 'pearler' of an idea then?!"

Once more the boffins were stood at the urinals.

"Did you read in the Times, that the bally cavalry were sat on their arses again at the Somme?" asked one of the other.

"Oh yeah, they're lazy bastards all right!" replied the other guy, buttoning up his fly.

"What do you say we come up with something that'll really fuck up the cavalry's brains?" queried the first guy, wiping his hands on his trousers.

"Like what, for example, a fast tank?" asked his chum.

"God, but you are full of absolutely fantastic bloody ideas!" enthused the first guy.

Off they went and started to beaver away at their drawing tables. In due course one stood up from his work. He grabbed the other fellow by the arm, pointing at his drawing and said, "Here James, take a look a look at this!"

James, confused, said, "Oh all right, if I must, whip it out then!"

The colleague, also confused now exploded, "WHIPPET! Fuck me how do you think up these names? It's perfect for this tank... fast as a whippet!" He slapped his pal, who was hurriedly re-buttoning his fly, hard on the back.

"Bollocks, I thought my luck was in!" James' mumbled.

So the Medium A. 'Whippet' was born, armed with three machine guns and a top speed faster than a man could run, it was soon seen running 'rampant' around the battlefields. The advent of these tanks created something of a race. The different nations involved in this conflict, not to be outdone by either friend or foe, were busy concocting their own designs. The French came up with vehicles such as the St. Chamond and the Schneider. The Germans spent most of the time repainting captured British tanks and throwing them back into the fray. But eventually they too came up with an example of Teutonic might in the shape of the A7V. This was a monster of a vehicle, cramming every available inch of space with a huge crew of eighteen men, it sallied forth into the maelstrom. Its future did not bode well, its huge bulk and slow speed made it vulnerable and unreliable. In fact an infantryman with body armour and a peashooter would have achieved more success. Looking at this machine, nobody could have possibly foreseen the massive impact that Germany would, in the future, have on tank design and tactics!

During the latter stages even the Americans, 'never one to be out done' had a crack at designing and building Tanks. They mainly copied our designs but, they were bigger of course! The war ended in 1918 with a bit of a fizzle, with it the tank race petered out too. As I've already explained, the Cavalry were now to be found at the War Office plotting the demise of, " Those fucking upstarts in the tank Corps!" even though the King intervened, the huge financial burden levied on the nation meant that our two friendly boffins were, 'put on the backburner'.

What of Germany? Well, the German army felt that they had been stabbed in the back by their politicians. "Ready to stop fighting the stinking Tommies?" Said a General one evening. "I should think not!" He continued while topping up his and his companions schnapps glasses. His companion, a disenchanted government official said; "What were we doing? The bastards had the Panzers, und we sat with unser thumbs up unser arsches! I will never let this happen again!"

The General responded with; "Fuck the world, we will schau them! What we need now ist a complete shit to lead uns to world domination!" Listening outside the door stood a diminutive greasy looking fellow, his hair a black oily slick swept over one eye, his moustache, now smaller in size since the shaving accident, a toothbrush sized bush under his nose. His name? Oh do come on! Adolph Hitler of course! He sneered; "Oh yes, we will show the world what a twat I can be!" In that instant the world's future was being re-written.

"Don't worry muffin -
those damn fools won't get me
to trade you in my sweet!!"

Now, under the terms of the Versailles treaty the allies had sought to ensure that Germany, would never be able to muster enough military might to once more become a threat. In theory this was great, in reality it had holes in it big enough to, strangely enough, drive a tank through! Hitler's rise to stardom brought with it money for armaments. His 'build agricultural tractors' in Sweden policy should have had us screaming in the stalls! After all, we got the damn ideas from tractors! But did it ring alarm bells? Did it hell. War? Unthinkable in the average British mind of the late 20's and 30's. Our men were back home, what was left of them! So, who wanted another war? Not the stupid Hun, we'd right royally whipped their arses in 1918, they wouldn't be stupid enough to start another one, would they?

It was this totally ignorant and blasé attitude in Britain that ruled the roost. Oh yes everyone acknowledged what an important part the tanks had played 'except the cavalry' of course. But now was a time for singing and dancing and long may it continue. If only it had, who knows what the modern world would now be like? British tank designers and builders such as Vickers were scratching their heads. James and Frederick, our two WW1 designers were now working for Vickers, their time at the W.O had come to an end.

"Ha....zee allies von't know vhat hit zem and, even if vee do not conquer zee vorld, imagine vhat a huge farm vee can have!!!!"

One morning while in the toilet James turned to Fred and said, "I've come up with a whizzo idea for a new Tank, it's got one turret and two engines giving it a top speed of forty mph!" "How big's the gun?" Enquired Fred. "It's a 20inch supplemented by two MG's!" Replied James. "Well, you can forget that as a fucking idea then, can't you, the bosses these days are only looking at designs which have a minimum of three turrets, a peashooter being in each one as a gun, an engine driving the tank at 15mph maximum and NO fucking machine guns!" Came the response from Fred. Having finished at the urinals they stood facing each other pondering, eventually Fred said; "James, put your fucking dick away!" James did as asked and they left. "Bollocks!" Mumbled James.. "Thought my luck was in!"

So it was that between the wars we as a nation fell behind in the race which was continuing, unchecked, behind the scenes. We even fell behind in the tactical race, even though our great minds such as Swinton were advocating the shape of things to come. As usual the Germans, in the shape of Generals such as Guderian, were stealing our ideas and seeing how they could fit in with their plans. We were playing on Salisbury plain with great ideas such as radio communication and inter-arm co-operation. The Germans on the other hand, were taking these same ideas and fully integrating them at an alarming speed. We were churning out a bewildering array of different tank types. We had everything from small two man, Carden 'Tankettes' through light and medium tanks to heavy and even heavier Tanks.

But all were a combination of moderately protected, poorly powered and dreadfully armed vehicles. Our design principles said that the size of the gun is governed by the size of the turret. But we were reluctant to build bigger tanks to facilitate the larger weapons required for effective shooting of other Tanks. We seemed to concentrate on 'Infantry support' Tanks, forgetting the possibility of 'Tank versus Tank' combat. Anyway, nobody had anything 'that we knew about' to beat us. Of course as the German military build up became blindingly obvious, peoples ideas changed somewhat. Suddenly Fred and James' life became quite frantic. One morning at the urinals, Fred said to James; "Hells a poppin', I've been told to build something that works! What shall I do?" James instantly replied; "Me too, I've come up with the idea of armour plating an Austin seven sticking a 2 pounder out the front and calling it a 'matilda'!" he said. "Fucking good idea James, and you're so full of them too!"responded Fred. "I think I love you!" Crooned James to Fred, but it was too late, the toilet's swing door was already settling into the doorjamb.

'Matilda' was born as a Tank, but it certainly wasn't based on an Austin Seven, it was a thickly armoured Infantry type Tank. It was impervious to all but the biggest German guns. The Germans actually quite admired it when eventually they came up against it. But as usual, its design was not conceived with tank combat in mind. When Britain declared war on Germany in 1939, it found itself faced with some stark truths. Firstly our tank force was woefully under strength for the task ahead. Secondly, our tanks themselves, with a couple of exceptions were, very inadequate for their allotted jobs. Our tactics were fairly well practised but, not as modern or effective as the German 'Blitzkrieg' doctrine. So here we were with our inadequate armour being hurriedly shipped abroad as part of the BEF, to France and to face the advancing, well equipped German army. The history books do say that the German army was possibly not as well equipped as the common belief says. I know it relied still, on large quantities of horse drawn power but, the spearhead, which after all counted most, was mechanised. The British army was deposited into a nearly hopeless attempt to halt the German flow.

3RTR was thrown across the channel at short notice with its tanks but with very little or, no ammo. Once our Regiment found its way out into the open countryside, due to confusion in the BEF command structure, it found itself isolated and unsure of what was happening. Never the less, once the decision was taken to evacuate the BEF, 3RTR distinguished itself by stemming the German advance, at great sacrifice to itself, and protecting Calais to allow evacuation. The remnants of the Regiment managed to just escape capture leaving its broken tanks and equipment strewn across the French countryside.

Throughout WW2 the design leaders remained, the Germans with their vast industrial might. The Russians though, had surprised the Germans when, the Blitzkrieg had run into the outstanding Soviet T34 Tank. This was designed to incorporate all the best features of the Tank. It was fast, well armoured and packed a sufficiently potent punch to be able to stop the average German Panzer in its tracks. What's more, it was simple to build and operate, cheap to build and very reliable. When one considers the vast logistical problems involved with the size of Russia, the tank was ideal. The Germans quickly realised that they now faced a problem large enough to make them think again. The answer? Capture a T34, ship it to Germany and let the boffins take a look. One day at the Krupps factory, stood two scientists, Jan and Friederich, at a urinal. " Shit, but ze T34 ve haf ist damn goot!" Exclaimed Jan. "Ja, but ve vill make somethink tvice as gut!" retorted Friedrich. He continued; "It cannot be so very difficult as, ze T34 vas built by stupid communistisch scum!" "But, it can be crewed by ze vomen!" explained Jan. "Ha, who needs ze fucking vomen!" Sneered Friedrich as he did up his trousers. Jan immediately said; "Ja, I agree, who needs ze fucking vomen, Friedrich I zink I luf you!" But as he turned it was too late,

Friedrich had left, the toilets swinging door already settling in the doorjamb. "Shiiiit!" Was Jan's only comment.

But in due course the Germans produced the 'Panther' and its big brother 'King Tiger' to beat the crap out of anything that got in the way, thereby joining the already successful 'Tiger 1'. Industrial attrition would eventually bring Germany to its knees. It was great having the best tanks in the world but, you need steel and an economy to build them, and oil, fuel and ammunition to run them. So even though they were the best tanks of their era, hammering forth and conquering all, there were, in the end, simply not enough of them to alter the course of the war. This was also combined with the Germans knack of 'over engineering' everything they touched. They had missed the fact that the T34 was simplicity itself. Consequently both the Panther and King Tiger were slow and expensive to build. I would argue that without doubt, Panther was the outstanding tank of WW2. Had it been built alone and without a confused Hitler prevaricating about also building King Tiger, it could possibly have turned the war around, if produced in large enough quantities! But it was not to be, and the war's outcome is confined to the history books. And thank god it ended in our favour!

Britain during the war, had frantically been trying to redress the balance. Relying on the lend-lease Tanks, such as the Sherman, from America, it was desperate to prove it could build a successful Tank. The odds however were not in our favour. The war thus far had taken its toll on our great nation. Some designs in the 'Cruiser' class had met with limited success but, also with their share of disaster. Later in the war having learnt lessons against the German Afrika Korps in the desert struggle. We seemed to pull back a little, but still a big failing was our lack of sufficient firepower. Not until we retro fitted the Sherman tank with a larger gun, renaming it 'The firefly', could we attempt to take on the 'Tiger' threat with any chance of winning! By the end of the war we had designed some fairly successful Tanks, the 'Cromwell' and 'Comet' being two noteworthy examples. The Comet actually served into, I believe the early 80's with the Irish army.

By 1945 Britain, having got its act together, had laid down plans for what was to be Centurion. This tank would prove to be the mainstay of our Royal Armoured Corps until the early to mid sixties. Its reliability and effectiveness becoming the benchmark for the other nations of the world. Too late for service in WW2 it was to prove itself in Korea and conflicts around the world, especially as it was bought by many nations, Israel having been a particular fan. Building on its reputation, Britain in due course decided to modernise and commissioned Chieftain which, even though it was dogged with many problems. The concept of a Main Battle tank came about as, even during Centurions era, we had experimented with heavy tank technology in the form of Conqueror, which was not a great success. So it was simple, one main tank with other tasks being carried out by 'specific to task' vehicles.

I have during the course of this book, highlighted some of Chieftains problems. But I don't wish to be unfair to what was essentially, 'not a bad old bus'. Its problems really only concerned its ability to move from A to B in a military fashion i.e. without breaking down. It always seemed unfair to us that, so much emphasis had been placed on its various systems but not enough on it's mobility. Fine I understand that our doctrine was based more on 'stay and fight'. But to stay we first had to get to where we were meant to be staying! Once there the fire control system was superb and, we were led to believe that our protection was second to none. But a chilling thought was that when boffins talk about 'survivability' they mean the weapons platform and not the crew inside. We knew we could sit and hit targets at ranges way in excess of our potential Soviet foes maximum range.

We knew also that Russian tank crewmen were recruited, at a maximum height of 5' 3". We also knew that Russian vehicles that were fitted with Auto-Loaders were unreliable as the machinery couldn't differentiate between the ammunition and the commanders forearm! Of course, the other thing we knew was that the Soviets had a lot of Tanks, so many in fact that we would have to kill four of theirs before we ourselves were killed. On the bright side we had also learnt that Russian tank crews had a propensity for drinking their vehicles' anti-freeze which was alcohol based!

So in the 1970's the world's status quo in the tank stakes was fairly even. Britain's Chieftain with its technical advances was mechanically, less than reliable but, fantastic at all the other arts of tank virtue, it's gun could hit a gnat at 3500 metres using its computerised fire control equipment, its armour was deemed impervious to all known types of ammunition and it's crews were the best in the world. Germany's Leopard 1 was adequate in protection, punchy in its firepower(the tried and tested British 105mm gun) and supremely efficient in its mobility, but only because it was the lightest tank of its type. American tanks came in a vast array of types and sizes but, their mainstay Tank, the M60 was mechanically questionable and the tank in general was undergoing massive refits to modernise its technology.

Israel with all its experience of relatively modern tank warfare in the middle east had been very busy. I feel that it is easy to forget the Israeli's and their contribution to tank warfare. At this time they were operating British Centurions but, decided to fit more efficient diesel powered units. They had modified the American Sherman into what became the 'Super Sherman'. They also used the Americans M60 and older M48. So as can be seen, Israel was invaluable in testing various designs from different countries and through battlefield experience, modifying the vehicles to optimise their salient features.

But, in a urinal somewhere in Israel, stood two boffins. The first looked at his colleague and said; "David I'm a bit pissed off with sorting out the cock ups of the other countries tank designers!" David replied, "Samuel, I know exactly what you mean, but what can we do? Design our own?" "Shit, David! Of course we could, We'll nick all the best bits off the ones we have and combine them in ours'!" Samuel excitedly replied and then continued; "we'll change bits round so they don't guess what we've done, like, putting the engine in the front instead of the back. Then in the back we'll put a compartment for carrying Infantry or wounded". David now chirped; "but what'll we call it, all the good names and numbers have been used already!" Samuel now pondered and then; "I know! we'll call it Merkava, the thick Westerners won't know it simply means Chariot!" David turned and said "Samuel, do you know how much I've always loved you?" It was too late, as the toilet door had already shut as Samuel rushed down the corridor, pencil in hand. "Bugger!" Was David's only comment. Thus the concept of Israel's MBT was born, and a very successful tank it is too!

The seventies passed, the eighties dropped onto the tank world like.. a big... dropping thing! Bang! The tank race took off again. It was started by NATO's German, British and American members joining together to develop a joint tank project. However the project was unsuccessful, apparently everybody concerned felt their own bits were best. The project broke up, each country taking their technology with them.

Britain then cruised for awhile until; the Germans launched Leopard 2, shortly followed by the Americans with their M1 Abrams.

At the MOD alarm bells rang. Boffins were seen running in every direction, buttoning their flies and departing hurriedly from the toilets, cries of "Bugger!" screaming through the air. As a throng gathered in the meeting room someone said; "What the fuck is going on?" The reply came loud and clear, "The fucking Yanks and Krauts have got the drop on us, brought out new tanks haven't they, the bastards!" "Bollocks!" chorused the gathered crowd. "What will we fucking do now?" Asked a guy with fifteen pencils balanced behind one of his ears. Another studious looking chap had been rubbing his chin in thought, then he looked up and said; "Well, we could be sneaky! Iran is, as we know a fuck up! But before the Shah was kicked out he paid us to develop that.. what's its name.... ah yes... the Shir Tank. I know there's a job lot of them laying around somewhere!" "Yes! In Leeds!" Interjected someone else. The government 'think tank' now buzzed with excitement, many suggestions flying around the room. Eventually one chap jumped up on the table top and calling for silence, made a statement; "We'll take the Shir and put Chieftains gun kit in the turret, change the number plates, make a few other modifications, paint it green and black and give it a name! What name though? Anyone need a piss?" When the crowd returned from the urinals, a name had been chosen, after much toilet debate and unheard declarations of love for each other. The name? Oh yes, Challenger of course!

The Challenger is without doubt the best British tank ever. It has achieved (not without problems), the nearest balance of characteristics in any British tank to date (I can't comment on Challenger 2), the Chieftain's steel being replaced by Chobham composite armour, Horstman suspension being superseded by Hydrogas suspension units and the BL L60 at last in the bin, the engine now being a thoroughbred Rolls Royce CV12 turbocharged power pack. Of course as I mentioned, the gun control equipment came from Chieftain, in which it had been great. But it had been designed for an MBT that on roads, was pushing it to get to 30mph. The gun's stabiliser had only to cope with around 20mph during travel 'cross country'; now it sat like a malignant growth in a 'new generation' MBT which could achieve around 30mph over bumpy terrain! The result was a mismatch of technology, which I'm glad to say has been rectified.

The engine and gearbox could now be replaced in well under an hour in battlefield conditions. This is a far cry from Chieftains cumbersome procedures for repairs. But, Chieftain was not yet dead! There was not enough money nor Challengers to replace the Chieftains in service! So back in the MOD toilets, someone came up with the cracking idea of retro fitting the remaining Chieftains with 'Stillbrew' supplementary armour. The first time I saw this I laughed. The front of the turret looked as if a YTS welding team had spot welded a huge metal bulge to the front of the turret. Oh dear, not the best of ideas!

Both Challenger and the 'Stillbrew' Chieftains were fitted with TOGS (Thermal Observation Gunnery System), now the commander and gunner had TV monitors through which to view the world and its targets. The Thermal sight head was able to read the ambient temperatures of its surroundings building a perfect black and white effect picture in the monitors! This system is impervious to all weathers, darkness, smoke and in some instances the terrain. A vehicle or persons, heat glows like a neon light on the screen. The accuracy of the picture enabling the crew to recognise a comrades or enemies face in the dark at immense distances. Warfare now is no longer dawn to dusk in a Tank, it is literally 24/7 (as the modern terminology expresses it!). This places more strain on the already exhausted men who man our tanks.

The future? Its now 2056, a shout goes out in the halls of the Department of Earth Defence, Whitehall, London; "Bloody fuck, the Saturnians have got a new Tank!" the reply echoes in the corridor; "Anyone need a piss?" Running footsteps are heard on the polished floor!

32. The Yanks are yanking their chains?

I've separated the American art of tank design into this, it's own chapter as they've made so damn many tanks, and, as with all things American – always bigger and better.

As the First World War rolled towards it's inevitable end. The war had attempted to drain the last of Europe's youth in the blood baths of the Western front, suddenly and quite unexpectedly, the Americans took an interest.

For a year or so they'd been watching as the first tanks lumbered through the morass of mud guiding the poor infantry onto their objectives with more than a fair chance of survival. Suddenly in Washington a little known group of 'project development analysts' sat bolt upright and exclaimed, as one, "sheeeee..it boy!"

They glared at each other and one chap shouted.. "If the president is gonna send our boys over there, they'll need some sorta protection!

Otherwise, chickadee chickadoo, our boys'll be comin a home in coffins!" Another analyst now chirped in… "that'll not be good for the president's re-election, we's a better be doin' somethin about this situation!"

They now pulled out various newspapers and sat idly reading and 'chawin baccy' the only sound being an occasional hiss followed by a ding as tobacco laden spittle shot from between their teeth into strategically placed spitoons around the seating area. One man suddenly looked up and said… "I know, we'll round up a bunch of reds off a reservation and send them over first! They'll soften up the hun and our gallant boys'll have a walkover after them!" This was met by disapproving 'tuts' and a flurry of hisses and dings! "hey boy" whispered a colleague to the outspoken racist… "they'll be votin before ya knows it… the president has to think in the future ya knows! Anyhows the limeys and frogs have been doin that for ages now so it's gonna be easier for us no matter what!"

One chap who, instead of chewing tobacco, sat pondering the New York Times while chewing his smouldering cheroot suddenly sat up and cleared his throat. "Hrrrmmmmpppphhhhh, hey boys I think our answer just came over the hill!" He now folded his broadsheet and turned it so all could see the picture he'd been studying. There, in all it's magnificence was a Mk V male pounding down on a trenchline with guns blazing. The reader continued.."Heyll's a poppin boys, we's gotta get us one of these... then we'll copy it and just make the sucka bigger!"

Everybody became most animated now jumping up and down hugging each other and dribbling tobacco stained saliva down the backs of each other's coats in their excitement. One chap even wondered whether anyone would care to join him at a urinal... "What boy?!" Came the response in unison... "you think we's are all homo-sexuells boy?!" And with that, as one they all jumped the poor unfortunate and beat the hell out of him.

So in due course the Yanks arrived in the hell of the Western front being led by their brand new tanks and yes they were... well, a bit bigger but, no better. Either way, the Americans came to Europe and in their parlance... "Beat the sheeeit out of them jerries!"

So, rid of the German threat of world domination and having ensured that 'Weeners' would keep coming from Germany for centuries in the future the American wave receded back stateside and once more the great eagle rested and watched the world.

One day however there was a 'future prospect of war, senior boffin armoured technology project development analyst' by the name of Christie who was reading a magazine about German politics. "Sheeeit on a stick!" he suddenly exclaimed jumping from his seat and running out of his office. He ran to the 'thinktank analysts room' down the corridor and smashed open the door. "Boys, we got us a problemmmm" he announced. "In this magazine it says Germany is building tractors in Sweden!" One brave bloke having cleared his mouth of mint flavoured 'chawin baccy' spittle enquired... "hey heiny so what's the big deal? The Versailles treaty only screwed up the Boche economy so they couldn't have an army or navy, NOT so's they couldn't do a little farming!"

Christie now continued, "No Chuck, this little feller Hitler is hiding something, probably tanks! I can a feel it in ma water, anyone wanna come to the urinals and check it out?" he now almost died in the face of the fists, boots and spittle accompanied by shouts of "hey ya fuckin queerboy leave us alone!" from his paranoid colleagues.

However in due course Christie got to play with his own design of tank. He was particularly interested in suspension systems having examined the dreadful systems employed in WW1. He was convinced that better suspension would increase mobility and higher speeds. So was born Christie suspension. It was radical and lo, he was right, it did the job very nicely. Suddenly tanks could achieve speeds which would raise expectations of shock action like the cavalry had once enjoyed. The American War Department? Oh yes they came to have a look and were even quite impressed then said, as they walked away... "YEAH Christie, we'll think about it, there's a good boy!" and strolled off spitting left and right in a most haphazard fashion covering the poor coloured cotton pickers as they toiled in the adjacent fields!

From seemingly that point on, America threw itself into designing and building a massive array of tank designs, the forecourt competition becoming as confusing as the automotive industry which built the huge and confusing variety of cars in an attempt to keep up with Mr Ford.

THEN... 1939 and WWWWOOOOOMMMMMMM-PPPPPP-HHHHHHH! Up went Europe again, in a cloud of smoke and belching explosions all over it's land mass.

In Washington meanwhile the President was addressing his defence chiefs... "Okay boys, this will not, I repeat, will fucking NOT become an American fucking war! But... just in case it does... we'll give the Limeys a few weapons on like a hire purchase scheme. That way we're trading for money... theoretically but... really we're helping them soften the naaaazi's ready for if we have to go (he broke briefly into song) 'over there, over there..oh the Yanks are comin the Yanks are comin' aaahhh that song brings back such memories"... "Mr President?" interjected one of the Generals. "Oh yes Walt, sorry I was just somewhere else a moment,... where was I? Oh yes... send some tanks and planes... not good ones mind just cheap crap so's it looks good but is about as much use as tits on a flatfish... okay y' all?" The response was unanimous... "Sure is Mr President crap it certainly will be, and it's on it's way!"

So with no more to do, the mighty American armaments industry swung into action and spewed forth tanks in their hundreds and in their thousands and.... they all headed towards blighty... almost like a potato blight. The British of course were really chuffed to see all these strange machines landing on the docks. Why? You ask, well, in general terms because Britain had fuck all tanks left, just about everything the British Army had was languishing, courtesy of the British Expeditionary Force, all over the French countryside after Dunkirk. In fact the Germans were busy turning most of it into novelty barbeques, or so rumour had it!

Either way, with Britain's armaments industry struggling and their tank designers having difficulty with the concept of guns bigger than peashooters, the Brits were mighty glad of these things looking like tanks and even having guns on them.

In the desert war against Hitler's Afrika Korps, some American designs even became popular with the crews, a light tank, the Stuart, even got nicknamed 'Honey' by a member of 3RTR, the name stuck as the tank was so popular. It didn't seem to matter that a shot from a German infanteer's rifle could almost open one up like a tin of 'bully beef'. Nor did it matter that it's fuel consumption alone would, in peacetime have altered an entire nation's economy. No, it was brilliant. The vaunted Sherman also became quite popular, even though Germans nicknamed them, between huge guffaws 'Tommy cookers' and even the Americans called them 'zippos' due to their propensity to catch fire... almost instantly, when hit, roasting the unfortunate crews to their deaths. At this point Britain was becoming wary, the Sherman's gun? "That may need to be a tad bigger to take on a Tiger!" said one Brit boffin and, upgunned by the Brits it was, to make a version called the 'firefly'. An apt name because against a King Tiger it would have been exactly like a firefly jabbing its blazing butt up against an elephants arse... ineffectually. Only when a bunch of Fireflys, a few Shermans, 2 tons of plastic explosive and a minefield and a demolition crew ganged up could a King Tiger really get stung.

Sure enough, one morning in Down Scratchett, a small Wiltshire Hamlet, the tromp of boots accompanied by a rousing chorus of "the Yanks are coming" announced the arrival of America's finest into World War Two closely followed by male screams of "lock up your daughters or there'll be a baby boom and we ain't got enough to feed ourselves let alone anyone else and... don't think you can survive on nylons.

Cigarettes and chewing gum!" From this point on though there were plenty of women who thought you could survive on those essentials.

The entry had also been hastened by the fact that Japan had pasted the American Pacific fleet at Pearl Harbour. Now that meant an all out assault on Emperor Hirohito's ally... Adolph Hitler.

In Washington, the 'there really is now a real prospect of war, senior boffin armoured technology project development analyst' department went into overdrive, spittle flew everywhere, one scared guy shouted above the others... " Fuck boys we've been caught sleepin on ma's porch here! Now our boys are over there fighting in the scrap we sent the Limeys! What are we going to do?" "Fuck 'em" came a bourbon soaked reply from a red faced sot laid back in a leather recliner, evidence of his mastery of spit trajectory laying round him on the floor, a whisky glass on his chest. He drawled on... "who gives a sheeeeit? I don't! We always think of something and I'm sure we will now... " He now passed out leaving the others to continue their in consternation over the vexing problem of what they would do about their tanks.

Meanwhile, back at the ranch where, Tonto disguised as a door, got his knob shot off! D Day was in full swing, all sorts of crap was going on, tanks carrying snorkels and massive skirts, behaving like boats and all sorts. Brave job they did too, in fact D Day was a costly but valuable victory. Most Allied tank crews however, as they came off the beach, met Herr Achtung Panzer and his rolling storm of armoured death and destruction. The only thing heard coming from behind the closed door in Washington was... "We's right in the sheeeeit now guys!"

But in the end the allies biggest winning factor over the Germans was moral courage, stalwart determination, the crumbling and inadequate German armament industry and a shit load of fighter bombers to support the swarming mass of tanks and other vehicles crawling over Europe towards Berlin like an army of ants. The Americans always said, "they's don't have to be great just build sheeeeit loads of 'em!"

So the Second World War took it's place in history. The world looked forward to a more peaceful future. America, decided that, it should however, remain in touch with the tank race. It had improved it's designs with examples such as the Pershing, okay it was the size of an aircraft carrier but only so it would be 'bigger and better' than anything else.

One morning the door to the office of the 'there really was a real prospect of war and we won it anyway but there won't be another, armoured technology project development analysts' burst open with such force that it caused a massive involuntary multiple hiss and ear bending DINGGGGGGG as 20 mouths spat huge wads of brown spittle across the room. An excited chap rushed in and asked all assembled "Boys, you heard we've gone into Korea!" "Sheeeeit!" was the chorus that greeted him, a lone voice continuing... "what'd we go and do that for?"

"Anybody need the lavatory?" came a voice at this moment. "Find that bastard and pile on!" came a shout as the poor unfortunate disappeared under the mass of flailing arms and even the odd chair as it crashed down amid screams of "queer" and "faggott".

They got away with Korea without having to do much development as technically the war didn't last too long and Britain with it's mighty Centurion stood solidly at America's side pounding the enemy with shot and HE. America's foreign policy has, since then, been build em and then build some more. Since the 60's they have however, calmed slightly choosing to build slightly less variety and more of one type. The world has now seen the M48 and M60 both also having been exported round the world. Then, up with the ill fated MBT 80 project between the NATO powers including Uncle Sam, unfortunately he couldn't make the appointment so the 'there really was a real war or two, we won anyway so there won't be another war... yet... but that doesn't matter cos we don't give a damn armoured technology project development analysts' department made the appointment, then everybody fell out with each other and, hoped, as they ran away, that the bits they'd stolen were the best bits.

The Germans and the Americans quite quickly developed and launched the Leopard 2 and M1 Abrams respectively and built them almost at the same time. In Washington, Chuck was putting together (spitting ferociously) a plan on how to beat 'the hun' to first tank produced. Someone however pointed out a slight problem... "Chuck, the fuckin gun is still the one off the Limey's centurion... it's small and old. The Germans are sticking a 120mm smoothbore gun on this Leopard and it then outguns the sheeeeeit out of us!" "It's okay Ricky" replied Chuck then continued... "I've got it all worked out! We'll wait till we get a good idea of what it's like then... steal the fucking plans then say we had it all along after that stinking MBT 80 project!"

He then added, the engine's gonna be sheeeeit hot on the M1 cos I've made it from a jet engine!" Ricky now chirped up "Fuck man, it'll drink so much gas it won't be cost effective!" Chuck was however, undaunted... "Sheeeeit, not a fucking problem pal, we'll arrange to invade Kuwait or Iraq, cap their oil wells, syphon off and no American will complain, their gas prices will be so darned cheap they wouldn't dare, you can suck my dick if it ain't so!"

Chuck was, shortly afterwards, found dead in the toilets, he displayed strange marks on his body that looked as if he'd been beaten to death by a mob. The only clue to be found was, daubed in red paint across his back, the word... FAG!

Soon after, one day the tanks moved swiftly into Kuwait!...

33. Go on, drive it then!

What's it like to drive a Tank? or, were you a tank driver then? These have got to be the most common questions I have, over the years, been asked. The answers are simply, Great and yes!

To become a tank driver is not as simple as books would have you believe. Sure, the manuals and military sales 'blurb' will tell the casual observer that, 'it takes only a few hours for a driver to become proficient!' But of course that's not the entire story. I agree it doesn't take long to learn how to accelerate, change gear, steer, brake and stop. But, as with everything there is an art to driving a tank that only time and experience can teach you.

'Tommo' redressing after prepping for a 'pack lift'.

Firstly, Accelerating and gear changing on Chieftain came hand in hand. If a driver accelerated and changed up through the gears too fast, the resulting mess could be considerable! The crew may suffer whiplash their necks snapping under the ferocious bucking of the tank as the gears were selected by the driver at maximum revs, in an attempt to pick up speed more rapidly. Also the turret crew could get badly scalded if the operator was finishing making a brew as the tank got underway. Changing down through the gears could be equally damaging.

Chieftain's gearbox was fitted with a governor, this controlled which gear could be selected at what revs. Therefore if a driver tried to change down with the revs too high, the governor would reject the driver's selection. A fine device when it worked! And considering that most experienced drivers disconnected it to enable them to have more control of the gears it was in fact, as good as useless. So the consequence could be, a driver changing down too quickly had the effect of suddenly stopping the tank on each gearchange. This could cause:

1. The operator to fly to the front of the turret interior bashing his body on the breech and other projections, probably spilling hot tea on himself in the process.

2. The Gunner to jolt his head forward against his sight, causing 'cap badge head', this being the imprint of his cap badge left in his forehead as it smashed into the sight. He may also spill a cup of scalding tea in his lap if he has just been passed it by the operator.

3. The commander to smash his head on the cupola breaking his nose, then spilling hot tea over his own crotch and the gunners head.

4. The driver to get a pain in the side of his head when the irrate commander had regained his senses, leapt out of his hatch, ran down the front of the turret holding onto his MG for support and kicking the driver in the side of the head!

Acceleration was therefore advised to be; accelerate, foot off the gas, change up, accelerate. This being as smooth and fast through the first three gears. Then building the revs higher and longer to facilitate a smooth transition through the top three gears. Changing down was; watch your revs, 'blipping' the accelerator a second before changing down a gear. The 'blip' raised the revs slightly and smoothed the change, or at least it did for experienced drivers.

Next, steering. We have already seen, through the 'in the house' incident what problems steering can cause. Chieftain had an 'epicyclic' gearbox. The design of this type of gearbox came from the American team of Merrit &Wilson. I don't know the exact details but the story I heard is this:

When the gearbox was designed and subsequently fitted to its first tank it showed a strange characteristic. If the driver selected no gear, but stayed in neutral, revved the engine and pulled on a steering tiller, the tank performed a 'neutral' or 'pivot' turn. This meant that one track moved backwards, the other moving forwards. The tank subsequently turned 360 degrees within its own length. Though not designed to do this, it has become an ultra useful feature, incorporated in all modern tanks. The designer of the gearbox apparently, tried to fathom out how his gearbox performed this feat, driving himself insane and subsequently into an asylum. I don't know if this is true or not but, I do know that no Driving and Maintenance Instructor, including my pal Lucy, could explain how it worked! As I've said earlier in the book, the system operated hydraulically, if the system wasn't functioning properly for example due to air locks in the pipe, the driver would be exerting even more pressure to the already heavy task of steering.

Braking and stopping was something of a chore. In front of the driver was the biggest brake pedal I've ever seen. One foot could have an effect but, more often than not, both feet would be needed for a relatively speedy response. Bringing over fifty tons to a fast halt as such, was nigh on impossible. Only with both feet and some nifty gear changing could the desired result be achieved. Once stopped, if required, you can apply the handbrake, this huge lever was connected to the brake callipers in the decks by a ratchet chain being 'cranked' on, pulling cables and through them the main brake pads onto the discs. There was a specified amount of pulls laid down as being the 'correct' adjustment for the handbrake. I can't remember any two tanks having the same amount of 'pulls' on the lever!

When I was learning to drive Chieftain at Tidworth I remember 'night driving' late one night on Salisbury Plain. Our instructor was my pal Dave 'Dai' Marsh. Suddenly, over the radio we received a message from our partner tank nearby. It had found a car parked next to one of the numerous tank crossing points across the main road that cut across our training area.

We pulled over to where our chums were. Dai dismounted and chatted to the other instructor. He then dashed back and resumed his position in the commanders hatch. He informed us that the car we could see (a Morris Marina, of all things) half-hidden behind a bush had a 'shagging couple' in it.

Well, that was it. How dare a pair go out, probably to a pub first, then stop off for a shag near where we were busy working?

Dai reached down and switched on the searchlight power controls. He opened the armoured cover of the searchlight, exposing the infra red filter. Therefore the 'white light' was not yet exposed. He now instructed the student in the gunner's seat to aim the main armament at the unsuspecting Morris. As we were doing this, the other panzer was doing the same. Then, after a radio countdown, both tanks swung open the IR Filter and…WHAM!

The Morris was lit up as if it were daylight, about 2 million candlepower of light ruining the lovers tryst. At the same time, Dai told me to move towards the car, revving the arse off the main engine. The other wagon followed suit and, even through the heavy condensation on the car's windscreen, we could clearly see, two white faces appear from behind the front seats. We were, by now, laughing like bloody drains. A shape fell over the front seat as the driver scrambled to start up and bugger off…pronto! The Morris coughed into life and expelled a huge pall of blue exhaust smoke as it exited onto the road in a fast but haphazard fashion.

When Dai and I chat today we still laugh about it.

Once a driver has mastered the skills involved with making the tank into a moving masterpiece, he must learn the other skills. He must learn how to maintain the vehicle and that includes not only the engines and gearbox, but also the 'running gear' namely tracks and suspension. This was taught to him on his Driving and maintenance course (D&M). The British policy on D&M has always been that a driver must know his vehicle inside and out. This is due to the fact that, in war you can bet your pants that when you need REME help, they wouldn't be available. So running repairs or 'bodges' in time of need could, and were carried out by the Tank's crew. Chieftain was classed as a 'dirty' Tank, crews returning from the tank park invariably looking like they'd completed a shift 'down't pit!' Replacing various parts as they needed replacing was an every day event for drivers. Steering brake pads were a favourite of mine. It involved hanging upside down in the gearbox compartment, removing the pads' retaining cotter pins then, prising the worn pads from their seatings and replacing them. Now that doesn't sound too bad until, you have to do it after a long route march when the compartment is boiling hot. In these conditions everything you touch burns your exposed skin. What, under normal conditions would take an experienced driver around twenty five minutes to complete, now took about an hour! This delay during an exercise could be very frustrating. Many was the time when, a tank commander with his experience, having got frustrated with a new driver would bawl, "get out the fucking way, I'll do it myself!" One trick we employed was to replace the cotter pins with safety pins from the first aid kit, this helped a great deal when changing pads.

The commonly agreed worst job for the driver was, to undo the Twiflex coupling in preparation for an engine or gearbox lift (pack lift). This involved the driver lying under the back of the Tank. First he would have to remove the large steel access plate from the rear underside of the hull. This, when being supported by one hand while undoing the securing bolts, was a heavy burden for the drivers arm. Having removed this 'belly plate', the driver would normally get covered in oil which drained from the hulls interior straight down over his face! The oil was the residue of wasted oil as it was poured none to accurately into the engines or gearbox filler caps. Or it may be the oil from a leak, either way it would definitely be there, right in your face! Through this hole the driver could now start to remove the Twiflex bolts. I mentioned earlier that the Twiflex coupling is a form of clutch drum joining the engine to the gearbox. It was of a considerable size, so the driver could only reach two or maybe three bolts at a time. So as he removed the bolts, he would have to turn the drum. This was damned hard as, there was simply very little to purchase on! Knuckles would soon be bleeding and tempers lost! Once the REME arrived and removed the offending engine or gearbox the driver would now be prepared for the ensuing scrum in the back decks. This was the normal 'spanner scramble' which occurred as soon as the decks had a big enough gap in them. The floor of the engine compartment would be littered with much debris, among which would be spanners dropped by drivers and REME fitters alike over the period since the last engine removal. Having finished the scrum and applied plasters as applicable, and with having completed the repairs or unit replacement, you could look forward to... putting the Twiflex back together!

The infamous 'back decks'.

One story I do recall about D&M was something that happened on the tank park in Paderborn. Whilst in SHQ we had a new chap called Scrivens (scribbo) join us. One morning I gave him a task we all loathed. Part of the maintenance tasks on the 'running gear' was to grease the final drives behind each of the sprocket wheels that drive each track. We would get an 'oddy' pump(a bucket sized container with a lid and pump) drop a can of XG279 grease into the pumps' body, connect its hose to the sprocket and pump up and down like crazy. The idea was to fill the final drive 'labyrinth' with grease for lubrication. This could take ages to fill, especially if you were fresh from driving a long distance. We would keep pumping, our arms taking on Herculean proportions until, grease appeared through a gap at the sprockets rear. Now, Scribbo got this 'nig' task, he duly grabbed the pump, checked its weight and realised there was already grease in it. He then connected it and away he went, pumping like the very devil were after him! I, meanwhile went to the LAD to check on a repair. Some twenty minutes later I returned to our hangar. Scribbo was there, he'd a look on his face like he'd suffered a hernia. He was pushing hard on the pump handle but it wasn't budging, 'Come on, put your fucking back into it!" I encouraged him. "It's probably the labyrinth blocked with mud, keep going, it'll free off in a bit." And having told him this, I left him to it.

About thirty minutes later I returned; he was now holding on to the Tank's rear bin with both feet on the pump handle, jumping up and down. The pump handle still stayed frozen solid! "Bloody hell! What the fuck are you doing?" I enquired, his beetroot red face looked wide eyed at me and he puffed, "I've been doing this for fucking ages! I got five good pumps in at the start and since then, not a fucking thing!" I inspected the rear of the final drive and everything seemed okay, but no grease to be seen! I now turned my attention to the oddy pump. I took off the lid and realised something was instantly wrong. Removing the pot of grease, I found that someone had put a pot of PX7 (battery terminal) grease in to the pump. PX7 has the consistency of cheddar cheese! You can't even dip your hand in, you 'smear' grease from the top and wipe it on battery terminals! I said to the shamefaced 'Scribbo'; "Didn't you check it was the right grease!" "Er, no! I thought it must be right 'cos it's in the pump!" came the reply. A clip round the ear, right grease into pump, he then proceeded to actually grease the final drive. That night he looked not only physically 'buggered' but also very embarrassed.

Having mastered and passed his D&M course, the driver could now, during exercise, practise the 'field skills' involved in driving his beast.

Ground appreciation was of paramount importance, for the weapons to be aimed and fired correctly whilst on the move, the driver must be able to look for the best ground to travel over tactically. When sat in a fire position waiting to move forward the commander will identify the next point at which he wants to stop and observe the land to his front. This 'hopping' forward, vantage point to vantage point movement is termed 'bounding'. The commander having identified his next bound, will now order the driver to 'jockey'. 'Jockeying' is simply reversing the Tank, keeping the gun and turret facing the direction of the enemy, then when out of sight from the far side of the hill to his front, the driver slews the tank and then pulls forward and either, reappears around the side of the hill or, crosses the hill crest at a different point to the one from which the crew were observing the next bound. This 'jockeying' manoeuvre is a simple tank survival measure. If we can see an enemy or potential place where they may be, it's fair to assume that 'they' could see us. Any observing weapons would have been targeted, their operators simply waiting for the target to expose itself fully. Therefore 'jockeying' can gain vital seconds during which the enemy loses its point of aim. During these seconds a tank can escape and continue safely on its way.

As the commander now tells him to move off, the driver pulls forward, smoothly accelerating and changing up through the gearbox. So now, as he accelerates away and emerges from behind the protective hill, the commander will have pointed out, and the driver will have picked up, the objective through his sight and be heading for 'dead ground', i.e. ground through which he can drive with a minimal chance that an observing enemy, may be able to engage or even see the Tank. As the driver skilfully guides his tank through the ground to his front, above him the turret will be a hive of activity, over the IC the turret crew will be chattering, identifying potential targets as they 'scan' the surrounding landscape. The commander may order steering adjustments if he sees an obstacle from his vantage point which the driver low in his cab, has not yet seen. The driver, fully reclined in his seat, can feel every judder, bump and shockwave caused by the movement of the vehicle. His immediate sight is very limited through his sight window, its width is governed to the extremes of the front wings to his left and right, the height of vision is from the glacis plate above him to, the top of his sight window. His depth of vision is what counts, he is looking at the ground, some fifty to a hundred meters to his front and making decisions based on that. He attacks humps and dips, if unavoidable, by accelerating and slowing using just the accelerator if possible. This minimises the rocking and swaying motion as the obstacle is negotiated. So, even though the driver retains the far objective in mind he has in fact, made his own set of reference points through which he will pass to reach that objective.

As he approaches the objective the commander will, if required, hand control of the driver to the gunner. As explained in an earlier chapter, the gunner will now guide the driver into the required fire position. 'Hull down' means that the top of the turret containing the commanders and gunners sights would be exposed over the hilltop, the rest of the tank remaining out of sight. The commander may decide to go 'turret down' in which case he would control the drivers movement so that, not even the turret would become visible over the top of the hills crest. The commander would however, be able to observe the landscape to his front beyond the hill. If the tank were now to remain stationary for some time, the commander would periodically order the driver to 'jockey', adjusting the fire position and not letting the enemy get 'too good a fix' on the Tank.

My Chieftain 'Flying 42' in BATUS.

That then was driving a Chieftain, what of Challenger? I never had the opportunity to really drive a Challenger on exercise but, I certainly had the opportunity to drive one on the driver training area at Bovington camp. My short excursion certainly was an eye opener. To start with it had no foot operated gear change, instead it had a small gear selection lever on the drivers right side. You selected gears as ratios using a gate type box. So the ratios were, as I remember them, 1st, 1st to 2nd, 1st to 3rd and finally 1st to 4th which, on an automatic car's gearbox would have been 'drive'. The vehicle would pull away fairly sluggishly in first, none of Chieftains neck snapping acceleration here! Drivers soon found that, to improve acceleration, they could, select 1st, rev the shit out of the engine keeping their foot on the brake, and then at the appropriate moment, release the brake throwing the tank forward at an acceptable speed. It should be remembered that Challenger weighs nearly ten tons more than its predecessor so therefore acceleration wasn't going to be that of a Ferrari! But, once the beast was rolling, what performance! 'Chally' skimmed at high speeds effortlessly across terrain that, in a Chieftain would have had the crew knocked unconscious. This was mainly due to the excellent performance of the new hydrogas suspension units.

A Challenger 'skimming'.

This suspension was so good we likened it to 'in our imagination' Aladdin shooting through the air on a magic carpet. It certainly enabled Challenger to maximise the power contained in it's Rolls Royce power pack. Challenger certainly seemed to also be a 'clean' Tank. Okay so drivers still returned from the tank Park looking dirty and dishevelled, but in nowhere near the state that they had when working on Chieftain.

Drivers were always looked on as being slightly 'Maverick' in their outlook on life. Isolated in their cabs they could become somewhat 'distant' in their approach to life. Certainly in 9 Troop at Tidworth, 'Switches' was such a character, he once on exercise found a child's, discarded toy police motorcyclists plastic helmet. When we stopped during any exercise thereafter, his tank would pull up, the drivers hatch would spring open, and there would be 'Switches', helmet on head screaming "Beeeeeee Deeeeeeeb, in true UNFICYP style. Chris Trevers, his commander, found it amusing to start with but, over a prolonged period of time, would find it frustrating and proceed to launch heavy objects at 'Switches'. Mick 'Ribbo' Ribton too, displayed an alarming tendency to single-mindedness. At every opportunity 'Ribbo' would attempt to put his tank and crew to the extremes of their capabilities. 'Ribbo' was never a loud person preferring instead to show his feelings more with actions than words. So, if while driving in a wood, a tree got in his way… SMANG… end of tree. If he had a saying it was definitely more a case of "Don't get mad, get even!" My mate Lucy was another driver with attitude. He always had the knack of being able to con anybody into doing anything! He was known within the Squadron as the 'king of the jelly'. He was the salt of the earth type who, when asked to could; 'sell sand to an Arab!' Unless like me, you knew him well he would lead you astray. The problem being that he would remain the picture of innocence while he was doing it! He also had a knack of getting good postings, the most memorable being 18mths in Oman as an advisor to the Sultans tank forces. At the end of this he was duly awarded the Sultans service medal.. a shame as, this medal wasn't wearable on British uniform. Well, not until Lucy got back to our Regiment and he instigated letters to the MOD which resulted in British troops being allowed to wear this Omani honour! I can just imagine the halls of the MOD ringing to the sound of people asking; "What's a 'good jelly'?" and, "What in the name of God is 'a jelly head' when it's at home?"

But, when all is said and done, our drivers had an excellent sense of humour. They were superb at innovation, this of course being necessary given Chieftains unerring knack of breaking down at the wrong time and in the wrong place! We could never work out why they always broke down in the middle of nowhere. We could, on a route march, drive through, fifteen towns, two kasbah's, a chorus line of dancing girls in a pub and… still breakdown in a swamp five miles later.

34. BANG!

"Target Stop!"

The Gunner, a job which only a few crewmen relish. The plus points of the job consist basically of, shooting lumps of metal at bigger lumps of metal. But even then, only during spells of intense range practise during each year. Some gunners would argue that these firing practises, more than make up for the long inactive exercise periods. The rest of the year, the gunners remain, unseen in the bowels of the Tank. They are unsung heroes who, quietly control the weapons systems, waving the main armament around the countryside like a massive, all seeing eye. This is of course, unless your gun kit is not functioning. Then the gun is placed over the back decks and crutched, you will then spend hours travelling everywhere backwards. At times like those I found a good book to be the best option!

The training is however, the verbally loudest course to be on. Everything from fire orders to loading drills are carried out at speed. And are accompanied by screaming and shouting as if to match the volume of the guns as they fire. Of course the shouting is to inject a sense of urgency into the drills required for killing the enemy. The speed of a gunnery engagement is, quite literally, the difference between life and death. An engagement's speed was always meant to be well under 20 seconds in duration, this, from my experience was very achievable!

Failure to successfully engage targets correctly or fast enough could drive the IGs (Instructor Gunnery) mad. They'd rant and rave at the poor crew, winding themselves into a frenzy. A notable IG was a member of A Sqn, Sgt Alan 'Lefty' Wright. He was noted for the changes in colour on his face as he got really stressed. His face would culminate in what A Sqn jokingly called 'State Purple enhanced'. Mike 'Will' Williams still ribs 'Lefty' about it today. Other 'old boys' from A Squadron, such as Andy 'Stavros' Fisher and Bob Jacobs, to name but a couple, are equally uncharitable in a good humoured way! Just as well... I'd hate to see 'Lefty' hit the heady heights of 'state crimson edged with purple ultra enhanced'!

I remember gunnery training well. Many was the time that we, laughed in a classroom at the antics of our chums during.50 Browning drills. The cocking handle on the.50 was designed in such a way that we had to pull it down and then backwards in one swift movement. The time would come when one of our 'smaller' colleagues would approach the gun. The 'DP'(drill practice) gun was mounted on an MG training stand, a metal framework with a mounting bracket on the top. This stand was free standing on the floor. The guy to practise the skills would stand with his back to the gun. On the command 'mount' he would turn, face the gun and carry out the next command. If he was starting from scratch the instructor would shout; "action" the pupil duly opening the breech cover and placing the start of a belt of 'drill rounds' in the bullet 'feed tray'. The next command; "load" would then be bellowed. The pupil would now simply pull the cocking handle back and release it reporting; "loaded", the breech block now carrying a drill round into the gun's chamber. Or at least, that was what was meant to happen! If the pupil was either very small or had difficulty in being ambidextrous it could result in hilarity. The cocking handle was on the left hand side of the gun, this could cause problems for some people. In trying to cock the gun they could start to move the gun and it's stand around the classroom! I've seen students with both feet on the stand trying to gain a foothold while they braced against the stiffness of the guns cocking mechanism. The cursing that accompanied these antics was hilarious. If the drill to be carried out was the 'stoppage drill' which, involved cocking the gun twice in quick succession well, that was absolutely amazing and could make tears of laughter run freely down our faces!

On the other hand, training on the GPMG was painful. The 'stoppage drill' was continually changing! 'Someone' in the gunnery world was always trying to make a name for themselves. The stoppage drill on this gun was confusing and, at times confusing. So somebody would look at this drill and think; "I know how to make it fucking better!" The end result naturally was, utter confusion. So when training in the room with the DP GPMG on it's stand, we never really knew which version of the drill was, at that time, 'in vogue'. The instructors all used however, the same terminology for the stoppage drill. As you worked through the various drills on the gun the Instructor would suddenly (and invariably) shout; "gun fires all day, gun fires all night, gun gets tired.... STOPPAGE!" At which point the soul 'behind the gun' would launch himself into the drill with gusto. Some instructors, to be fair, did try to vary the speech, the substituting of "stoppage" with "sausage" was a favourite but, of all the instructors so, that too soon became boring.

On a range firing point at Hohne.

While in his seat during exercise or ranges, the gunner's eyes are continually glued to his sight. In the sight is contained, a bewildering set of aiming marks: ' The Graticle Pattern' which he must use to accurately engage targets. While on exercise or, during range battle runs, this can prove problematic. You see his sight is looking in magnified detail, over 2000 metres away, therefore he can't see the terrain to his immediate front. So if the driver should hit a bump unexpectedly the gunner stands a fair chance of 'wearing' his sight! The ride in a gunners seat can be particularly uncomfortable, especially at night. You quite literally have nowhere to go, the commander is jammed in behind you and, to your left the massive breech of the 120mm is bucking up and down like a kicking mule. To your right are instruments and controls which seem intent on injuring your body. In front of your face the sight is rocking back and forth in time with the gun. But, there are people who love this atmosphere, its main plus point being; you are dry and can be moderately warm. When all is said and done I personally found the gunners seat very tedious on exercise. When selecting targets and simulating engagements, it was very frustrating to go through the motions without the 'nearly' orgasmic delight of making the gun actually go bang!

But ranges, now that is a different matter! You can feel the buzz of excitement in the turret as you sit waiting for a fire order. Then it comes;

"HESH tank ON!" screams the commander indicating the target to you. He does this by using his controls to put your aiming mark in the area of the target you are to engage.

You, having seen the target, yell "On!" and use your gun controls to place the 'ellipse' in your graticle pattern around the target.

Having done this you report "Lasing" and push your laser switch to emit a laser beam onto the target. In the second or so it takes for the 'bounceback' of the beam from target to your sight you push the switch in the opposite direction and hold it there. The fire control computer, having calibrated the distance to the target, now moves the ellipse up the graticle pattern to a distance reading mark, the stabilised 120mm now heaves and 'drives upward' to lay on the aiming mark. The ellipse is now once more, around the target. On the other side of the turret your loader has now howled "Loaded" having completed the loading cycle. You now excitedly bellow; "firing now!" and press the trigger. The muzzle of the gun now belches flame and smoke which blocks your vision. The entire tank rocks with the force of recoil and the turret is filled with the motion of the breech moving backwards and then 'running out'. The loader is clanging another round into the breech followed by the bagged charge behind it. The breech snaps shut and "Loaded!" is once more reported. Meanwhile the obscuration to your front is clearing and, you can see the red glow of the projectiles trace element as it falls towards the target. SMACK! The trace hits the target. "Your immediate reaction is to shout; "TARGET!" The commander concurs by shouting "Target stop!" Engagement over, you scan for another target to be presented to you. At the end of each Troop's session they would dismount and wait for a debrief from the IG (Instructor Gunnery) who would tell them all about their good and bad points of the engagements.

As I said previously, I find it hard to get excited over my experiences as a gunner therefore I can't really remember many humorous anecdotes about the job. Canada was definitely the best place for gunnery. While sat waiting for targets to be presented, one of the gunner's favourite pastimes was 'Gopher Lasering'. It must be remembered that there were warnings about the use of lasers. When a gunner pressed the laser button the laser beam that was emitted, was a charge of around 32,000 volts! The effect on a human (apparently) could lead to sterility or, if hit in the eyes, blindness.

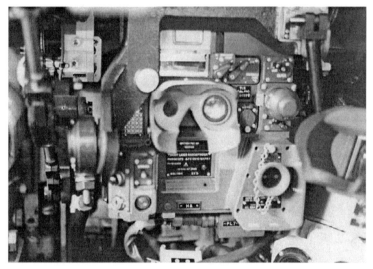

Chieftain gunner's sight.

These effects however were nothing compared to the effect such a beam would have on a Canadian Gopher! Just picture the scene, a Gopher is sat upright atop his burrow entrance. The bored gunner in his tank spies this guardian of the underground world! The graticle is placed on the Gopher and the laser button depressed. The Gophers world now lights up and the Gopher is heavily fricasseed. The gunners would compete to see who could prompt the best reaction from the dying rodents. They could vary from, simple rolling over and expiring to, fairly acrobatic leaping and charring manoeuvres. Of course for the laser to be lethal the range had to be fairly short. A gopher at longer distances would incur a scorched arse and dive immediately for shelter, cheating the hunter of his prey!

Lucy (centre) looks on as his gunner argues that
he could, in fact, hit a barn door at fifty metres!

I remember once at ranges in Lulworth, a tank commanded by John Percy sustained a 'misfire' on the 120mm. John duly changed his flag to yellow and proceeded to wait the allotted 30 minutes as per the drill. His gunner, Alan 'Woody' Woodcraft trapped below in his seat, waited nervously for the drill to be completed. About 20 minutes later the 'misfire' turned into a 'fismire' and the gun went off with its normal explosive reaction. The effect however was, that it so shocked 'Woody' that, he was up, clambering over the commander and out through his hatch, running from the tank before John had even realised what was going on! Sat waiting behind the firing point all that we, in the assembled throng, could see was two minutes after 'Woody's' departure, John's head appeared from his hatch shouting "Where the fuck is my gunner?" This had us rolling on the ground in fits of laughter! We discussed long and hard the feasibility of what we had just witnessed. After all, we couldn't comprehend how 'Woody' had achieved this feat of acrobatics, John Percy wasn't even a chap of small stature! So for the gunner to have physically climbed past him and exited through the small hatch seemed, simply impossible! 'Woody' for his part remained silent about the whole affair.

The other mishap that could befall a gunner was, in his excitement to shoot a tank target, he would let loose a hail of MG fire! This would have been okay had the commander not been expecting the main armament to let loose an explosion. The gunner on his fire controls could, by means of a switch, select either 'main' or 'co-ax'. If, during the excitement of an engagement, the gunner selected 'co-ax' the result could be catastrophic, well for the gunner anyway! As the trigger was pressed the rattle of MG fire would be heard. Two things would now happen, firstly the gunner would flinch, and desperately try to select main in a vain attempt to cover up his mistake! Secondly, the gunner would try to make himself as small as possible in his compact workspace, this was because the commanders instant reaction would be to verbally abuse the gunner. This abuse may be accompanied by physical violence in varying degrees from, a clip round the back of the head to, blows and kicks to the gunners general body! Either way it would be felt by the gunner that, this form of error would not be tolerated. Once more, this violence was a form of 'Tank park' discipline not, bullying. At the end of the day we are talking about, potentially the difference between life and death. If during an engagement with an enemy Tank, the gunner decided to 'sand blast' the opposing Tank's paintwork with MG fire, the enemy commander would make sure that our tank was 'cosmetically' altered forever. That would have been 'it' for us, bringing the curtain down on the rest of our lives prematurely!

"Scrubbing" the gun.

Gunners on exercise always got the tedious tasks, for example on replens they would always be despatched from the tank with the water cans for refilling. During hide routines at night, the Troop's gunners and drivers would provide sentry duties in all weather while, the commanders and operators, inside the turret, stood radio watch! Strange then that, some of the most sullen characters I knew were... Gunners! But most, like us all, were chaps of infinite humour who enjoyed pranks and jokes with the best of us. When a gunner was experienced enough and deemed suitable, he could progress through his trade to become a 'Gunner Mech' and in time a Gunnery instructor. Once gunners started this career progression they became known as 'cassette heads'. This dubious title was given as, they always seemed to know gun drills etc. as if they were a repetitious tape recording. But, of course that was the nature of gunnery, everything by the book, following laid down procedures and drills!

35. "Wilco, out!"

Oh dear, this could I fear, become a long chapter as, signals was my bread and butter trade, eventually I would end up at The Royal armoured Corps Signal School in Bovington having qualified as a Signals Instructor. But that story is not for this book, you'll be glad to hear! I shall endeavour not to make this chapter too long, but it may be difficult as I have so many experiences as an operator and loader.

From very nearly, the start of my adult Tanking career I was an operator more than any other job on a Tank. I explained earlier in the book how I was 'Stan Janner's' operator. My baptism was fairly rough; I had to quickly learn from 'Stan' that a vital part of the C42 radio's tuning drill was a hammer or, other fairly heavy object. This fact had been omitted during my training but to finally tune in the frequency required, you had to get a needle to 'swing' and centre on a spot on a dial. This was notoriously difficult, turning knobs, watching intently as the needle swung to and fro, resolutely refusing to stop on the bloody spot! 'Stan' quickly explained; "Malc, get the needle near the spot, pick up the hammer and smack the radio hard just above the dial!" This he demonstrated to me and, my tuning difficulties were over as, the needle miraculously dropped, as if dead, onto the spot!

Of course, tuning a radio was not even half the battle for an operator. Voice procedure, this title was for many operators and commanders enough to bring them out in a cold sweat! How do you speak on a radio? It appeared that for some people this was extremely difficult. You are not allowed to refer to anything in clear speech. A concept that, especially for officers, was very hard to comprehend. If I were to try writing and explaining the vocabulary used in the signals 'dictionary' it would easily take up a whole book on it's own! But I shall attempt to explain messages as I go. For example all letters are sent as per the 'Phonetic alphabet' e.g. A is 'Alpha', B, 'Bravo' and C, 'Charlie' etc. Numbers are said as they are, Zero, one, two and three and so on. Zero is however written thus; Ø. Therefore a radio Callsign e.g. T4Ø would be read and spoken as; Tango four zero, not, Tango forty. So from now on, for the uninitiated, please try and read any messages as I've explained. I will endeavour to be careful in what I explain as, many of the terms and phrases I use may be in use today and I would not like to compromise any security aspects of the modern soldier's security.

"Noddy suited" on radio watch.

As the years progressed it became increasingly difficult to speak in 'clear speech', more and more information requiring 'encoding'. When I started my career the codes in use were known as 'Slidex' for worded messages of standard format, and 'Mapco' for encoding map references. These codes were eventually superseded by a single code known as 'Batco'. This is all I am, for obvious reasons, prepared to explain about codes used by the Army. But the reluctance of some people to use codes due to the speed required for action to take place in response to an order could lead to hilarity. For example we never referred to a tank on the radio as 'Tank'. Instead all references to vehicle types were made in 'veiled' speech. For example a vehicle was simply known as a 'Callsign', why then would officers try and categorise them further. The favourite when operating in a mixed battle group was 'Heavy' and 'Light' Callsigns. Christ, it wouldn't take the brains of an Archbishop to work out that 'Heavy' probably meant a Tank! So trained enemy 'intercept' operators who scanned the frequencies 'information gathering' could easily start to build up a picture of what they were facing!

All forms of Order giving are placed into standardised format, thus facilitating the ease with which they can be encoded. To the enemy this would then appear as a meaningless mass of numbers and letters. Slang is severely frowned upon as, if it's used by a particular unit to refer to certain objects or occurrences; this would be used by the intercept station to identify certain units by this method. People however used names and words in the false impression that they were legal! A good example would be the word for radio, 'means'. As I explained in a previous chapter 'means' was accepted as a word shortening the phrase 'means of communication', in other words a radio! This was in fact not necessarily an 'illegal' word but, I never really understood why it should be used. If you wanted to get someone to communicate with another tank we were hardly using bloody 'pigeon post' were we?

When talking on the radio if you ended a section of a message with the word, "Over", this meant you were expecting a response from the other person. If ended with "Out", you had terminated the conversation. When orders were given, the recipient, if all was understood and he was willing to comply, would answer "Wilco, out". This was subsequently found to be 'insecure' as "Wilco" inferred that someone had just been given an order. Therefore "Wilco" became outlawed. "Roger" meant that you understood the message that had been transmitted to you, as opposed to it meaning that you were about to commit an indecent act on a fellow crew member! Some people became 'nervous talkers' chatting away on the radio net as if to reassure themselves that all was well. When 'Clansman' radios first came into service, 'blowing into the microphone' became common place. Operators would do this as if to reassure themselves that the radio was indeed working. This was because the radios were now silent, gone was the constant 'mush' sound of the old C42 droning in your headset. The C42 was also prone to losing its frequency so, it seemed very strange with the new radio that, there wasn't a procedure for constantly re-tuning the radio. This led to a feeling of insecurity for 'older' operators who now had to accept change in their everyday lives!

At this point I would like to give you an example or two of how bad voice procedure could have been.

Regimental Command radio net

This net normally has people who are very angry, stressed and confused on it. But every so often the Colonel himself may get on the radio in an attempt to restore order to the chaos and calm people down, albeit he may have selected the wrong radio to speak on, I have attempted to change actual callsigns in a bid to maintain security.

"Hullo all stations this is Tango 99, today has been a massive success, you are all personally to take a pat on the back from me....."

"Hullo Tango 99 this is Ø, you have the wrong means selected over!"

Undeterred by the interruption the CO continues unabated:

".... it's been a long, arduous exercise for both you and your machines so we need our well earned rest.... "

"Ø, WRONG MEANS OVER!"

".... before we fall back to our hide locations tonight, I wish to congratulate you all on a spiffing performance".

"Tango 99, this is Ø that was long winded and watch your security. Cut it out. Out!"

"....today was long and we have another long day ahead of us tomorrow. Thank you for your efforts and goodnight."

Not only Senior officers have problems with voice procedure, another example could be a young Regimental Intelligence officer while on radio watch late at night in Command Troop, the Colonel has departed on one of his vehicles, the Colonel uses different callsigns when he's on different vehicles:

"Hallo Echo 1Ø Alpha this is Ø, what er, where and what Callsign will you.... er,...you.... er what Callsign are you using to.... um.... oh bollocks....er,... wait,... um... out!"

"Hallo Echo 1Ø Alpha this is Ø, what tank   or.. um.... er what Callsign are you.... to um.. to er?"

"Echo 1Ø Alpha, I'll be using Echo 64 Over."

"Ah.. er...um... thank you, Roger out."

A Squadron radio net, the OC ordering a 'quick attack':

"Hallo all stations this is Ø, orders.... I envisage a wide blitzkrieg movement cutting the enemy off from their rear echelons and reserves and blowing a huge, gaping hole in their lines...."He is interrupted by an unknown Callsign thinking they are chatting on the IC;

"Ere, I thought this was meant to be a fucking quick attack?"

"Fuck knows! Are you managing to write all this crap down?"

The REME now interrupt the message flow:

"Hallo tanks this is your mechanics. The tank belonging to Corporal Paul 'Bish' Betteridge, Third Royal Tank Regiment is broken down at grid 234594. it'll probably take us a good two hours to sort it out, out."

Control hearing the glaring cock up made by the REME now chirps in;

"Hallo Mike 73 Bravo this is Ø, watch your security. All grids and reports should be in code. Out!"

Another Callsign now breaks in un knowingly;

"Christ almighty, did you see the size of the tits on her by the petrol station?"

The OC is now, after all the interruptions, once more heard still giving orders!

".... and turning their line of advance so that we can begin to chase the enemy away eventually achieving the final victory which we so richly deserve..."

Outside, the war carry's on and on and on until, an unknown Infantry unit 'breaks in' on the net:

"Yankee 16 Charlie this is Ø send combat report over."

"Hang on... ssssh.....was that for us?" floats out across the air! There follow repeated attempts to get a combat report until Ø decides that Y16C can't hear him so he decides to resort to checking the communications;

"Yankee 16 Charlie this is Ø Radio check over."

"Na, no fucking way was that for us." the wayward station unconsciously says.

"Don't fucking know. Anyway Sarge, Fancy a beer?"

"Yankee 16 Charlie this is Ø NOTHING HEARD OUT!"

Now, these are only fanciful ideas but, similar occurrences did happen while on exercise! Each tank Squadron had a Squadron Signals NCO in SHQ. He was constantly involved in fighting to maintain radio discipline! The reality was of course that within our Regiment radio security was, in fact, very good. This was mainly down to Command troop and each Squadron's signals guru. Some Troops thought that while exercising during the day, SHQ could only exert verbal pressure for any slackness while talking on the radio. When a friend of mine, 'Killer' Lewis was Signals NCO however, that all changed. One day a Troop Leaders operator kept using slang and being cocky on the Squadron net. His bad luck was that the following evening, the Squadron went into a 'hide' together. 'Killer' immediately left his tank in search of the offender. Having found him and threatened him with horrific physical

~ 246 ~

violence should he re-offend, the operator became 'strangely quiet' on the air ever after!

Command Troop 'Hiding'.

The other tasks involved in the operator's busy routine were loading (I've already covered this subject), food manufacture and 'brew' making. The operator, next to the commander, was also normally the most experienced man in all facets of Tanking. So you would be expected to, not only do your own job but, also help and advise on the other jobs involved in the crew. In a relatively short period of time I had become proficient in 'brew making' while the tank was bucking up and down, travelling across rough terrain. I could also work minor miracles with tins of compo rations, the BV, slices of bread and a knife! It has to be said that hygiene within the turret's confines was not a primary concern. 'Butties' were normally slices of bread containing margarine and the allotted filling but, they would also contain a smattering of oil or diesel from the operators grubby hands! The BV and it's boiling water could be a demon, if left unattended with cans of food inside, prolonged heat could cause the cans to explode.

One day on Soltau, 'Nosher' Cadman, 'Bert' Hammond and I were conferring in a wood. 'Bert' had left his operator 'Luigi' Lomax preparing a meal in the turret! We were studiously looking at 'Nosher's' map when from 'Luigi's' turret came a loud but muffled 'CRUMP' followed by angry shouts of "fucking hell!" and "what a fucking mess!" Steam was seen rising from the turret hatches at high speed. Then 'Luigi' appeared out of the loaders hatch his face and uniform looking red. The red hue was due to the fact that two tins of baked beans in the

BV had exploded! The lid of the BV had been blown off the casing, and a shower of beans had been in hot pursuit, the inside of the turret now having been truly pebble dashed with the contents. 'Luigi' too, had been covered in the beans and also the boiling water! 'Bert' now gained a look on his face like the devil incarnate, "what the fuck has that muppet Luigi done now?" he exclaimed as he strode off towards his Tank. It was as he strode towards the vehicle that 'Luigi' appeared, 'Bert's' immediate reaction at the sight of his operator was, to fall on the floor laughing. But his mirth was soon replaced by anger and frustration when he realised that his parka had been in the turret, this was now also covered in food! 'Luigi' was cleaning the turret for days in his attempt to remove all traces of that meal!

Loaders take great pride in their abilities as housekeepers of the turret. I remember while operating for George Brighty I was the proud owner of a chrome coffee pot. I had kept this pot safe for many years and it was my pride and joy. Until Jeremy Taylor was our gunner anyway! One day as we were advancing up a hill, George and I were sat with our heads out of our respective hatches. As we advanced towards the hill's crest to our front, the gun's stabiliser aided by Jeremy, was attempting to remain pointing meaningfully at the expected objective beyond. This meant that Jeremy was using his controls to depress the gun's muzzle as he, through his sight, kept his aim on the target. Then over the IC Jeremy said; "Bugger this, I can't get the gun to go any lower!" "Wanker!" replied George having looked down at the front of the tank to ensure that the gun had room to depress. This it did but, still Jeremy was complaining at the gun's lack of movement. I looked at George who motioned that I should go down and take a look at the problem. As I descended into the turret the problem became immediately obvious. Next to Jeremy's head, on top of the 120mm breech, jammed between it and the turret roof was… my tall coffee pot! It was however, no longer tall, in fact it had taken on the dimensions of a deep pan pizza! Having asked the question of whether he had seen my pot, only to receive the reply "I didn't think to look at the breech!" To say I was less than amused would indeed, be an understatement! The verbal and physical abuse I now launched at Jeremy was immense, it even included the throwing of a 'dummy' HESH round over the top of the breech, hitting him in the neck! Nobody, I mean nobody, was allowed to touch my coffee pot, let alone destroy it! The pot had obviously become dislodged from its stowage position during one of 'Zippy' Wellington's more 'bumpy' forays across country earlier that day. All operators had something, a secret weapon, with which to add that 'special something' to the crew's life. Mine had been that damned pot, I mourned it as if someone beloved had died! Jeremy for his part, showed no remorse whatsoever! The bastard! How dare he? I LOVED THAT COFFEE POT! George understanding my bereavement, tried to console me with our favourite fruit gum teddy bears! I was however not so easily mollified and, for the rest of that exercise, Jeremy was doomed, Swarfega filled sandwiches, cold meals, dreadful brews and any other amount of horrors I could inflict on him! The moral of this story for all tank crews being, don't piss your operator off!

Radio watch, this was normally a boring affair during the night. Once into a hide the night routine would be established, the gunners and drivers would stand guard while the operators and commanders shared sitting in the turret listening for messages. It was, as I said, boring as, darkness was normally a time for radio 'silence'. So you would, at the allotted time for your 'stag' be woken by a guard, pull on your boots and get in your turret switching on your radios. The guard was responsible for waking the radio watch as we were not allowed to leave the radio unattended lest we miss a message. So the sleeping places on the back decks were always allotted to the same people. The normal sleeping arrangement was; on the 'Jenny' deck; the operator, on the main engine deck; the driver, the armoured engine 'T' piece under the gun; the gunner and finally the commander would sleep on the gearbox decks. This way a sentry knew who and where the next sentries and radio watchers were sleeping. If any change was made, for example the driver may choose to sleep in his cab, it was his duty to inform the sentry who would be waking him! I remember once 'Swilly' Winsor, decided he would sleep elsewhere, my resulting search awoke the entire crew who, were less than pleased! I eventually found him in a turret basket snoring his head off. By the time he'd got up and come to where I was waiting to hand over my duty to him, an extra half hour of my sleep time had passed. When he found me I was stood on the front wing of my tank attempting to 'beat off' a viscious wild boar and it's family with my SMG. They had 'come a foraging' for food in our hide. 'Swilly' was immediately by my side trying to scare off these intruders. This took another twenty minutes! But there was no way that we, would go face to face with these damned animals, they were truly dangerous!

But radio watch was good for some things namely reading and writing. There was little or no time in our busy lives for relaxing with a book or sending news home to loved ones. So radio watch was a good opportunity to sit in a damp turret putting pen to paper. Damp? Oh yes the turret at night would drip with condensation where what little warmth had been gained during the day, combined with your breath would cause every metal surface to run with water droplets. This could in the worst instance be magnified in storms, by rainwater leaking in through the hatches. So there I'd sit, my filthy hands rubbing dirt across the damp writing paper leaving a mess through which, the letter's recipient would have to try de-ciphering my scribble! I apologise to all the people to whom, I sent such letters. But hey, at least I thought of you!

The operators life could, become quite frantic at times. He would perch on his side of the turret, scribbling down messages like a 'man demented' attempting to decode these messages and passing the information to the commander as quickly as possible. The commander to be fair, would also make sure that he wrote down the message so that nothing would be missed. If this was happening while on the move it could be utter chaos as, the movement of the vehicle could cause the operator's chinagraph pencil to snap. We used these pencils to write the messages on plastic sheets saved from MG ammo boxes during range periods. Their use was invaluable as they seemed impervious to water thereby making them 'all weather' message pads.

This entire tank parlance is fine but what of the control stations themselves? Once I had passed my Control Signallers course, I mentioned earlier how I'd spent time in RHQ Command Troop. I found myself one night, during an FTX sat in a ferret in a wood with Steve 'paps' Papadopalous, on top of a hill. We were of course, soaked to the skin as there was a raging storm attempting to blow us clean off the top of the hill. Command troop had departed about an hour earlier, heading for another position, leaving us as a rebroadcast station between them and the rest of the Regiment. As the troop moved through the darkness we could hear, over the command net, that they were trying to contact the RSO. We found this strange as surely he was in the convoy in his ferret, all they had to do was stop and walk over to him and speak!

Suddenly, looming through the trees next to us at high speed came what looked like an immense bat! As the figure neared us, we realised that it was the RSO, his soaked and glistening poncho flying out at each side of him like huge wings! The Lieutenant, shall remain nameless, but had lived in South Africa for some time, and was renowned for wearing a monocle and perpetually carrying his 'ashplant' even on exercise. The 'ashplant' was carried by all RTR officers in place of other Regiment's more traditional canes. This was a tradition carried on from a very muddy WW1, when one day an officer had snapped the branch from an ash tree and used it to test the ground's firmness in front of his advancing Tank. At a later date we 'kidnapped' his 'ashplant' snapped it, wrapped it in a first field dressing as a repair and returned it anonymously to his person. It nearly brought the poor chap to tears!

Anyway on this night the luckless officer had totally missed everything as.... he and his driver had been asleep. Not even the roar of the departing troop's vehicles had roused them from their slumber. He was now asking us; "Where the bloody hell have they all gone?" We duly gave him the grid reference of the troop's final resting place that night and, five minutes later off he sped, but to us it looked like, in totally the wrong direction! The radio was alive for hours with the RSO trying to contact the troop, but eventually they met, apparently the Colonel was not impressed at the RSO's antics.

The day H drove... A Sultan Command Vehicle at 60mph!

In command troop a real bugger of a job was operating in the back of a Sultan command vehicle. Sat with piles of radio gear, paperwork and bodies, claustrophobic would be a good word to use. If all this junk didn't injure you as you sped cross-country, the large mapboard hinged from the vehicle roof would. Once in a location, attempting to contact anyone could, if the RSO had selected a particularly bad 'comm's' location, be extremely frustrating! I remember one day 'Polly' Pinder was on radio watch desperately trying to contact the RQMS, radio check requests were continually transmitted. In the end frustration took over, with a scream 'Polly' leapt from the back of the Sultan and, ran into the middle of the woodland glade in which we were situated. He then cupped his hands to his mouth and bellowed into the sky;

"Fucking hallo Tango 55 Alpha this is fucking zero, can you fucking hear me?"

Obviously the only reply he was going to get was from us in the form of belly laughs at his performance. Ten minutes later, having regained his composure, 'Polly' returned to his duty, on the loudspeaker we could suddenly hear a message booming out;

"Hallo zero this is Tango 55 Alpha, have you been trying to get me?"

"Aaaaarrrrrrrggghhh!" Was 'Polly's only response sailing to our ears.

So the operators life on exercise would be a busy one, keeping the crew happy and well fed, keeping the tank in touch on the radio, practicing his map reading skills atop the turret, ensuring the BV was always kept topped up and on the boil, encoding and decoding messages and, if he was experienced enough, conferring with the commander on tactical issues honing his skills in preparation for the next step in his career path, the commanders seat!

36. "Make it so number one!"

I have used Star Trek next generation's, Captain Jean-Luc Picard's saying as the title to this chapter on purpose. His coolness when all is going horribly wrong is a testament to all British tank commanders, with but a few exceptions.

The tank commander is a master at 'keeping all his balls in the air at the same time!'

The commander while in barracks had specific troop duties to fulfil dependant on his rank and title. The Troop Leader, if an officer normally receives duties, which take him away from the troop and tank park life. Senior NCOs normally administer the troop in all matters from vehicle servicing to discipline. This is the bread and butter of the Troop Sergeant or in his absence the Troop Corporal. It could get slightly confusing as corporals could be Troop Sergeants as lance corporals could be Troop Corporals. This was due to the posting regulations that were in force. For example a Regiment had a quota of places for the rank of sergeant. If a sergeant went on posting for a year, even though he was 'detached' he was still held on 'Regimental strength', so no corporal could be promoted to take his place. Even though this rule applied, a corporal could be equally well qualified to carry out the Troop Sergeants role. Therefore he would be 'job promoted' into the sergeants position. A lance corporal could therefore easily find himself as Troop Corporal.

Once on exercise the Troop Leader would appear from nowhere assuming his duties amid much good humoured chorusing of; "who the fuck are you? Do we know you?" Most officers I'm sure would have rather spent their time with us, rather than the 'other duties' they were designated to by their superiors. The simple fact for them was that, there never seemed to be enough officers! The Troop Leader normally had the most experienced crew, though not always as, the Troop Sergeants and Corporals normally designated who would crew what Tank. Wouldn't you, given half the chance, keep the best for yourself? Each crew would normally spend many months working and living together, a good commander like a father, keeping his siblings working and playing together in harmony. Or at least as good an amount of harmony as possible, after all we remained individuals to a degree, so friction at times of stress was an inevitable consequence of living together in such confines. But no matter what friction was boiling from time to time, everybody remained mates with each other.

So what makes a good tank commander? I can only give my opinion, hopefully not as a reflection on my abilities. The Royal Armoured Corps saw the qualities required as follows:

A sense of awareness, this means that he must be able to grasp the 'broad brush' picture of what both, friend and foe are doing.

Leadership, a tank commander must adopt his own leadership style but always lead from the front, always be prepared to show the way and give clear and precise orders. Strive only for perfection from both himself and his crew.

Speed of response/anticipation, tank commanders must be able to keep up with the sometimes, chaotic speed of armoured warfare, he will only achieve this by maintaining flexibility through his ability to read any situation, reacting to it quickly and using his initiative!

Knowledge, not only must the tank commander know his own crew and vehicle capabilities but, he must understand the capabilities of other units supporting him and, he must also have an excellent understanding of his enemy and his capabilities.

Commonsense, This to me is vital; I saw many so called 'intelligent idiots' who, though very brainy at theory were, totally inept at transmitting their thoughts into actions. A commander must apply his gut instinct at what is the commonsense thing to do, it will normally prevent accidents of potentially catastrophic proportions!

These then, were the qualities that helped qualify a man to become the ultimate poseur, a tank commander! Possibly the only thing missing from the list is the quality I have tried to express in this book; a sense of humour! Leadership is a fine balance of motivation and mutual respect. I for example was a great believer in 'don't ask someone to do something that you wouldn't do yourself'. This was not difficult because to be selected to go on the 3-month commanders course, you had to be proficient in every tank trade. There is no point being a commander if, when asked a question, you don't know the answer! Leadership must be combined with a sense of humour so that, in times of stress when a crewman asks you a question which is so stupid as to be unbelievable, or he makes a huge mistake, you can laugh, point him in the right direction, give him an answer which makes him feel valued, and carry on with what you were doing and stay unruffled. After all, you are the most senior person on the crew and morale would suffer badly if, at the drop of a hat, you continually kicked the crap out of those who you depend on!

I remember when commanding in Canada, 'Nosher' insisted he gave me an experienced operator (who shall remain nameless!), as my gunner and driver were relatively inexperienced. I myself was commanding for the first time at BATUS, 'Nosher' therefore decided that the operator, being trusted, would leave me more time to concentrate on the other two. First day on scheme we went to 'action'. I changed my flag to red and we made ready to move forward and engage any targets. I spotted our first target, issued my fire order, heard 'Smudge' Smith, the gunner's response, and "Loaded!" came from the other side of the turret loud and clear, then 'Smudge' shouted "firing now" and.... bugger all happened! 'Smudge' immediately reported, "misfire!" I looked down at the rear of the breech to check that all was in order. There, where the FNA (firing needle assembly) normally sat was, nothing, 'nichts,' 'nada', bugger all, except a hole that is! I immediately verbally assaulted the loader accusing him of being the 'spawn of Satan', requesting that he immediately; "fit the fucking FNA you fucking goon!" He cooperated with my request and, we started the day's firing. Needless to say he had just committed probably the biggest sin possible for a loader!

For the rest of the exercise I found myself worrying about what he might do next. So much for my 'experienced' loader! Later that exercise we sat through the 30 minute misfire drill only to, at the end of the wait have our operator, gingerly open the breech, while we sat, crapping ourselves with anxiety lest there be a smouldering bagged charge sat smiling at us! We needed not to worry as he'd been loading so fast that, in his own confusion, he'd actually forgotten to load a bloody charge! That incident really got me going and the abuse and the flare pistol, which flew at him, must have really hurt! Did I say never lose your cool? Maintain a sense of humour?

'Bombing up' in Canada.

Infantry, 'grunts', 'no-hopers' or whatever you may call them. A subject that I hold dear to my heart, never ceasing to wonder how sometimes they could be so stupid with only one bloody head each! Once more in Canada, our troop was placed with a company of 'grunts' as 'intimate support'. Our duty being to accompany the Infantry as they stormed an 'enemy' position. This simply involved us moving slowly forward firing at the position providing cover for the 'grunts' as they ran alongside us in the final assault. I'm sorry did I say 'simply'? Nothing in reality could have been further from the truth! As we slowly advanced the Infantry fell behind us while practicing their 'fire and movement' drills. As I sat observing their antics through my vision blocks in the cupola, I became aware of a sound similar to that of a hailstorm. Suddenly, one of my glass vision blocks 'crazed' and cracked. I strained my neck round and looked out of a block behind me. There, behind us was a section of Infantry, spraying us with liberal amounts of MG fire! "Fuck me", I exclaimed angrily, continuing with; "those twatting idiots behind us are shooting at us!"

'Nosher' the MLB- Mad laughing bloke!

The Infantry mentality had expressed itself in the form of; "Well, it's 56 tons of steel, it don't matter what we do, it won't hurt them fuckers!" They were of course right, it didn't hurt us but that night our attitude changed. As we parked in the Squadron leaguer we set about getting ourselves ready for the night routine. As we removed our sleeping bags from the rear bins, we were covered in a cloud of duck down, all our bins having been riddled with bullets. The tool bins were also looking like tea bags! We were to say the least, a bit pissed off! But, as the saying goes; don't get mad, get even, and boy did we get even!

The very next time we were placed with the Infantry Company we had already formulated a plan. The troop had set up a totally 'illegal' chatter net using our 'spare' radios. The troop leader had pre-briefed us that on this assault we would already have 'sabot' rounds sat in our 120mm breeches. On the radio command we would, slow down and come to a halt, which we duly did. The 'grunts' inevitably caught us up and would have overtaken us except the safety staff made them 'go to ground' next to our Tanks. They were staring up at us wondering why we had come to a stop. Then our troop leader started his countdown and, when the command "Fire" came through, all three of our tanks let rip with a three-gun salvo of main armament! The effect of the pressure release from the muzzles of our main armaments combined with the explosion's decibel quota was, devastating. The Infantry were rolling on the prairie in agony, holding their ears and some, even having nosebleeds, great! The desired effect was achieved, then as we advanced forward once more the Infantry suddenly found themselves with our six MGs spraying bullets over the tops of their heads. Strangely enough; we didn't suffer from 'friendly fire' again that exercise.

Sat in the commanders seat, I often visualised real war scenarios. Would we have come out alive? How long would I have retained all my crew members without injury? The answers to these questions and many more, I was, luckily never to find. I like to think that my qualities as a commander would have been good enough to keep my crew alive. When I was on my commanders course, a year after I started commanding! I did well in all the subjects taught. On my final report the officer in charge of the course did however, say that I shouldn't become prone to impetuosity! This was a reference to my actions during a TEWT. On the day in question we were taken to a 'grassy knoll' near Bovington camp. The Major in charge of the tactics phase set us a task.

"Okay chaps, in front of you is the valley, on the far side at the top of the hill is an enemy position!" He rasped, pointing out the landscape ahead. He continued: "The position is manned by a company of Soviet infantry supported by two T62 Tanks, you are a Troop leader, and using the dead ground to best effect, you are to plan a troop attack on the position!" Having paused for effect, he now added; "I want you to go to town on this one, use your imagination and create a dashing armoured attack mowing down the enemy!"

I sat and considered the problem, my creative juices surging through my mind. After the allotted ten minutes 'thinking time' the Major asked each one of us in turn for their plan. Many plans were put forward receiving the Major's attention and critique as to the potential success rate of the plan. My turn came and I stood up flourishing my hands in the air, pointing and waving my plan into life.

"I've got my troop sergeant left and corporal right with me as fire support from this position sir!" I explained, the Major's brow furrowed, "Riiigghht!" He hesitantly replied. I bashed on regardless; "my sergeant will carry out a left flanking manoeuvre, down the valley swinging back up towards the position from the dead ground. As he crests the hill he will engage the T62s which he'll see and MG the Infantry! Meanwhile the corporal will flank right along the valley, then cut up the hill behind the wood taking up a position to cut off any retreating enemy as they run from the wood! Meanwhile I'll be pasting the position with direct fire from this firebase!" I finished the attack explanation with a bending of my knees and a wave of my hands as if accepting applause on stage as, the final curtain dropped.

The Major, his face a picture of confusion now replied;

"Yeeeeessssssss, and then of course corporal C, you'll not have forgotten your writing pad will you?"

Confused I stuttered; "For what sir?"

He then shouted, "for writing to the families of the poor fucking bastards that you've just allowed to be murdered, you clot!"

I looked bemused, surely it would have worked? How could it have failed? The Major now explained why my plan would have failed. I had split the troop up and sent them individually to their doom without their comrades to support them. It was then explained that my impetuosity was reminiscent of the 'charge of the light brigade' mentality of the 19th century. This was however, the only negative point in my report. I feel that my career as a tank commander was fairly successful. I could map read to a high standard, hit targets with my crew and, keep my tank moving though breakdowns were 'a plenty!'

Breakdowns, good grief, I quickly lost count of how many times I was left broken down in some god forsaken part of the countryside. It didn't matter if it only took the fitters twenty minutes to find us, it felt like twenty hours. While waiting we would be trying every trick in the book to fix ourselves and resume our place in the battle. I remember once in BATUS, we were ready to depart on exercise from the dustbowl onto the prairie late one afternoon. Our tank was a gem, clean (even in the engine compartment), serviced and ready for action. 'Tommo' my driver started the engine and its reassuring thumping sound filled my ears. The Squadron moved off with us in the middle of the snaking dust cloud that the tanks created. Then, after only about a mile; "Malc... all me warning lights have come on!" Tommo's voice rang in my headset. This was suddenly followed by a loud metallic clang from the back decks and we came to an abrupt halt.

The REME, bringing up the rear of the column, soon arrived and stopped at our side. After much conferring and scratching of heads, it was announced; "Well Malc, your engine's fucked!" Even I could have told them this piece of startling information! Apparently the engine had somehow seized which was a blow to morale as it had only been fitted two days before our arrival. Either way, we were unceremoniously towed back to the dust bowl and, that night a fresh engine was dropped into the gaping cavern of our engine compartment. The problems didn't end there though! Before we left again, our radio packed up, and having no second or 'spare' set, we had to wait until the following lunchtime for a replacement.

But during that time we were visited, by two vehicles from a nearby Canadian reservist unit. The vehicles were armoured cars, the 'Grizzly' and the 'Cougar', we took up the Canadians offer to have a drive of these beasts and, in due course, having given them a good 'thrashing' on the prairie, we announced them as excellent. We did of course, allow them a quick drive of Chieftain around the dustbowl but, no higher or faster than third gear! Sadly their visit was soon at an end as was our delay in leaving for the wide open prairie.

Our tank with it's new heart in place, performed magnificently for the entire exercise. We became known as 'Malc's magnificent men in their flying machine'! This was due to the fact that our tank seemed to be faster than anyone else's. As the saying goes, 'all good things must come to an end' and so it was with that 'Med man'.

L-R, Grizzly, Chieftain, Cougar

We received 'endex' over the radio and the Squadron headed for BATUS. As usual we were zooming along in the column 'playing' at overtaking 'Nosher' to annoy him then dropping behind only to overtake again. Then, quite out of the blue, 'Tommo' sang out; "Malc, my temperature gauge is showing hot!" I turned in my hatch to see a huge plume of white smoke being blown from the engine decks, accompanied by a sickly sweet burning smell, it could only mean one thing. A bloody coolant leak! "Okay Tommo, pull the fuck over and we'll have a look", I reluctantly ordered. Our head on rush for BATUS, washdown and cold beer was now, well and truly halted. I climbed out of my hatch, jumped onto the back decks and started to open the armoured deck covers. Once access to the compartment was gained 'Tommo' and I lifted the radiators to the upright position and inspected the damage. By now our trusty fitters had stopped, jumped across to our tank and were also looking for the problem. Our coolant tank had split a weld seam, coolant was pissing out everywhere.

The REME solution was, to give us all their full water cans and, instruct us to "top up and motor on". This was a favourite cure with the REME, it meant that it couldn't be fixed there and then so, in the case of a leak, we would simply pour more of whichever fluid was required, into the appropriate orifice, and keep moving, refilling as many times as necessary, in order to get to our destination. In this instance the REME too, were in a rush to get back to camp so, they weren't about to start a major repair at this stage. So we, as ordered, topped up and motored, like a bat out of hell, on! The last we saw of our trusty steed was the engine being removed at the workshops in BATUS. I always wondered how many engines and with what regularity, BATUS used in a training year.

Map reading, many people struggled with map reading, I however didn't really have any problems. The standard tank commander's map was an Ordnance Survey 1 in 25,000 scale map. I once came unstuck on ranges because the map was a 1 in 50,000 scale map. Whereas, on the normal map I was used to what speed and time it took to pass through a grid square, this map with it's huge squares completely screwed up my mind. We seemed to be whizzing across the map at such a speed that, I simply couldn't keep up.

I was used to having my map folded neatly, changing sides at a leisurely pace as we moved through each grid square. This bloody map however, soon took on the proportions of a ship's sail as we flew down the road. I fought in vain with the thing, and then... the wind ripped it in half and, took one half off behind me with great speed. Somehow I managed to find my way to our destination as, luckily the remainder of the journey was contained on the surviving half of the map. This map reading game was fine on Chieftain but, Challenger now, that was different. Suddenly commanders not only had to worry about where they were on their map but, they had to worry at twice the speed! Challenger simply flew along so, keeping up with the landmarks and distance travelled caused some people problems.

Map reading really 'became fun' when 'closed down', the landscape took on a whole new meaning when viewed through the commanders episcopes! Mixed in with this was the other tasks associated with the command function. Keeping an eye on the guns position by means of the traverse indicator (a small dial with a representation of a tank in it and a moving needle for the 120mm), this showed the commander which way the turret was facing in relation to the hull. The radio would be chattering away in your ear, the vehicle would be bucking around like a wild thing, controlling the crew looking for targets and keeping an eye on the rest of the tanks in your vicinity. Constantly twisting and turning in your seat, having eyes in the back of your head, operating the gun and turret controls, having had only two hours sleep each night after night, interpreting order after order as it's passed to you, translating your map to the ground outside as it rushes by, accelerated by the close, dark interior of the Tank. All these and many more tasks kept the commander's mind and body busy. By the end of an intensive training period it's no wonder that I used to feel exhausted.

After an exercise we would return to barracks and, our first hot shower, sometimes for many weeks, was a luxury. Many of us found that a thirty-minute bath, followed by a twenty-minute shower and finally a further thirty minutes in a fresh bath would, remove most of the diesel, oil and grime from our bodies. Oil and diesel however, had a knack of staining our hands after prolonged contact. It could take days or maybe weeks for the stains to be removed. By then of course we would probably be back on scheme again! That of course doesn't mean that we didn't wash, we did and as regularly as possible. But a daily or more commonly, two or three daily wash in cold water does not make you a shiny clean boy! The inside of a tank can smell like nothing on earth, but of course you won't notice as, you are for that time, part of the smell inside the steel enclosed interior. After a prolonged period 'closed down' to open the hatches and smell fresh air could, make you want to simply 'close down' again as you'd become more accustomed to the vehicles stench than the atmosphere outside. We all truly became part of the Tank, another piece of machinery plugged by the radio's 'umbilical' cords into the Tank's systems.

Never the less, it was a fantastic feeling to be part of the machine, part of the team that made it function as what it really is; a massive Queen of the battlefield, an awe inspiring offensive weapon. And to command such a leviathan, well what can I say? Simply, fucking awesome!

37. Paderborn, end of an era

Our time in Paderborn was coming to an end. It had been decided that we were to become an 'extra' armoured regiment in BAOR. We would move to Hemer near Dortmund to take up station. Our move would happen in 1987 but, not before we moved to the UK for fifteen months. This was due to our new barracks having to be converted from Infantry to tank use. We would take up the duties of RAC Centre training regiment at Bovington with one Squadron being stationed at the gunnery school in Lulworth and another – 'F' Squadron being formed and then detaching to the sovereign bases in Cyprus.

Maintenance and clowning during Staff college Demo.

Before this would happen we had a load of 'living' to do in Paderborn. C. Squadron had to perform a 'Staff college demonstration' at Sennelager before a crowd of military dignitaries and students. This was a combined Army and RAF demonstration of our tactical prowess. Some of the spectators we heard were Russian! To us it mattered little, it simply meant that we would once more have to 'bull' up the Tanks. This we did and the demonstration was a great success.

Another event I participated in was with the German tank training unit at Augustdorf on the other side of the Sennelager training area. I was 'jellied' into this as I spoke German. 'Luigi' Lomax also found himself with me. We were to provide a Chieftain for visitors to inspect on the German's annual open day. Their CO had asked if we could do such a thing. Our answer was yes. When I heard the news my immediate thought was, "shit, a Chieftain in the middle of all those new Leopard 2's". By now we had all seen the new Leopard on FTX and had been impressed at its performance. Of course this would mean more 'bulling' of our 'old fashioned' Tanks. Or would it? We were told that to save us some work a 'base workshop' overhauled Chieftain with all the latest modifications was due at our barracks the day before the German's open day.

This tank would be diverted on its transporter and we would meet it at Augustdorf early on the morning of the open day. Oh joy, no cleaning and painting to be done! We would have aTank straight off the production line, nothing could possibly go wrong, or could it? The morning of the open day arrived, 'Luigi' and I travelled to Augustdorf. There, as promised was our tank still on the transporter. All we had to do was start the engine, reverse it off the transporter and park it in the allocated space. We started it all right but we couldn't engage reverse gear. "Bollocks" shouted I, "try again Luigi" I continued, Still no joy. By now the German troops, having parked their Leopard's nearby, were coming to have a look at Britain's armoured might. How embarrassing, our tank for all it's revving of engine, would simply not move. "Fuck this for a barrel load of fucking monkeys" I now stormed as I climbed onto the back decks. I threw open the gearbox decks and reaching down behind the gearbox, pulled on the lever manually to engage 'emergency reverse' as the electronic gear selection was obviously not working. This done we drove the tank off the transporter and, after some more antics in the back decks with the gearbox lever, managed to park the Tank. We then traversed the turret to 'gun front', switched off the engines and sat waiting for our guests. The German troops seemed fascinated by both our tank and our ability to 'troubleshoot' our way out of trouble. We showed them as much as we could in an informed tour of our facilities.

In return a German tank platoon leader invited us to view Leopard 2. We were escorted through the fence surrounding the Tank. And invited on board, we climbed up to see what this tank was made of. We were then taken for a drive which impressed us mightily, this finished, the Leopard was once more secured behind it's fence. No other visitors that day were allowed on or in the Leopards. 'Luigi' and I felt very privileged indeed to have been so honoured earlier that day.

Things had, over a period of time, changed in Paderborn. Our old Geordie friends the '5 & 9's (15th/19th Kings Royal Hussars) had moved on to pastures new. In their place an Infantry unit moved in. Suddenly the city centre at night had changed. We had always gone out in pairs but, to the Infantry leaving barracks for a drink, a pair meant a group of ten! The first weekend the 'grunts' were in station two of our guys were hospitalised. They had committed no offence other than to meet up with a bunch of infanteers who were worse for wear. Drink is a dreadful thing, our guys were set upon and severely beaten. When news of this reached our ears, the matter would have to be settled the following night. This was carried out by Tankies entering town 'en masse' with blood lust in their eyes. Once the infantry had been taught a lesson by our tough, hardened veterans, things settled back to an air of normality. But it would be fair to say that Paderborn simply wasn't the same after that. This was a sad affair with the Infantry as we were not a Regiment given to inter unit violence, but once riled we were not a force to be toyed with!

Killer in 'pre Gym warm-up' mode!

Once more I was not to be involved in the Regimental handover, this time to the 5th Inniskilling Dragoon Guards. Instead I found myself returning to Bovington prior to the Regiment as I had to attend a Signals

Instructors course for three months, afterwards rejoining my Squadron at Lulworth. But, before I left Paderborn there were goodbyes to be said. Firstly I wished farewell to my favourite pub 'the movie star' which C.Squadron had adopted as it's second Squadron bar. It was sad as I'd made many friends both German and British within its portals. The owners, a German and a 'Brit', laid on a bit of a spread for me which was touching. My final goodbye was heartbreaking, I had to say a fond and loving goodbye to my two German sons who, after a disastrous attempt at marriage to a German girl, I was now to leave behind without even knowing when or if I would see them again. Marriage and tank commitments just didn't, for me anyway, seem to work.

My farewells said, I loaded up my car and headed for the UK. I eventually saw my chums again at Lulworth and Bovington. I had the role of tank Troop Sergeant at Lulworth and thoroughly enjoyed the experience of controlling 22 MBTs along with my now, old friend SSGT 'Killer' Lewis as my troop leader.

Tank Troop Lulworth – display team!

As the Regiment settled into it's 'non combat' role the days rolled into one another interspersed with visits to our friends and family at weekends.

That didn't last as he was in due course promoted to Squadron Sergeant Major, and a fine one he was too. I decided that, now with age and other priorities in mind, I would try to get a posting to stay in the UK. This I in due course did, remaining for the final eighteen months of my career at the RAC Signal School.

During this time I decided that it may be time for an 'old sweat' to move on and start something fresh. It was a sad day for me when I handed in my uniform and ID card. There was none of the feelings of ceremony and pride that I'd had fifteen years earlier when I'd joined. Only a feeling of sadness that I'd never achieved my ambition of becoming a Senior NCO, Sabre Troop Leader. I had always said that if I reached that point I would have achieved what I'd dreamt of. But having reached that point I would have nothing left to achieve. Even the post of SSM would have been for me, the end. I wanted to be with the guys, living and breathing the early mornings first whiff of diesel fumes as we headed out of the protection of a wood. But as with all facets of life, things change and along with them, your manner of prioritising your life. I'd always been a '22 year man' but somehow without even realising it that had changed. I would now be a 'civvie', and as when I'd joined the Army at 16, this would now for me, be a new adventure!

So, all my equipment handed in, on the 1st April 1990, I departed Bovington camp and headed for a whole new adventure … Civvy street!

Epilogue

What then have I achieved in this book? Well, I hope that I have reawakened happy memories in my Third tanks comrades. I hope I have given an insight into tank life to those among you who always wanted, but never had the opportunity to live on a Tank. But most of all I hope that I have given you all something to have a laugh about.

Through all the mishaps and jokes that I have related I would however, like you to remember that Soldiering is a very serious profession. It would be simple to think that we all just got pissed and had a great time. But these anecdotes are only a few of my experiences over fifteen years. I could not hope to relate fifteen years of my military life in a book. I have only selected a few memories with which to try and raise a smile. I have not mentioned any of the memories I have over the deaths of comrades other than 'Taff' Cousins. Nor have I dwelt on the less colourful events in the army such as long wet nights spent on barracks guard duties.

But all of these events, like the ones quoted, happened. They are equally as important to me as the humorous ones in this book. Who knows? Perhaps, if this book really gets published and, if there is enough demand, I may really write Armoured Farmer, Return of the jelly! When I join my old chums at a reunion we 'pull up a sandbag', 'swing a lantern', sit and 'chew the fat' over the good times we had. Although time has marched on, when I see these men, all with our hair now tinged with grey (apart from the cocky bastards who dye their hair!) I know, that given a pair of black overalls, we would not have changed a bit. When all is said and done, once a Tankie, always a Tankie.

In 1992 our beloved 3rd Royal Tank Regiment ceased to exist in all but our memories, and that I feel is what's important, our memories. As we grow older the biggest part of our lives becomes our ability to remember, after all there's more behind us than in front! I once said to 'Lucy' Taylor that I would write a book one day, this I have now done. I have not set out to offend anyone and hopefully this is the case, we were all bonded together by our ability to laugh at anything and everything. We were young; death was something which, at that age meant nothing. We were invulnerable to everything. Why? Well because come what may, we knew that we were the best at what we did; Tanking in all its glory and hardships.

Here is a ditty I penned in honour of the dreaded Chieftain engine failure:

The breakdown!

So it was that we donned the Tankie's black overalls,
Looking smart and from the girls receiving whistles and cat calls,
And proudly on each shoulder we wore the Brunswick green flash,
Twas for love of the 3rd tanks and chums....not for the pitiful cash!
For we lucky few joined the 'Westcountry's own' the Third of track,
'Armoured Farmers' was our nickname and humour we didn't lack,
True comradeship and trust from each other we won,
An' scrump by the gallon we drank when work was done!
In late '76 forth from Fally to Blighty we did sally,
Alpha Squadron did in Warminster dally,
But Beer and Benylin aided them to prove,
To the Grunts that they - really could move.
Bumble and Charlie proved that in Tidworth they could motor,
Though MOD money was slashed like gutting a bloater,
Labour tried really hard to scupper our chances,
Us wishing for spares - QM Tech avoiding our glances.
While Command and Support in Swingfire and CVRT did roam, Taking
off their RayBans only at weekends and when at home,
The roar of their engines and the clouds of departing dust,
Clogging our throats at their passing and they certainly we cussed!
Oh, the heady days of the rolling Salisbury Plain,
Inevitable L60 breakdowns making it hard for us to stay sane,
The roar of the engine and smell of burnt derv,
Gave us as Tankies guts of steel and plenty of nerve.
But then it would come a loud chug and a clank,
Followed by silence broken only by a cry of "This is fuckin wank!"
As the engine's lube system became rapidly external,
It seemed our frustration may well be eternal.
Into his mic our Sunray did openly scream,
For fitter assistance did he shout while venting a spleen,
In due course Tiffy and his team from afar would appear,
Laughing and shouting as they drew near.
On our decks they slowly would climb,
And scratch their heads they would for a time,

Then after tests and whispers huddled while in a ruck,
A verdict then came forth, "It's shagged and we don't give a fuck!"
Then off in their wagons they shortly sped,
Leaving our commander to do nought but scratch his head,
"For your new pack we'll send the FRT" Tiffy had uttered,
Our response – "You Wankers!" we muttered.
In due course our new engine we received,
As into our back decks the FRT it noisily heaved,
Then some time later into life it coughed and roared,
Our commander now, no longer looking peeved and bored.
He now looked at us and held out his cup,
"Lads - Genny and BV on and let's brew the fuck up!"
And so it was that our breakdown into history did pass,
None of us for the Chieftain's L60 giving a fat rat's ass.
But, one thing for us all remained fixed and for sure,
And nothing could from our belief us cure,
The Black and Green of the Third of Track were Tankies pure,
And our great brotherhood's fellowship would forever endure!
Fear Naught!

Before I finish, I should like to finish on a high note so here's a joke I once heard, many moons ago:

A veteran of WW1 is sat, his young grandson on his lap, in front of the fire:

"What did you do in the war grandad?"

"I was in the trenches son"

"Did you kill any Germans grandad?"

"Oh yes, I killed Germans son, well apart from one that is!"

"Why, what happened grandad?"

"One day I was in an attack on a German position, involved in hand to hand fighting, when faced with this Gerry I remembered my Instructor telling me to first, punch the enemy till he was dead, like this; punch, punch, punch." He showed a demonstration with his fists. He then continued;

"This I did except, he wouldn't die!"

"Cripes, what happened next grandad"?

"Well the next step was to load bullets in my gun and shoot the German like this... Bang, Bang, Bang!" He demonstrated with an imaginary gun.

"Did he die grandad?" Asked the now excited youngster.

"No he didn't Jimmy, no he didn't."

"So what did you do grandad" enquired the little chap.

"Well Jimmy, I turned and ran like buggery away from the Gerry, and all the way back to my trench, all I could hear was the bloody Gerry coming behind me going... TANK, TANK, TANK!"

Finally I should like to say that the one thing that I had at sixteen years of age, set out to do in the tanks was to become a man. The 'Armoured Farmers' had made sure that, indeed fifteen years later I was finally that ... a man!

But then...

Reuters 08:00GMT 06-01-2007

A rousing cheer for the MOD today, rose in the air! In line with the new recruitment policy the reformation of 3RTR has been announced. Raising the maximum enlistment age from 26 to 33 combined with soldiers being able to serve under normal conditions till the age of 55.

This has meant that re-recruitment of Tankies into the Third can now mean direct assembly of 'Senior Members' into a newly formed Regiment alongside the 'Sabre' ranks of 3RTR, the new formation will be known as the SDFTF or to give it it's full name - The Stone Dead F*cking TTTwwaaattttssss & Freeloaders.

An MOD spokesman claimed that:

A. *This would have a positive 'mentoring' benefit to younger members of the Regiment enhancing retention of Soldiers beyond the 3 years of average service.*

B. *Another perceived advantage of the SDFTF would be the reformation of a 'Logistics & Stores' section under control of Full Corporal Dennis Adams a folklore hero of 3RTR who has served (unkillable) since the Regiment formed in 1915, only forestalling his service in 1992 when he was 'temporarily laid up' with 3RTR's colours in The Church of St Peter-upon-Cornhill. The forseen bonus of this reformed SDFTFL&S would be - huge savings to the MOD Armour budget as it would become (once again) nigh on impossible to get any spares or equipment requests fulfilled by this stalwart of Storemanship who's cap badge motto was 'Fucking Naught'.*

The spokesman finished by adding there was only one slight doubt about 'older ex members of the Regiment re-enlisting'. That was whether they would now be able to master the new technologies of the modern Armoured Corps? A nearby passer by, a giant 7foot tall chap sporting a handle bar moustache and RTR tie, overhearing the interview now interjected - "Take it from me mate, we'll have a beer, tie the technology tight in Don10 signal wire and then hit the fucker with a hammer! Everything will work just fine!" And with a wink and a grin he wandered off to the nearby 'Enlist today' office.

There are no ex- 3rd Tankies, only 3rd Tankies!
Forever Green! Fear Naught!

Thanks to 'Good CO' and all for their help in advertising my book on www.arrse.co.uk!